About the author

John Gledhill is Emeritus Prc logy at the University of Ma of the British Academy and UK Academy of Social Sciences. He was chair of the UK Association of Social Anthropologists from 2005 to 2009, has served on the executive committees of the World Council of Anthropological Associations and the International Union of Anthropological and Ethnological Sciences, and is co-managing editor of the journal *Critique of Anthropology*. He is the author of *Casi Nada: Agrarian Reform in the Homeland of Cardenismo*; *Neoliberalism, Transnationalization and Rural Poverty*; *Power and Its Disguises: Anthropological Perspectives on Politics*; and *Cultura y Desafío en Ostula: Cuatro Siglos de Autonomía Indígena en la Costa-Sierra Nahua de Michoacán*; and editor of *State and Society* (with B. Bender and M. T. Larsen), and *New Approaches to Resistance in Brazil and Mexico* (with P. Schell).

THE NEW WAR ON THE POOR

THE PRODUCTION OF INSECURITY IN LATIN AMERICA

John Gledhill

Zed Books
LONDON

The New War on the Poor: The production of insecurity in Latin America was first published in 2015 by Zed Books Ltd, The Foundry, 17 Oval Way, London SE11 5RR, UK

www.zedbooks.co.uk

Set in Monotype Plantin and FFKievit by Ewan Smith, London NW5
Index: ed.emery@thefreeuniversity.net
Cover designed by www.roguefour.co.uk

A catalogue record for this book is available from the British Library

ISBN 978-1-78360-303-9 hb
ISBN 978-1-78360-302-2 pb
ISBN 978-1-78360-304-6 pdf
ISBN 978-1-78360-305-3 epub
ISBN 978-1-78360-306-0 mobi

Printed and bound by CPI Group (UK) Ltd, Croydon, CR0 4YY

MIX
Paper from
responsible sources
FSC
www.fsc.org   FSC® C013604

CONTENTS

MAPS

ACKNOWLEDGEMENTS

The research on which this book is based was carried out with the support of a three-year Major Research Fellowship from the Leverhulme Trust. I am sincerely grateful to Leverhulme for its generous support of my project, while absolving the Trust from any responsibility for the arguments and conclusions that I present in this work.

In the course of this research I enjoyed the support of three excellent research assistants. Daniela Miranda and Thiago Neri helped me with interviews in Salvador, Bahia, and Lourdes, Sommariba Silva assisted me with my work in Michoacán. I thank them all for a job well done. During my absence from Salvador to complete a final year's teaching at Manchester University, I have been kept up to date with developments in Bairro da Paz by means of reports from members of the research team directed by my wife, Dr Maria Gabriela Hita. They are Marietta Bomfim, Emilly Mascarenhas, Cleane Pereira and Cleide Souza.

In Chapter 5 I use a small amount of material from earlier research in Michoacán funded by the UK Economic and Social Research Council, the Wenner-Gren Foundation for Anthropological Research, and the Mexican National Council for Science and Technology (CONACyT). I thank these funders once again for their support, once again stressing that I alone am responsible for the arguments presented, and El Colegio de Michoacán for its long-standing hospitality and wonderfully stimulating intellectual environment. I am also very grateful to CIESAS Sureste for its support during my visits to Chiapas.

During my last stay in Mexico I enjoyed the personal hospitality and friendship of Andrew Roth and Cristina Monzón in Zamora, Jesús Prado, Raquel Abarca and family in Guaracha, José Luis Escalona in San Cristóbal de Las Casas, and Margarita Zárate in Mexico City. I am truly grateful to all of them for receiving me in their homes, and to all the other academic colleagues and friends in Mexico City, Michoacán and Chiapas who provided the conviviality and intellectual stimulation that has always made visiting Mexico such a pleasure. It is always an equal pleasure to spend time with academic colleagues at the Federal University of Bahia. I enjoyed opportunities to present early results from this work in conferences and seminars in Brazil, Mexico, Argentina, Austria and Spain, and to publish some preliminary analyses in Portuguese and Spanish. In this regard, I would like to register my special thanks to José Luis Escalona, Andrés Fabregas, Adela Franzé, Alejandro Isla, Anete Ivo, Salvador Maldonado, Daniel Miguez, João Pacheco de Oliveira, Dolores Palomo, Mariano Perelman, Brigida Renoldi and Laura Valladares.

The content of this book reflects the willingness of many people to talk frankly with me and to allow me to carry out participant observation in their communities. Special thanks are due to the leaders and members of the Permanent Forum of Entities of Bairro da Paz, not all of whom are completely convinced of the value of academic research, but have without exception always welcomed me not simply to observe but also on occasion to participate in their deliberations.

Finally, I would like to thank Mariela for her love and support, which is more important to me than I can express in words on the printed page.

1 | SECURITIZATION, THE STATE AND CAPITALISM

> Our government is as corrupt as ever, but obviously some things have got better for us. When did you ever see a campesino wearing a wrist watch? (Peasant farmer, Mexico, 1983)

> It's fairly quiet around here. Well, we get the extortion calls on the phone, but there have only been a few cut-up bodies that they left in bags outside the cemetery and they weren't people from here. We have their protection. (Family in the same village, 2012)

This is a book about what states do to people when they define them as a threat to the security of the rest of society. It is also a book about why states so often not only fail to resolve the problems that the people themselves see as threats to their security, but actually compound them. My argument does not, however, suggest that the causes of these problems can be located simply in national or regional conditions and histories. Transnational and global processes are extremely important, and they are both geopolitical and economic in nature. This complicates the issue of thinking about politically feasible ways of making things better than they are now. For example, we might answer the assertion of the US Department of Homeland Security that it has a right to participate in the reinforcement of security at Mexico's southern border with Guatemala (Isacson et al. 2014) by saying that the conditions in Central America that have created a 'humanitarian crisis' of northwards migration are in part the result of past US intervention in that region. Yet the domestic politics of immigration inside the USA and the state of Central American societies are related to economic processes that are far broader in scope, and deeply anchored in a complex and interlocking chain of power relations. Although some of the corporate actors in these chains, such as mining companies, agro-food transnationals and hedge funds, may be susceptible to campaigns to clean up their acts in terms of social responsibility, what we have surely learned since the 2008 crisis is that it is a challenge to secure even modest reforms to the most scandalous aspects of contemporary capitalism. When it comes to what Latin America might expect in the future, the scenario, as reflected, for example, in the 'vulture' hedge funds' legalized predation on Argentina, remains discouraging.

There is, however, still a lot that Latin America can do for itself whatever the US imperial hegemon tries to do. This is a guiding assumption of a book that focuses principally on the countries with the two largest economies in the region, Brazil, a country that is itself of continental scale, and Mexico. In recent years, the Brazilian government has placed its bets on a heterodox economic strategy that allows real wages to rise,[1] and become a major force on the world diplomatic stage that emphasizes its independence. Mexico has more or less done the opposite. But Mexico's destiny does not have to depend on its proximity to its *gringo* neighbour, even if the assumption that it does guides the thinking of its current government, headed by Enrique Peña Nieto of the Institutional Revolutionary Party (PRI). Returning to power in 2012 after twelve years in which the presidency was in the hands of the right-wing National Action Party (PAN), the PRI government outdid its pro-business predecessor in its plans for letting *gringos* profit from the nation's oil and opening the door to new foreign investment with a 'reform' of the country's labour laws that was not good news for workers. But both Brazil and Mexico have one thing in common. Whatever economic advances they have achieved in recent years, they both suffer from serious problems of violence, and it is this that makes them so central to any discussion of security issues in Latin America. As Arias and Goldstein (2010: 20) point out, Latin America presents 'an immense diversity of forms of violence', which I will unpack for these two particular countries in the course of my analysis. But as the title of the book suggests, I will do this with a particular focus.

Much of the violence I examine has the characteristics of 'new wars' as defined by Mary Kaldor (2012), in contrast to the 'old wars' based on military conflicts between states. Kaldor emphasizes a blurring between violence carried out by states and other political actors competing for power, and violence on the part of 'private' groups, such as criminals and paramilitaries. It is often difficult to separate out economic and political motives, 'private' and 'public', and, because of the significance of transnational connections, the 'local' and the 'global'.

In referring to a 'new war on the poor', however, I am borrowing an expression used by anthropologist and physician Paul Farmer (2003). Farmer is known both for his personal humanitarian work and for his insistence on the need to understand 'structural violence', a term he borrows from Johan Galtung, the Norwegian sociologist who was one of the founders of peace studies. Structural violence is about the 'machinery of oppression' embedded in social orders, which includes racism and gender inequality (Farmer et al. 2004: 307). For Farmer, the concept is necessary not simply because it is not always possible to pin the blame for suffering on specific social actors, but also to avoid a romantic overestimation of how successfully 'oppression' can be 'resisted' by those at the receiving end of it.

I am sympathetic to Farmer's arguments, but I think it is important not to allow a diffuse account of structural violence to obscure the historical connections between specific situations and the actions of identifiable actors that I illustrated above in the case of the relationships between the United States and Central America. What I aim to do in the ethnographic parts of this book is avoid the dangers of excessive abstraction by exploring how large-scale processes and relations work themselves out in local contexts that are populated by people who are socially heterogeneous, often conflictive among themselves, and not necessarily agreed even on how to deal with a common enemy. It is important to explore actor subjectivities and what might shape them (which is seldom something that is directly 'visible' in ethnographic data), keep the plurality of 'violences' in view, and explore how multiple forms of violence intersect and what the effects of that intersection are. Nevertheless, although the anti-romanticism that Farmer advocates is salutary, it is important to recognize that 'the oppressed' do have some capacity for collective 'resistance' and self-organization, since, as we will see, state security interventions may not only refuse to build upon that capacity in a democratic way, but actively seek to undermine it as potentially threatening to the power relations that the state seeks to maintain or expand.

As a preliminary window on to what those power relations are about, I turn first to questions of poverty reduction and social mobility in Latin America, which at first sight appear to be the more positive aspects of developments in the region over the past decade, despite the fact that indigenous and black 'Latin' Americans remain relatively disadvantaged.

Poverty, inequality and social mobility

Advocates of the free market economic policies usually termed 'neoliberal' might seem justified in citing Latin America as proof of the success of their ideas. Chile, turned into a laboratory for neoliberal 'shock therapy' by the military coup that ended the democratically elected left-wing government of Salvador Allende in 1973, has enjoyed four decades of sustained growth that have lifted the country's per capita income beyond that of Brazil and Mexico. Chile also ranks higher than both Brazil and Mexico in terms of the United Nations Development Programme's Human Development Index (HDI), at number 40 in the world, compared with Brazil's position at 85, and Mexico's at 61 (UNDP 2013). The standard HDI adds life expectancy as a measure of health, and mean years of schooling as a measure of education, to income statistics. Chile's score is 0.819, not that far off the 0.875 HDI score of the United Kingdom, which is ranked number 26 in the world. However, the UNDP also offers an inequality-adjusted HDI measure. When inequality is factored in, Chile's HDI score falls from 0.819 to 0.664, whereas the UK's score descends only slightly, to 0.802. Both Brazil and Mexico also suffer major declines when their HDI scores are inequality-adjusted, from 0.73 to 0.531, and from 0.775 to 0.593, respectively.

Social inequality and inadequate investment in quality public education and healthcare lay at the heart of the mobilization of students that rocked the right-wing government headed by business-man Sebastián Piñera in Chile from August 2011 onwards, opening the way to the re-election for a second term of centre-left president Michelle Bachelet in March 2014. Similar issues dented the popularity of Brazil's centre-left president, Dilma Rousseff, in mid-2013, when what were predominantly students from middle-class families took to the streets to protest against the rising costs of public transport, and question the costs of hosting the football World Cup and parallels between corruption in FIFA and corruption within Brazilian politics. Defenders of neoliberal economic policies might argue that their very success provokes a crisis of rising expectations among the upwardly mobile, made particularly ironic in the Brazilian case by the success of the governments led by the Workers' Party (PT) in reducing not simply poverty but also social inequality relative to the levels produced by the neoliberal restructuring of the economy during the 1990s, following the 'lost decade' of crisis in the 1980s.

The PT administrations led by two-term president Luiz Inácio 'Lula' da Silva had reduced the number of Brazilians living in poverty from 37.5 per cent to 20.9 per cent of the population by the time Dilma Rousseff entered office in 2011, more than halving extreme poverty, to 6.1 per cent (CEPAL 2012). Under Rousseff's own 'Brazil without Misery' programme (*Brasil sem miséria*), direct income transfers to poor families with children aimed to eliminate extreme poverty entirely. Yet the real measure of the success of the PT governments was that the creation of more jobs that paid living wages and offered social security benefits enabled many poor families to move out of dependence on poverty alleviation programmes altogether. This had a significant impact on levels of social inequality.

The Gini coefficient of inequality in income distribution in Brazil was 0.604 in the early years of the 1990s, falling to 0.587 by the end of Fernando Henrique Cardoso's second term as president in 2002, and reaching 0.5687 by the end of 2004 (Ivo 2008). Although this was still a high level, the tendency to reduction in inequality of monthly income was evident for all regions, and for both men and women, in the 2007 figure of 0.534. The annual pace of reduction was increasing, leading some analysts to suggest that Brazilian income inequality could converge with that of western Europe within a decade (Suarez Dillon Soares 2008). By 2011 the Brazilian Gini had fallen to 0.501, although the gap between the Brazilian inequality figure and the UK's Gini index of 0.34 in that year remained large (IGBE 2012). Nevertheless, as the gap between rich and poor in the UK has continued to increase, along with the number of families obliged to resort to food banks, *O Globo* newspaper's London correspondent, Vivian Oswald, was inspired by an interview with Oxfam's research director, Ricardo Fuentes-Nueva, to write a piece suggesting that, however imperfect Brazil's government might be, it was at least to be praised for trying to move the country in the opposite direction to that favoured by the British Conservative–Liberal Democrat coalition (Oswald 2014).

Brazil's efforts compared favourably with those of Mexico. Figures published by the Economic Commission for Latin America and the Caribbean in 2012 did show that poverty measured in terms of income levels had also diminished in Latin America's second-richest country, but only by 4.1 per cent, while extreme poverty or 'indigence' had actually increased, standing at 13.3 per cent in 2011 in contrast to 12.6 per cent a decade earlier (CEPAL 2012). Although the multidimensional method of poverty evaluation used by the Mexican government's National Council for Evaluation of Social Development Policy (CONEVAL) showed small improvements in some areas between 2010 and 2012, including access to education and health services, income-based indicators of poverty and indigence in Mexico had continued to deteriorate, leaving more than sixty million citizens below the official poverty line (CONEVAL 2013). Furthermore, as Mexican sociologist Julio Boltvinik has consistently argued over the years, even accepting the narrow normative terms of reference of official poverty measures when it comes to asking fundamental questions about what kind of societies we need to construct in order to offer all who live in them an opportunity to realize their full potential as human beings, the official Mexican poverty statistics suggest that only 20 per cent of the country's population live comfortably, without suffering from any form of vulnerability or deprivation (Boltvinik 2014).

In Brazil social mobility ended during the two decades of neoliberal structural adjustment. Industrial centres such as São Paulo experienced the same kind of downsizing of workforces as deindustrializing cities in the global North, but without having the blow moderated by the kind of social protection that most workers in the old centres of the capitalist world economy still enjoyed (Guimarães 2006). The children of former industrial workers, a minority of the labour force, found their own employment prospects restricted to low-paid service sector jobs and work in general became more precarious (Druck 2011). Under Lula, however, unemployment fell, real wages rose, and social mobility resumed (Pochman 2009). This process continued under the first Rousseff administration, laying the basis for the president's re-election by a narrow margin in October 2014, even though economic growth had slowed considerably. Almost twenty-four million Brazilians, mostly young and many black, ascended into the 'C' class of persons, with earnings in the range between four and ten times the minimum wage. It is, however, sociologically misleading to describe this group as a 'new middle class' as distinct from an upwardly mobile working class. Entry into the world of mass consumption through the generalized extension of consumer credit, and even access to state-subsidized home loans, does not erase the accumulated social advantages that the 'old' middle classes acquired through private primary and secondary education, easier access to free public higher education, and membership of social networks that ease entry into professional careers (Souza 2009). In a society in which differences in lifestyle are maintained through residential arrangements and use of public space, and prejudices that link race and class remain significant despite affirmative action programmes and changing public sentiment, 'feeling' middle class is not the same as having the ability to consume more goods and services that results from a higher disposable income. Inequality has been reduced in terms of earned income, but not capital, which has important non-economic dimensions everywhere (Bourdieu 1989).

We already know from the experience of the global North that it proved difficult to sustain the continuing intergenerational social mobility and ever-rising living standards that seemed possible during the long boom that followed the Second World War and the apparently successful Keynesian management of capitalism. Thomas Piketty has argued that the principal structural transformation of this period was the growth of a true 'patrimonial' or propertied middle class, in a context in which the 'shocks' created by two world wars had reduced the extreme concentration of capital that had characterized the developed world up to 1910 (Piketty 2014: 260–1). Even so, this  was a middle class whose 'capital' consisted of owning a home (whose value likely appreciated over time) and retirement savings. The poorest 50 per cent of the population still owned 'practically nothing' (ibid.). During the unprecedented period of growth that occurred after the Second World War, income inequality also diminished. From the 1970s onwards that process went into reverse with the beginning of the redistribution of income back from labour to the owners of capital that David Harvey (2007) sees as the essence of 'neoliberalization'. Piketty's point, based on an analysis that starts in the eighteenth century, is, however, that low rates of economic growth are the historical norm. Once the rate of return on private capital exceeds the rate of growth of income, output and labour productivity, wealth accumulated in the past grows more rapidly than wages, wealth concentration increases, highly paid entrepreneurs become rentiers, and property-less workers fall ever further behind (Piketty 2014: 571). Piketty argues that as the emerging economies 'catch up' with the old centres of capitalist accumulation, and their growth also slows, this tendency will become a global challenge.

Capital as wealth in the twenty-first century is not what it was in the previous era of high wealth concentration, since landed property has become less significant as a source of rents while rents arising from new kinds of financial markets have become increasingly important. In the era of 'financialization', any good or service, including mortgages and student loans, can be converted into a tradable asset ('securitized' in the financial sense). A good deal of current wealth is generated by increases in the value of financial assets and the ability to participate in financial investments that bring especially high rates of return through trading that is essentially speculative. These trends are socially problematic in various ways. Financialization can create price instability in the increasingly globalized markets for commodities that are essential to human survival, notably food (Van der Ploeg 2010), along with housing and energy. Rapid price hikes have catastrophic implications for poor families. Members of the middle and working classes lack the opportunity to participate in the kinds of activities that are generating further wealth for the already wealthy, even if their purchasing power is not actually falling, and it is often falling severely for the most vulnerable families as labour market restructuring continues through innovations such as zero-hours contracts. Middle-class people and better-paid workers are vulnerable to financial market turbulence because their own stake in these markets is in the form of debt, or pension schemes that can be restructured to their disadvantage. The large-scale holders of capital, including those who command the fabulous salaries and bonuses paid in the financial sector itself, and information technology entrepreneurs, now have better opportunities than ever to pull ahead of everyone else, and to pass their advantages on to their children.

Joseph Stiglitz (2012) has argued that the ultimate price of inequality in the global North is a stifling of truly dynamic capitalism and erosion of public confidence in democratic politics. Emphasis on the problem of wealth distribution clearly resonates strongly with the claim of the 'Occupy' movement that the societies of the global North have become societies run by, and for the benefit of, the '1%'. Like the Spanish 15-M movement, the *indignados*, Occupy reflected the way that crisis had disrupted the traditional economic expectations of young people from more privileged social backgrounds and fostered disillusion with representative democracy. In the case of the United States, Occupy protesters found it difficult to bring poor working people and people of colour into their movement, although they did make efforts to do so (Nugent 2012). Even if movements such as Occupy can be seen as expanding the horizons of political democracy by adopting political practices that promote grassroots decision-making, the difficulty of sustaining them demonstrates the magnitude of the challenges that changing contemporary capitalism presents. It is possible that movements that begin by critiquing existing political parties may contribute to the revival of electoral democracy. Replicating the decision to enter electoral politics of some of the left-wing leaders of the Chilean student movement, a group of Spanish *indignados* led by political science professor and TV presenter Pablo Iglesias decided to form a new party to contest the European parliamentary elections in 2014. Despite being only four months old, *Podemos* (We Can) won five seats and captured 8 per cent of the votes cast, on a platform that included higher minimum wages, lowered retirement age, guaranteed minimum income, nationalization of private companies rescued from bankruptcy with public funds, and an end to European Union border controls and tax havens for corporations. Yet Podemos took votes from established parties of the left, and the main political winners from rising inequality and falling economic security in Europe seemed to be right-wing populist xenophobes and fascists.

The '1%' concept also appealed to US trade unionists faced with a crisis of membership, ever stronger legal impediments to organizing formal sector workers, and extreme difficulties in reaching part-time and immigrant workers. Richard Trumka, head of the American Federation of Labor-Congress of Industrial Organizations (AFL-CIO), the largest union in the USA, has also invoked the findings of Thomas Piketty, linking wealth disparity to the remorseless downward pressure on real wages that has remained a central feature of the US economy under Obama (Jopson and Harding 2014). The challenges of the situation that he faces has led Trumka to advocate for legalization of undocumented workers and against the mass incarceration of men from the Afro-American and other ethnic minority communities, a move that represents a considerable shift from the AFL-CIO's position in the twentieth century, and reflects its embrace of a 'community unionism' model that favours links with other kinds of rights activists and environmentalists. Yet these kinds of reformist proposals have secured little real traction in US politics.

This book follows the tradition of Marxist thought in treating capitalism as a system of social relationships that is inevitably contradictory in its workings, but whose logic needs to be unpacked by delving analytically beneath the surface of things and the kinds of understandings of the world that come to seem 'natural' to most social actors. But it is not a book that attempts to advocate any bold utopian future. All that I seek to do is to explore some of the contradictions of 'actually existing capitalisms' that gravitate around questions of security, thinking about what might be done within the existing balance of social and political forces to avoid some of the more catastrophic consequences for the people that I will discuss in the case study chapters that form the core of this work. As the quotes at the beginning of this chapter suggest, even Latin Americans whose material standard of living has improved over the past fifty years have to contend with threats to their personal security that are serious, even if they are not without historical precedent. In the next section, I review ideas about 'human security' that have become central to the conventional international development agenda, highlighting how some analysts have tried to give them a more radical edge, although the general tendency promoted by the international development apparatus has been towards their domestication. I then go on to explore the less attractive side of the coupling of ideas about security to ideas about social and economic development, a coupling that defines poor people as a threat to the security of the rest of society, turns social protest into a threat to national security, and victimizes people who try to solve their problems by crossing national frontiers without documents. This coupling is made through the process of securitization, whose negative consequences are the principal focus of my analysis.

The human security paradigm

In its 1994 Human Development Report, the UNDP launched a new proposal for the development of the countries of the global South based on the concept of human security (UNDP 1994). In relation to traditional models of national and international security, the UNDP proposed a shift of focus from states and their interests to people and their interests (Buzan and Hansen 2009). The potential radicalism of the UNDP concept lies in its insistence that the security of people is not only menaced by civil conflicts and violence, but also by environmental degradation, racial and gender discrimination, unemployment or precarious employment, poverty and hunger. The human security framework opens the door to defining the state as part of the problem that people may face in achieving personal security. States may fail to establish the rule of law or pervert it, they may restrict freedom of expression and the legitimate activities of political parties and civil associations, and they may invoke 'states of exception' that are justified in terms of supposed threats to national security as a pretext for suspending the basic rights of their citizens.

Connecting questions of violence and conflict to the deprivation produced by poverty, the human security paradigm proposes a holistic approach to finding solutions, arguing that people can only fulfil their potential as human beings if they are liberated from both fear and want. It is not possible to resolve personal security problems by providing a person with a job if that person is going to die prematurely from malnutrition or from a disease that cannot be cured for lack of hospitals, or if that person is likely to be murdered on his or her way home from work by criminals, paramilitaries or a member of the local police force or military. In this perspective, human security is menaced by unjust political, economic and social structures, externally sponsored military interventions that cause civilian 'collateral damage', and by domestic conflicts linked to the struggle for power and control over economic resources. Although the immediate emphasis is on guaranteeing everyone physical security and so-called 'basic' necessities, human security stresses the need for everyone to attain 'dignity' as a precondition for welfare. This not only makes it necessary to eliminate all forms of social discrimination but also lends itself to the principle that work itself has to be 'dignified' and intergenerational social mobility a possibility open to all. As the examples in this book will confirm, large segments of humanity have their right to security as defined by the UNDP violated on a daily basis.

The UNDP's work on human security made an important contribution to the formulation of the eight Millennium Development Goals agreed by the leaders of 189 countries at a UN-sponsored summit meeting in New York in 2000. What was actually agreed through a series of subsequent meetings and consultations on practical measures for attaining these goals was, however, inevitably watered down considerably through the need to create an internationally acceptable consensus. For example, although the policy documents talk about poverty eradication, the agreed objective was simply to reduce extreme poverty by a half before the end of 2015 (Cornwall and Brock 2005). Even governments that had not actually managed to attain all the existing goals, including the Mexican government under Felipe Calderón of the PAN, accepted publicly that it would be desirable to be more ambitious.

The same process of diluting proposals to achieve international consensus among state actors is apparent enough in the case of the human security concept itself. One of its advocates, who argues for a more ambitious approach, Sakiko Fukuda-Parr (2003), contends that the human security paradigm provides the best framework for confronting the totality of risks provoked by economic globalization and for treating them in a holistic way. She points out that transnational organized crime and the trafficking of persons and organs do not fit very easily into the established frameworks for tackling poverty reduction and the resolution of civil wars and international conflicts. The instability of global financial markets provoked by the financialization of capitalist accumulation has reinforced the negative impacts of labour market restructuring on the security of employment and income (and even, as I pointed out earlier, increased the likelihood of working families suffering hunger when food prices shoot upwards). The conversion of home loans into financially 'securitized' assets to be bought and sold between institutions that have no incentive to be responsible lenders within the logic of financialization also threatens to deprive workers of the relatively small part of the value of their accumulated labour power that they succeed in saving or investing in a home. The problems of epidemics and diseases of poverty that re-emerged as a result of the structural adjustment policies of the International Monetary Fund (IMF) and World Bank are not simply national. Viruses do not respect political frontiers and migrate easily between continents as a result of air travel. The increasingly grave problem of shortage of water is not simply national either, since the way a country manages its water resources can prejudice neighbours dependent on the same sources. Climate change offers a paradigmatic example of the global interdependence of threats to security. The environmental price of the high levels of consumption (and waste) of energy sustained in the old and emerging centres of accumulation in the world economy is also paid by residents of regions that do not enjoy the same standard of living. Most consumers of drugs in the global North escape the violence that exists in the regions where the drugs are produced. Controlling these risks requires a strengthening of international cooperation. Yet the most inclusive institution for promoting such cooperation, the United Nations, finds it hard to negotiate workable consensuses, especially when proposed measures are regarded as contrary to the interests of the United States and the transnational corporations that habitually receive the backing of the US government.

In the case of US policy on the international drugs trade, the historical record suggests that geopolitical 'reasons of state' sometimes override what might appear to be the government's responsibility for domestic public health. There is now abundant evidence that the Central Intelligence Agency (CIA)'s clandestine operations to fund the arming of the 'Contras' against the Sandinista government in Nicaragua with money acquired from illegal sales of weapons to Iran, after the US Congress blocked direct funding, led the agency to work against the efforts of the US Drug Enforcement Administration in Mexico and made a significant contribution to the growth of the Mexican cartels (Hernández 2012). More generally, it remains difficult to discuss the responsibility of the global North for the economic, social, political and environmental problems of the global South in a way that could change the basic posture of an international development apparatus in which Northern interests remain dominant. The tendency remains one of locating both the problems and their causes within the global South itself. Within that framework, there is a notable selectivity in any diagnosis of situations in which the national state itself is a cause of human insecurity. Fingers are pointed at 'anti-democratic', 'failed' and 'terrorist' states more or less in line with the foreign policy of the USA and its allies. Attention is diverted away from countries such as Saudi Arabia, despite its role in financing international terrorism.

As a consequence of this selectivity, it is difficult to dismiss the criticisms of the human security paradigm that have been made by East Asian states (Acharya 2001). These include criticisms of Western interventions in the internal affairs of sovereign nations that are justified on 'humanitarian' grounds. Some might dismiss East Asian postures as hypocritical: the region is hardly a paragon of international collaboration for collective security in the light of the tensions that now exist between China, Vietnam and Japan, and the Chinese also now have to face up to the consequences of being an external actor in the conflict in South Sudan. Nevertheless, leaving the Iraq and Libyan disasters aside, it has become increasingly difficult to see even what many once judged successful humanitarian interventions as having worked out well in the long term. The settlement imposed upon Bosnia was premised on the highly debatable assumption that ethnic conflicts were 'primordial' and that pacification would have to be achieved by a political solution that reproduced ethnic divisions (Kaldor 2012: 43–5). The creation of a costly superstructure of cantonal governments – intended to be transitional but still in place two decades later – was not simply an economic burden and a recipe for inefficiency in vital tasks such as job creation in a country with an unemployment rate now over 50 per cent (Smale 2014). It also led to the expansion of an illegal economy of vast proportions that principally benefited the political class, just as the civil war itself had proved good business for those who commanded paramilitary forces (Kaldor 2012: 56).[2] Although ethnic politics has continued to be attractive for those at the top, about the only positive sign in the dismal economic panorama that faces ordinary Bosnians is that ethnic identities and divisions have been transcended in street protests that denounce both the corruption of the politicians who pocketed the lion's share of the reconstruction aid that the 'international community' supplied, and also the European Union for sponsoring the intervention and then washing its hands of the resulting problems. As one banner in a February 2014 protest eloquently put it: 'I am hungry in three languages' (Borger 2014).

The Bosnian intervention was a failure in terms of the human security paradigm for various reasons. It reinforced the ethnicization of politics, produced a political regime that remained part of the problem instead of offering solutions, and failed to reconstruct an economy that could offer mass employment, leaving Bosnians dependent on the illegal and informal modes of livelihood that received the protection of ethnic nationalist political parties (Kaldor 2012: 70). This suggests that there should be a connection between 'freedom from fear' and 'freedom from want', or between security and social development, but the issue is the kind of connection that is made and the motives that lie behind it. As we will see in the next section, there is a relationship between security and development that was integral to classical counter-insurgency wars designed to halt the global spread of communism, and this is a relationship that has been revived in other kinds of 'pacification' projects related to contemporary processes of capitalist accumulation. First, however, I want to review an approach to security and development that does not embrace the human security paradigm.

In its 2011 World Development Report, *Conflict, Security and Development*, the World Bank defined insecurity as 'a primary development challenge of our times' (World Bank 2011: 27). Although the report recognized that 'global economic shocks' can also be a cause of violence, its main focus was on how criminal violence, civil conflict and 'failed states' prevented achievement of any of the Millennium Development Goals in some countries and tarnished advances towards greater prosperity in others. Perhaps surprisingly in the light of its mission, although less surprisingly in relation to the way the Bank pursues that mission in practice, the report preferred to focus on the perspective of 'citizen security' rather than 'human security'. Citizen security relates to the rights that citizens of a society should normally expect the national state to guarantee them (and by definition does not explicitly address the rights that non-citizens in problematic categories such as undocumented migrants might expect a state that is not their own to guarantee them). Citizen rights include protection from threats to personal security and freedom from fear. They also include political and civil rights, and the right to use and enjoy property. The latter right is important because it assigns the state a duty to protect private property rights in a way that might, for example, justify violent forms of police action should that action remain within the boundaries of the legally defensible.

That means, for example, that when police in Brazil use what some would see as excessive violence in evicting homeless families with children from an empty building in the name of the rights of its proprietor, they are acting within the parameters of citizen security. The wider issue of rights to housing that might be part of a human security agenda is not relevant. The citizen security paradigm is also compatible with the policies of mass incarceration of poor people of colour that are characteristic of both Brazil and the United States (Wacquant 2009). The emphasis in citizen security is therefore back on the state as guarantor of public order, although it is an emphasis that stresses the state's responsibility to uphold the rule of law, defend political freedoms, and create conditions that protect rights of lawful assembly and association in civil society. The citizen security paradigm stands squarely in the liberal tradition. It can be invoked by those who seek reform of judicial, prison and police institutions. Yet the principal focus in the World Bank report was on the threats posed to citizens by criminal and other non-state actors that are violent. The Bank was especially impressed by Colombia's efforts in the field of citizen security. Yet as anthropologist Austin Zeiderman (2013) has shown, in a striking demonstration of the limitations of the citizen security paradigm, some Colombians experience difficulty in claiming the state's protection simply as citizens.

The government of President Álvaro Uribe faced a serious legitimation problem, since it was widely impugned for human rights violations in its campaigns against left-wing guerrillas and for assassinations of trade unionists. Uribe attempted to improve his image in liberal humanitarian terms by creating protection and assistance programmes for people who had suffered forced displacement, either by the guerrillas or by paramilitaries (ibid.: 74). In Bogotá citizens could successfully claim support from these special assistance programmes only by proving themselves directly at risk of losing their lives as a result of death threats from criminals or paramilitaries (ibid.: 76). But the state's claims to offer help to 'vulnerable' people offered them another route to claim rights. Recent arrivals found it difficult to find anywhere affordable to rent, and often deliberately squatted in zones of high environmental risk from landslips, often encouraged by older settlers who had turned recruiting newcomers into the zone into a business (ibid.: 75). They could be evicted from the areas that they had invaded by the police, but were generally not evicted if they could convince the police that they really were displaced people. If they could then convince the authorities that they lived in an area where their lives were threatened by landslips, they might get a housing subsidy to resettle in a safe location. Yet since local government resources were limited, they faced a filtering process that sought to limit access to humanitarian programmes on the grounds that claimants were not at genuine risk of losing their lives but dishonestly exploiting the state's 'generosity' towards the vulnerable. Access to state support was not, in practice, based on citizenship rights, but on the successful 'performance' of being a person vulnerable to threats to life (ibid.: 77).

This was a challenge, since the state had to reject most claims. So in 2008 a group of displaced people decided to occupy a city park to protest against the government's failure to provide them with the humanitarian assistance that they were guaranteed by law (ibid.: 78). The numbers in the park soon swelled to more than a thousand. The government responded by doing everything in its power to discredit the leadership of the protest, which was accused of manipulating people for its own ends and even exploiting young children in a despicable effort to win undeserved public sympathy. It looked for a while as if the protest would be ended by force, but then came the swine flu epidemic. The protest could now be presented as a threat to public health, and a *cordon sanitaire* was placed around the park (ibid.: 80). The mayor's office declared that over a hundred people in the park displayed symptoms of respiratory problems and promised that those who left would be given hospital treatment. But most stayed put, and United Nations High Commission for Refugees staff were called on to mediate, in a welter of government accusations that people were being prevented from leaving by the opportunistic leadership. The UNHCR eventually negotiated a deal in which what was now around two thousand displaced people would receive a range of benefits, including long-term housing solutions and food support, if they were willing to leave. The government agreed, because it could now do so without legitimizing the 'illegal' occupation of the park by the protesters, or abandoning its insistence that they were gullible people being misled by unscrupulous, self-interested agitators. The protesters thus finally secured the benefits that they had been trying to claim as displaced people, but could do so only after being reclassified as a public health risk. Their efforts to act politically as citizens had been rejected as fraudulent, so that they could only secure support under what Zeiderman terms a biopolitical[3] rationality of public security, by becoming carriers of a virus that could contaminate other Colombians who did not experience the same difficulties in claiming their rights as citizens (ibid.: 82).

Given that forced displacement could be seen as a consequence of 'state failure' in World Bank-speak in the first place, the state's 'generosity' towards this inconvenient part of the national population might seem a somewhat inadequate response to the underlying problems. Yet what is significant about this example is that the 'inconvenient' enjoy a distinctly second-class kind of citizenship, and often find themselves placed in the morally invidious position of having to hustle and lie in order to 'perform' their 'vulnerability' appropriately. They are exploited by the rent-seeking of people who are not displaced, but some displaced people themselves are drawn into doing the same thing, a situation that is also typical of undocumented migrants who find themselves in the limbo of trying to get by in a country in which they do not have citizenship rights. The citizen security model simply does not work for these kinds of 'inconvenient' populations.

In this Colombian case, the people in the park secured humanitarian assistance only when they were turned into an object of 'securitization', redefined not as 'vulnerable' people deserving protection, but as vectors of health risks that threatened society as a whole.

It is not, however, simply these kinds of populations which become objects of securitization, and securitization is not simply biopolitical in its rationality. As we will see in the chapters to come, other kinds of 'inconvenient' segments of national populations, such as the people who live in irregular settlements (*favelas*) in Brazilian metropolitan cities, have also been presented as threats to the welfare of society as a whole. Actions to remove poor black Brazilians from urban centres were often justified on grounds of public health hygiene in the past (Chalhoub 1996). Under the military dictatorship, the growing mass of poor rural–urban migrants produced by the development of the capitalist economy were not considered capable 'citizens' at all, but objects of social development interventions that would eventually enable them to act as citizens (Caldeira and Holston 2004). Today, however, *favela* residents are considered to possess the capabilities of being citizens, and state interventions are justified in the name of freeing them from the armed dominance of criminal gangs in order to restore their effective enjoyment of their full citizenship rights. Although many people who live in *favelas* are relatively poor, these populations are, as we will see in the next chapter, much more socio-economically heterogeneous than the term 'poor' would normally suggest. Yet they are 'inconvenient' in a contemporary capitalist context for a number of reasons that are unconnected with the presence of criminals in these communities, reasons that boil down to the principle that capital accumulation can be enhanced through the removal of barriers to its penetration of the spaces that these inconvenient populations occupy, and barriers to its ability to extract the maximum profit from selling goods and services within them. This is a hidden agenda behind the 'securitization' of *favelados* as a problem for the city as a whole and their 'pacification' through a militaristic form of police occupation that often fails to deliver on its promise to respect the rights of these Brazilian citizens.

Securitization and the development–security nexus

Ole Wæver and his colleagues at the University of Copenhagen School of International Relations (Buzan and Hansen 2009) introduced the term 'securitization' into security studies in the mid-1990s. Their approach was constructivist. When an issue is 'securitized' it passes from the realm of ordinary politicized questions, becoming an issue that threatens the very survival of states and their citizens, defined not as individuals but as the collective object 'society'. Because theirs was a constructivist theory, the Copenhagen School paid attention to the problem of who has the power to define an issue as one of security. Although they argue that in principle anyone can do this through an appropriate discursive strategy, they reach the reasonable conclusion that some actors have rather more power to do so than others. State actors have to be high on the list, at least in countries where the public retains some confidence in the ability of their government to defend their country and its citizens from attack or everyday threats to individuals' ability to go about their lives in peace. Government efforts to securitize social problems may also receive considerable support from mainstream mass media, although they may also be criticized by independent media, and in political democracies party interests may also provoke critiques from unexpected quarters, especially during election periods. It is also fairly apparent that, at the global level, the governments of the North Atlantic powers and their allies have been especially active in promoting the securitization process. Nevertheless, we should remember that China proved supportive of the post-9/11 international security agenda for its own reasons, such as the repression of the Falun Gong spiritual movement.

Although I will pay some attention in my own analysis to the discursive level of securitization, I am more interested as an anthropologist in how social situations shape the way that different kinds of social actors think about questions of security, the role of the police and the prison, and what and who constitutes a threat to personal security and why. I am also interested in questions such as what shapes the behaviour and subjectivities of those who are charged with maintaining public order. Why, for example, would a policeman who lives in a poor community give someone who appears to be in a similar social situation a gratuitous beating, and why would a guardian of public order who is a person of colour add racist abuse to the gratuitous beating of another person of colour? I am also very unenthusiastic about restricting the frame of analysis to 'society'. This is not simply because, as will already be apparent, I regard the construction of specific segments of a larger society as 'threats' to the whole with profound scepticism, as a likely source of social injustice and possible cover for the implementation of hidden economic agendas on the part of more powerful interests. It is also because some major problems with securitization relate to the transnational and global relations generated by capitalist uneven development and the logic of maintaining the capitalist accumulation process. Maintaining capitalist accumulation today involves both the continuing extraction of resources and the continual expansion not simply of the proportion of the world's population that participates in the capitalist market economy, but also the number of areas of social life that can be turned into sources of capitalist profit. It also involves dealing with 'inconvenient' populations that are currently supernumerary to those processes, Marx's 'relative surplus population'.

A useful way into these issues is provided by work in critical security studies that focuses on what Mark Duffield (2010) calls 'the development–security nexus', a perspective that also provides a critique of the human security paradigm in the forms in which it has been appropriated by the international development apparatus. Duffield begins his discussion with data on the rising number of kidnappings and killings of aid workers over the last decade, a situation that has prompted the construction of fortified compounds to protect aid workers and new measures to ensure their security when they leave these enclaves. This reflects the way that aid and economic development projects have been harnessed to counter-insurgency operations in countries like Iraq and Afghanistan, which makes it increasingly likely that resentful locals who do not like being under military occupation will see them as agents of an imperial apparatus rather than people trying to 'do good' (ibid.: 54).

The harnessing of development projects to counter-insurgency is not something new. As Duffield points out, it was the British who coined the famous phrase 'winning the hearts and minds' of the people, when they were fighting the military wing of the Malay Communist Party and its principally Chinese Malay rural peasant supporters from 1948 to 1960 (ibid.: 60). In this case, development interventions were designed to produce a particular political outcome, a post-colonial state dominated by ethnic Malays, and part of a strategy motivated by geopolitical interests, fear of the expansion of the communist bloc. Although this was also the pretext in Latin America, insurgencies there were generally a response to domestic social injustices and oppressive and often ethnicized systems of class domination. I explore this theme in more depth in Chapter 4, which looks at the Mexican 'dirty war' in Guerrero during the 1960s and 1970s, and the counter-insurgency operations in Chiapas that began after the Zapatista Army of National Liberation (EZLN) declared its rebellion against the Mexican state and global neoliberalism in 1994, still continuing today in a 'low intensity' form. Yet although 'subversives' are still being persecuted, the geopolitical spectre of communist expansion has become a thing of the past, whatever new anxieties may be being provoked in the United States and Europe by China and Russia as rival powers on the global stage. Today's 'global' security threats are more focused on transnational organized crime and terrorist networks, 'failed states', civil wars, the international movements of displaced people as refugees, and other forms of migration from the global South to the global North, although it is often difficult to make the distinction between 'economic migrants' and 'refugees' that is central to Northern immigration control. This is another sense in which the focus of security has shifted from states to people, constructed as 'dangerous' through securitization.

Duffield argues that 'poverty reduction' in the global South is a self-interested strategy on the part of the global North designed to contain this long list of new threats. It is based on the assumption that it is poverty which lies behind 'state failure', experienced as loss of government legitimacy, civil wars and the growth of organized crime and terrorism (ibid.: 56). Development aid has become linked to the promotion of 'peace and stability', with new funding streams becoming available for conflict resolution and reconciliation measures (ibid.: 57–8). This has led to a major structural reorganization of foreign interventions in conflict-ridden countries. UN missions are increasingly based on an integrated command structure that links humanitarian NGOs and development agencies to political and military missions. This model is not simply for countries devastated by civil wars or under foreign military occupation, since it has also been applied in the Caribbean (ibid.: 58). The problem with this shift is that NGOs and development workers in general may lose their 'non-political' humanitarian identity, especially where donor-funded NGOs are licensed by the UN to 'build state capacity' and extend the reach of the state into people's lives. Whereas James Ferguson (1990) argued that the international development apparatus was able to 'depoliticize' interventions that were economically unsuccessful but effective at extending the reach of the state into society by presenting them as 'technical' solutions to problems of 'lack of development', contemporary development interventions are more frequently seen as politicized by locals because they are visibly about building or rebuilding the kinds of states that the donor countries want to see (Duffield 2010: 59). The kinds of states that the donors want to see are principally states that are stable. It does not seem to matter whether they are states that are democratic, or whether they are states that coexist with large illegal 'shadow economies', providing they manage things in a way that promotes political stability. This is, as we have seen in the case of Bosnia, a potentially contradictory strategy.

Many of the 'new security challenges' that the security–development nexus is concerned with are products of neoliberal structural adjustment programmes. These policies have eroded the capacity of rural people to survive economically, along with tendencies such as the production of biofuels and 'new agricultural commodities' in the global South for 'just in time' delivery to consumers in the global North at the expense of local subsistence production (Van der Ploeg 2010). In the urban context, what used to substitute for the welfare state in the global South, networks of mutual aid between kin and neighbours, was also steadily eroded by the squeezing of household incomes in many countries, including comparatively rich countries such as Mexico (González de la Rocha 2004). The 'human security' paradigm reflected growing awareness that life chances and the possibility of securing a sustainable livelihood had deteriorated for the losers in the neoliberal capitalist transformation of Southern economies. Half the population of Africa continues to live in extreme poverty and has yet to benefit from the higher growth rates of recent years. Yet that growth has reinforced the perception that a better life might be secured by migrating. So Duffield argues that the international development apparatus's embrace of human security is about trying to keep people from moving by making local life just a bit more sustainable, a policy complemented by ever-increasing border security in the countries of destination, the Fortress Europe syndrome (Duffield 2010: 66). Development aid is designed to restore a level of 'self-reliance' to the poor of the global South that will make it sustainable to exclude most of those people from the societies of the global North. It is not about bringing higher levels of social protection to the global South itself, although the human security approach is not inconsistent with states doing more if they have the capacity to do so. It is about ensuring that 'basic needs' are met so that Southern poverty can be contained, reproducing global differences in life chances (ibid.: 56). The development–security nexus therefore seeks to manage a polarized biopolitical divide between North and South (ibid.: 67).

This liberal-humanitarian style of development seeks to create the conditions under which 'adaptive self-reliance' will accomplish this goal. Yet it is far from clear that limited development aid dampens rather than stimulates desires to advance further in terms of material lifestyle through migration, and it may make investing in migration more viable. Furthermore, the international development apparatus tolerates only 'safe' or 'approved' forms of adaptation. Duffield's examples of approved forms of self-reliance include 'NGO audited micro-credit projects' and planting legal crops instead of narcotics (ibid.: 67–8). The problem is that illegal shadow economies are likely to offer much more attractive alternatives. It is their attractiveness as an alternative which has led to their transnational expansion. Not all ways of achieving 'adaptive self-reliance' by means that are technically illegal are threatening to anyone associated with organized crime. A good deal of small-scale smuggling across international borders of the kind that Gustavo Lins Ribeiro has described for the tri-border area between Paraguay, Argentina and Brazil is simply a way in which poor people manage to make a livelihood on the margins of the contemporary capitalist order (Ribeiro 2006). Such 'economic globalization from below' makes a positive contribution to maintaining a globally polarized system run on neoliberal capitalist principles. If maintaining that system relied on development aid alone, the world would be even more dangerous than it is.

But as I will show in the following chapters, it is difficult to isolate the 'harmless' illegal economy from more socially damaging criminal economies – that is, control the development of forms of adaptive self-reliance that take perverse forms that are in reality more damaging to citizens in the global South than they are threatening to societies in the global North. Another problem is that although poverty and unemployment may be part of the explanation for the emergence of extremely violent movements opposed to 'Western Modernity', such as Boko Haram in the north of Nigeria, they are not the whole of the story of what is driving these kinds of 'security threats', which implies that the palliative development assistance on offer from the 'international community' is unlikely to contain them (Adesoji 2010).

The military dimension that the international development apparatus has been acquiring has also become increasingly central to the public security policies of Brazil and Mexico. Although the enforcement arm of the Brazilian police was already organized as a corporation subject to military discipline, army units have participated in the occupation of some of Rio de Janeiro's larger *favela* complexes. In Mexico, the 'war' against the drug cartels, coupled with the 'capture' of local police forces by organized crime, has provided the pretext for deeper military participation in policing. The targets of such policing actions have extended beyond criminal organizations to include civil movements that cannot reasonably be read as 'insurgency' against the state, as we will see in Chapter 5.

Although it is necessary to understand what is happening in Mexico in political as well as economic terms, the internal deployment of repressive force is related to efforts to crush resistance to 'neo-extractivist' modes of capitalist development. These have become central in most Latin American countries, irrespective of apparent differences in ideological orientation such as Bolivia's official promotion of 'Good Living' as an 'alternative development' paradigm (Bebbington and Humphreys Bebbington 2011). Renewed state interest in raw material exports, particularly minerals, and linked to growing Chinese demand, is justified by 'progressive' governments on the grounds that the revenues generated will help to fund poverty reduction programmes. The Brazilian government used the larger 'national interest' to justify its support for the controversial Belo Monte hydroelectric dam scheme, despite its negative impacts on the previously protected indigenous populations of the Xingu National Park. Although local communities are often split on whether they want to accept mining projects or not, and indigenous people do not always oppose forms of 'development' that will transform their environments if they take a form that they perceive as beneficial in terms of their own aspirations (McNeish 2013), the neo-extractivist turn has been associated with a good deal of repression of movements opposing projects or demanding compensation for environmental damage. The irony is that states that seem very 'capable' when it comes to suppressing resistance to transnational capitalist projects often seem far less 'capable'

of providing their citizens with personal security from the everyday violence of criminal gangs and kidnapping and extortion, problems which have now reached proportions that are provoking further rounds of population displacement from some regions as well as diminishing the quality of life of those who stay put.

This is another paradox that this book will explore in detail, but there is a more general way in which repressive violence relates to the way in which capitalism produces 'inconvenient' populations. Brazil's mass incarceration of poor, predominantly black, men, has resulted in its being considered the paradigmatic Latin American example of a US-style 'penal state' by sociologist Loïc Wacquant (Wacquant 2009). Mexico actually has a slightly higher rate of incarceration than Brazil, at 196 per 100,000 compared to Brazil's 193 per 100,000, once again made up mostly of poor (and often completely innocent) citizens, although neither country even begins to compare with US rates of 737 per 100,000, or for that matter Russia's 615 per 100,000 (BBC 2014).[4] Wacquant's penal state is directly linked to neoliberalism, defined both as a regime of capitalist accumulation and a mode of 'governing' in the Foucauldian sense. Wacquant describes it as having a 'left' hand which is 'feminine', oriented to managing the consequences of economic precariousness through social development interventions, and a repressive 'right hand' that is essentially about 'punishing the poor'. Some Brazilian scholars have already extended this conception of the Janus-faced logic of a neoliberal 'society of control' to the *favela* 'pacification' programmes of Rio de Janeiro (Arantes 2012). Wacquant's framework reminds us of some uncomfortable truths about 'liberal' modes of development. One is that even the 'gentle' interventions of social workers in poor communities may be directed to producing 'docile' neoliberal subjects adapted to the lower niches of the labour market. Nevertheless, his ideas seem to fall short in a number of key areas, leaving aside the fact that Brazilian 'authoritarianism' in neoliberal governance replicates long-standing historical patterns. Wacquant describes the neoliberal state as a 'Leviathan', whose contradictions lie principally in conflicts between distinct 'bureaucratic' factions within it, given that the penal state enjoys as much backing from centre-left as from centre-right political parties within electoral democracies. He does not pay sufficient attention, in my view, to the permeability of the state to private interests, including organized crime, nor examine the way that the state itself is responsible for the expansion of the illegal activities that have come to permeate its own institutions. This is especially important in Mexico, but by no means irrelevant to Brazil, whose police are susceptible to 'capture' by a wide variety of interests, as I will show in the next two chapters. The nature of Brazil's democratic system, with its plethora of parties, is also an important issue. Governments built on coalitions need to make substantial concessions to private sector interests. One example would be the way in which the first Rousseff administration was obliged to make concessions on environmental legislation to the landowner lobby led by Senator Kátia Abreu of the Brazilian Democratic Movement Party (PMDB), the PT's main coalition partner at federal level.

The development–security nexus is therefore relevant to a wide variety of contexts beyond international development in war zones. It is, however, of more than casual significance that the domestic security processes that this book analyses are often presented officially as a kind of war and experienced by the people who are the objects of these state security interventions in precisely those terms.

The structure and methodology of the book

Chapters 2 and 3 are devoted to public security in Brazil, with particular emphasis on the *favela* pacification programmes adopted in Rio de Janeiro and the state of Bahia, in the Northeast region, although I also consider the case of São Paulo, which has not followed this approach. I have conducted ethnographic fieldwork in Salvador, Bahia, working with a community organization that was created with the support of a research team from the Federal University of Bahia in one of the city's largest (and most combative) irregular settlements. This ethnographic work is the basis for Chapter 3. The discussion includes the perspectives of serving police officers as well as community residents.

One of the principal issues to emerge in the course of these first two chapters is the relationship between 'the rule of crime' and the 'rule of law'. The official justification for new forms of police intervention in irregular urban settlements is that the state needs to regain control of territories that its previous neglect delivered into the hands of armed criminal gangs, in order to allow residents of such areas to enjoy their full rights as citizens under the rule of law. Yet everything turns on the nature of the relationships between the official justice system, the police, and residents. Regular experiences of police violence and corruption can make domination by criminals the lesser of two evils for some residents, and as Gabriel Feltran (2010b) has shown for São Paulo, residents may prefer the official justice system for some purposes and the alternative normative system offered by criminals for others. In this discussion, I follow Ben Penglase's insight that 'insecurity' is co-produced by the violence of both criminals and state agents (Penglase 2009), in order to explore the shifting dynamics of these relations in different settings, and to highlight how potentially positive proposals to transform the policing of poor areas have been undermined in practice by three structural constraints: a class-biased logic of securitization; the subordination of considerations of social justice – including the rights of poor people to personal and economic security – to neoliberal logics of urban development; and a failure to embrace fundamental reform of a police system that is a legacy of the dictatorship and still serves the interests of the socially and politically powerful in informal as well as officially legitimized ways.

Chapters 4 and 5 are devoted to Mexico. Once again I pursue the issue of the 'co-production' of insecurity by different violent actors, and discuss why people might prefer to rely on criminal organizations for justice and protection than rely on the official institutions of a state that has rarely delivered 'the rule of law', and often administered the law in a way that deepens social injustice. I will show how and why, in the case of Mexico, it has become increasingly difficult to draw clear lines between the worlds of crime and government. Desperation in the face of this reality has driven some Mexicans to attempt to see to their own security by creating armed self-defence forces, making them targets for new kinds of repressive state intervention. My discussion shows that there are partial historical precedents for more recent developments, but I also seek to highlight what is new and a product of state transformations linked to neoliberal capitalism.

Chapter 4 deals with the social and political impacts of counter-insurgency wars in the states of Guerrero and Chiapas. In the case of Chiapas, I also consider the role of non-drug illegal economies in alleviating crisis, and the contribution of US-mandated securitization of Mexico's southern border to deepening crisis for Central Americans already subject to abuse by Mexican state agents and criminal gangs during their passage northwards. I have some personal ethnographic knowledge of these regions, but this chapter is mainly based on the research of others. Chapter 5 is devoted to the state of Michoacán, and draws on my thirty years of research experience in that part of Mexico, although I have made use of the research of others here too. The Mexican part of the book inevitably pays considerable attention to drug cartels, the diversification of their criminal activities and, in the case of Michoacán's Knights Templar cartel, their transformation into mafia-style organizations. I chart the recent history of community police and self-defence groups (*autodefensas*) in Michoacán, an issue that is also important in Guerrero. Throughout this discussion I offer a critical analysis of the role of the state in the production of insecurity, which reaches something of a climax in my analysis of the *autodefensa* experience.

The concluding chapter offers a synthesis of the implications of the case studies for a critical analysis of the human consequences of the securitization of social problems. In revisiting the question of human security, and the negative consequences of repressive interventions, I also return to ways in which capitalist accumulation processes foster new forms of suffering in the name of security.

My ethnographic work employs the extended case method developed by the Manchester School of social anthropology (Burawoy 1998; Handelman 2005). A problem with extended cases, especially cases located in different countries, is that the researcher cannot be present in person at every significant moment in the development of the processes being studied. I have supplemented information that I gathered directly via interviews or participant observation with information from other sources, including newspaper reports, which I have been collecting into a database on a daily basis since beginning this study in 2010. This material is used principally as a source of information of an unambiguously factual type, interpreted in a way that is informed by my ethnographic research. But I also occasionally draw on journalistic analysis of issues. Although anthropologists sometimes look down their noses at journalists, and there is often much to criticize in media representations, there is also much to admire in the efforts of investigative journalists to explore the murkier side of power relations and the activities of violent state and non-state actors. This applies to both Brazil and Mexico, which remains one of the most dangerous places in the world in which to practise that craft.[5]

All names of persons in this book whose identities are not in the public domain are pseudonyms, and all translations from Portuguese and Spanish are mine.

2 | VIOLENCE, URBAN DEVELOPMENT AND THE PRIVATIZATION OF PUBLIC POWER IN BRAZIL

I begin this chapter by observing an apparent paradox. Under the federal administrations led by the PT, poverty in Brazil has been significantly reduced, along with unemployment. The lifestyles of many working-class Brazilians have improved as a result of rising real wages. Yet national indices of crime and violence have increased. Using data provided by the Ministry of Health, sociologist Julio Jacobo Waiselfisz (2014) calculated the national homicide rate in 2012 as 29 victims for every 100,000 inhabitants, the highest since 1980. Although there are regions of Brazil, including São Paulo, in which more people die in traffic accidents than are murdered, this is generally not the case. Brazil's homicide rate is fifty to 100 times greater than that of Japan and other advanced capitalist countries. It is higher even than the official homicide rate in Mexico, although there are regions of both countries where the national murder rate is much less than half the local rate (Damián 2014). Homicide statistics exercise a powerful hold over the social consciousness of more fortunate Brazilians. Members of the established middle classes are more likely to be victims of armed assault than to be murdered by criminals, let alone to die as a result of 'stray bullets' from exchanges of fire between criminals and police (Penglase 2011), although murder associated with robberies (*latrocínio*) is perceived to be on the increase even if the absolute number of victims remains relatively small.[1] Yet the fact that the meanings of violence are always socially constructed, and that what statistics really tell us needs to be unpacked more, does not diminish the importance of the fact that most Brazilians, irrespective of social class, do feel that their country has a serious public security problem.

Although my own ethnographic research has been carried out in Brazil's third-largest metropolitan city, Salvador, Bahia, the principal focus of this chapter is on the two cities that are bigger than Salvador, São Paulo and Rio de Janeiro. Bahia has become considerably more violent than the states in which the other metropolises are located, ranked fifth nationally in terms of Waiselfisz's calculations of homicide rates for 2012, with 41.9 murders per 100,000. Rio de Janeiro was below the national average with 28.3 and São Paulo even lower at 15.1. São Paulo's rate had risen relative to 2011 because of special factors discussed later in this chapter, but both cities had seen a major decline in murder over the past decade, 50 per cent in Rio and 60 per cent in São Paulo, which, even after the 2012 increase, remained, on this measure, the second-least violent region of the country after the southern state of Santa Catarina (Waiselfisz 2014: 9). In 2011, according to the Mexican NGO *Seguridad, Justicia y Paz*, 40 of the 50 most violent cities in the world were located in Latin America, 14 of them in Brazil (Consejo Ciudadano para la Seguridad Pública y Justicia Penal, A.C. 2012). Maceió, capital of the state of Alagoas in the Northeast region, was in third place, with a lower homicide rate than San Pedro Sula, Honduras and Ciudad Juárez, Mexico, but, together with Belém, capital of Pará in the Northern region, more violent than Acapulco in Mexico, the Venezuelan capital Caracas, and Cali and Medellín in Colombia. Salvador had moved from 29th to 22nd place in the ranking since the previous year. By 2013 the same organization placed Salvador (including its Metropolitan Region) in 13th place, with a homicide rate of 57.51 per 100,000 (ibid.). Although this rate hardly compares with San Pedro Sula, with its 187.14 murders per 100,000 population, or Caracas and Acapulco, now in second and third place with figures of well over 100 per 100,000, of the cities higher than Salvador in the ranking, only Caracas, Fortaleza and Guatemala City had population sizes comparable with the 3,884,435 inhabitants of Salvador and its Metropolitan Region. In absolute numbers, 2,224 people were murdered in Salvador during 2013, compared with 2,037 in 2011.

The number of homicides in the state of Bahia increased by 242 per cent between 2010 and 2012, bringing the total number of murders to almost six thousand statewide. Although 439 fewer Bahians were murdered in 2013, Bahia had the highest absolute number of homicides of any Brazilian state in that year.[2] In the case of Rio, news on homicides up until the end of 2013 focused on the apparent success of new public security policies based on the installation of Pacificatory Police Units (*Unidades de Polícia Pacificadora*, UPPs) in reducing murder rates in *favela* communities, a policy that the PT state government of Bahia also decided to implement, three years after Rio initiated its programme. At the end of 2013 homicide rates in the twenty-nine Rio *favelas* occupied at that time, with a total population of more than a quarter of a million residents, had fallen to 8.7 per 100,000, a third of the national average, and in seven of the occupied *favelas* there had been no murders at all during the year (Rocha et al. 2013). Nevertheless, in the course of 2013 there had been an increase of 16.7 per cent in murders in the state of Rio de Janeiro, which has a population of over sixteen million, along with an increase in robberies and thefts of vehicles: the number of robberies, 60,796, was equivalent to 5,000 people being assaulted per month (Martins 2014). This raises questions about the contribution of *favela* pacification to the larger problem of public security. Furthermore, deaths within *favelas* began to increase again during 2014 as a result of a rising number of confrontations between police and traffickers in communities with UPPs. Traffickers fired on police and soldiers not simply in reaction to police 'mega-operations' against the drug trade but also with the apparent intention of reaaserting their place in communities that appeared to have been successfully 'pacified'.

Since the Rio programme has been running longer than its Bahian equivalent, there is more evidence to reflect upon, although significant differences of history and context also need to be taken into account. The analysis offered in this chapter will lead me not simply to consider the unintended consequences of Rio's public security policies but also towards arguments about *favela* pacification that see the process as having agendas other than that of contributing to the overall reduction of crime and violence. Indeed, thinking solely about the impacts of the programme on violence obscures some other important social consequences of pacification for *favela* residents.

Unintended consequences are also important in the case of São Paulo. That metropolis does not have a pacification programme for the urban periphery but it is the home of a major crime organization, the First Command of the Capital (*Primeiro Comando da Capital*, PCC). Some Brazilian journalists now see the PCC as a developing mafia-style organization that is building its networks nationally beyond its home state, including in Bahia. As we will see in more detail later in this chapter, the PCC does share some organizational practices with the Sicilian mafia. Yet as Jane and Peter Schneider (2003) show in their analysis of Palermo, and I will re-emphasize later in this book in my discussion of Mexico, what makes classical mafias powerful is their capacity to penetrate 'legitimate' society and politics. In Sicily, mafias not only contributed to the reproduction of a 'subculture of violence', but formed dense networks with politicians and bureaucrats. The Schneiders document how these 'legitimate' actors become conflictive 'pieces' of an internally fragmented state as they respond to the demands of these backstage interests. In the Palermo case mafias also forged relationships with 'respectable' private sector interests, such as bankers and real estate developers. A key variable in the comparative study of mafia-style organizations is therefore the extent and the depth of their penetration of society and politics. Both the PCC in São Paulo and Rio's militias, discussed in the next section of this chapter, enjoy relations with actors beyond 'the world of crime'. The scope of these relations is less extensive than that achieved by the Mexican crime organizations discussed later in this book, but they are important for building a comparative perspective on the contradictions of Brazilian public security policies. Brazil's biggest metropolis may have a lower homicide rate than Salvador or Rio, but this does not validate the state government's faith in solving the problem of crime by mass incarceration, in increasingly privatized prisons (Leahy 2013). Paulista patterns of violence reflect the particular kind of influence that the PCC enjoys over the 'world of crime', and the complex relationships of antagonism and collusion that have emerged between the PCC and official law enforcement agents.

What is common to all three of these metropolitan cities, and to Brazil as a whole, is the way that definition of the first priority of public security as that of controlling violent criminality makes it seem imperative to maintain a police that is capable of armed repression, and even to use the military to support civilian policing. Although there is widespread recognition that repression alone is not an adequate strategy, it still seems unthinkable to many, not least to the soldiers of the military police, that it should not remain integral to everyday police work, given that criminal gangs are heavily armed and dangerous. Because of structural problems in the police corporations themselves and the nature of Brazilian society and politics, this produces many contradictions, as will become clear in the discussion that follows.

Understanding patterns of violence

São Paulo's homicide rates appeared to be on a strong downward trend in 2011 (Waiselfisz 2012). Yet by early November 2012, a daily spate of execution-style killings had produced a 90 per cent increase over the homicide rates during September and October of the previous year, making the total monthly death toll more than double that registered in Ciudad Juárez at that time (Leblon 2012). By November 2012, the body count in Ciudad Juárez, the Mexican city that had been number two in *Seguridad, Paz y Justicia*'s world ranking the previous year, had fallen substantially relative to the peaks associated with the spectacular *narco*-violence that made Juárez so notorious from 2009 through 2011. The authorities attributed this to the transfer of security from the Federal Police to a reformed municipal police force commanded by a retired soldier, Julián Leyzaola. Leyzaola's iron fist (*mano dura*) approach moved violence away from the city centre to peripheral low-income neighbourhoods, although it also provoked growing complaints against the police for human rights abuse and extrajudicial executions (Patterson 2012). By 2014, however, a different form of order was being established in Juárez. The old conflicts of the era of Felipe Calderón's presidency between the Juárez, Sinaloa, Gulf, Zetas and Beltrán Leyva cartels for control of this vital node in the transmission of drugs to the United States became a thing of the past. The Sinaloa cartel agreed a non-aggression pact with the group now dominant in the city, La Línea, professional killers who had worked for the Juárez cartel founded by the Carrillo Fuentes family. La Línea then began a campaign of extermination against members of youth gangs that had previously carried out contract killings on behalf of the cartels, but had now become completely unruly, selling drugs on their own account, engaging in robberies, extortion and kidnap and abuse of young women, and, most important of all, killing for no business-related reason. Leaving the dismembered bodies of their victims on the streets to send a message, the 'professionals' of La Línea were engaging in a 'cleansing' that would make it easier to get on with mainstream criminal business (Esquivel 2014b).

Even this simple comparison shows us that one-dimensional quantitative measures, such as number of homicides per 100,000 inhabitants, cannot capture the way the nature of lethal violence varies at different times and in different places. It may involve a variety of violent actors, whose relationships with each other and the state may also be crucial. As we will see in the next section, the new cycle of violence in São Paulo that began in July 2012, in many ways replicating an earlier outbreak of violence in 2006, was triggered by an escalating confrontation between the police and the PCC and the breakdown of backstage agreements in which 'legitimate authorities' were also implicated. Reduced violence in Ciudad Juárez, in contrast, reflected a return to an older scenario of violence between local gang members and extrajudicial killings by police in poor neighbourhoods that was probably closer in nature to the violence that occurs on the urban periphery of Maceió in Brazil. But in Juárez, further changes in patterns of violence after the reorganization of the public security apparatus also reflected readjustments within the world of organized as distinct from disorganized crime. It is therefore important to understand the particular social profiles of homicidal violence in different places – that is, which groups are most directly affected by the specific forms of violence that lie behind the statistics, in terms of class, zone of residence, gender, race or other social variables.

What Briceño-León and Zubillaga (2002) termed 'the young man from a marginal neighbourhood' figures as a central actor in accounts of contemporary scenarios of urban violence not simply in Latin America, but also the United States. Situating their discussion in the context of this wider literature, Alba Zaluar and Christovam Barcellos (2012: 21) argue that 'exhibitionist hyper-masculinity' emerged in Rio de Janeiro 'in the social context marked by armed conflict and "lots of money in the pocket" favoured by the trafficking of drugs'. 'Unable to construct their masculine identity through work, education, property and the consumption of durable goods as manual workers could up to the middle of the twentieth century', these men do so by displays of physical force and 'orgiastic spending' that make them 'a menace to their neighbourhoods and persons who surround them' (ibid.). Nevertheless, Zaluar and Barcellos also observe that what explains the increase in homicide rates in the *favelas* where they live is the easy availability of large quantities of firearms (ibid.: 22). This situation reflects the proximity of a seaport and airports, as well as the poor security of military armouries (Zaluar 2010: 16). Police and soldiers have been significant contributors to the supply of illegal arms to criminal groups historically (Misse 1997: 7). Yet as Zaluar points out, despite peer pressures, only a minority of adolescents participate in this hyper-masculine culture of violence in the Rio *favelas*. Her research team in the Cidade de Deus *favela*, included in the UPP programme, calculated that around 1 per cent of the population was 'somehow connected to the drug crews' (Zaluar 2010: 20). Furthermore, they showed that if the focus is on the risks of being a victim of homicide, a more complex account of the ecology of urban violence is necessary.

In 2009 the homicide rate averaged over all Rio's *favelas*, 34 per 100,000, was lower than the rate in the municipality as a whole, which was 52 per 100,000 (Barcellos and Zaluar 2014: 4). This suggests that the presence of drug gangs provided some security to the residents. Between *favelas*, rates ranged from 22 to 44 (ibid.). Barcellos and Zaluar show that, other things being equal, the greatest risk of death occurs on the borders of territories controlled by rival drug trafficking groups. Beyond the deaths that occur in shootouts associated with territorial invasions by different gangs and police incursions, it is dangerous for a young man who is a 'soldier' in one faction to cross into the territory of a rival group (Zaluar and Barcellos 2012: 21). This is not simply a war between 'bandits' and police. Furthermore, there is a third force in the struggle for territorial control over *favelas* in Rio de Janeiro, the groups called 'militias'.

Extra-official paramilitary organizations run by off-duty or retired police, firemen and soldiers, which also enjoy the patronage of local politicians, the militias first began to appear in the eastern zone of the city, in more recent settlements with a high proportion of migrants from the north-east of the country (Barcellos and Zaluar 2014: 6). By 2010 their expansion had still not reached the *favelas* closest to the city's central avenues, but the development of the militias had now contributed significantly to the reduction of the number of *favelas* controlled by the biggest criminal network, the Red Command (*Comando Vermelho*) (ibid.). The militias expel the traffickers, which may provoke a spike in homicides in the area at the moment of their conquest of the territory, but once they have taken it over, they enforce disarmament of the population (ibid.: 5). Although this is to reduce the possibilities of future resistance to their dominion, which not only constitutes a permanent 'protection racket', but also involves profiting from 'tolls' on sales of goods and services such as bottled gas and cable TV (Zaluar and Siqueira Conceição 2007), it also has the effect of reducing the likelihood of deaths from inter-personal violence between residents. Barcellos and Zaluar found that the militia-controlled areas had lower rates of mortality than the areas controlled by armed drug gangs, and offered the following explanation in terms of strategies used for occupying space:

The militias do not occupy the *favelas* only, but their entire surrounding area, which becomes a lucrative source of income through the legal or illegal trade in goods and services like transportation, electricity, water, and leisure activities. Furthermore, the militias also employ other forms of coercing residents, like expelling people linked to drug trafficking, collecting firearms, torturing people who commit crimes deemed unacceptable, and so on. (Barcellos and Zaluar 2014: 8)

With the addition of the UPPs to the scenario, there are now three forces competing for territorial control over the poorer areas of Rio de Janeiro. Barcellos and Zaluar estimated that, in 2010, the militias controlled *favelas* with a total population of around 422,000 inhabitants, while the three main criminal networks controlled 557,000 *favelados* between them, and the UPPs 142,000 (ibid.: 3–4). Four years later the only actors losing ground were the traffickers, which itself changed the dynamics and spatial patterns of violence further, as some of the criminal actors began to resist the police within the *favelas* occupied by UPPs and others moved across Guanabara Bay to Niterói and the municipalities of the Baixada Fluminense.

Although the frontiers between territories controlled by drug traffickers are 'hot spots' of homicidal violence in Rio de Janeiro, this still leaves the wider pattern of violence in Carioca society and the rest of Brazil to be explained. Although drug trafficking is central to patterns of violence, other kinds of crimes, such as theft of vehicles, bank robberies, assaults on buses, kidnapping and extortion, are also increasing. Physical violence tends to be central to all of these crimes. A victim who 'reacts' to an assault (even through a gesture of anger rather than active resistance) can easily get killed, especially now that more assaults involve guns, often in the hands of teenagers. Sexual crime, including trafficking of minors for sex tourism, and rape inside and outside domestic contexts, much of which remains unreported, is another major preoccupation.[3] Although the principal focus should remain on men, disturbing patterns of sexualized violence are emerging among female as well as male adolescents as young as fifteen years of age in poor neighbourhoods, including stabbings motivated by jealousy over unfaithful boyfriends. In Bahia, a fourteen-year-old girl was tortured by three other adolescents of fourteen, fifteen and seventeen years of age for having sex with the boyfriend of one of the aggressors. A participant in the event made a video of it on her cell phone, which was posted on the Internet by another girl not present at the time.[4] Since both participation in drug trafficking and sexual activity begin at a young age, one might speculate about connections, connections that were explicit in the case of two young girls in Salvador, aged sixteen and thirteen, who were tortured and beheaded by members of a gang in a neighbouring community on the suspicion that they had conspired with the gang of their own neighbourhood to lead their rivals into a trap (Eça 2011). Neoliberal capitalist cultures of production of the self through consumption may also play a role in the escalation of violence, not simply by creating desires that many individuals cannot satisfy without participating in the illegal economy, but also by their remorseless promotion of sexuality as a lifestyle imperative and marketing tool.

It is, however, important to recognize that violence is nothing new in Latin American societies and that much of it has been meted out historically by elites in the name of 'order and progress' and 'social cleansing'. The first hill settlement to be named a *favela* in Rio de Janeiro was occupied by soldiers who had fought in the war of extermination against the millenarian community of landless peasants, former slaves, indigenous people and social bandits founded by Antônio the Counsellor in Canudos, in the backlands of Bahia, in 1893. *Favela* was the name of a local species of tree that was abundant in the hills surrounding Canudos (Da Cunha 1984: ch. 4).[5] The oligarchic and militaristic government of the First Republic failed to make good on its promise to provide land in the capital for the discharged soldiers. For many Cariocas, nothing much has changed over the years. Rio still has a serious deficit of affordable housing for poor people. Scheduled demolition, in preparation for the World Cup, of the Favela do Metrô, close to the Maracanã football stadium, left some of the existing residents who were to be relocated still living among the rubble because their new homes were not ready, and delays to the redevelopment of the site allowed new squatters to move in (Phillips 2011). The squatters were still there in June 2014, the month that the World Cup was due to start, hoping that if the redevelopment had still not taken place, it never would (Wrede 2014). The scale of police killings of poor young men of colour is disproportionate. Although it is always justified on the grounds that the subject resisted arrest in a manner that threatened the officer's life, human rights activists frequently encounter evidence that victims were shot at close range in extrajudicial executions. This aspect of the policing of *favelas* reinforces the idea of continuity in a racially exclusionary politics of urban space (Costa Vargas 2013: 278–9), despite the fact that a significant number of *favela* residents have succeeded in achieving social mobility through spatial mobility over the years (Perlman 2010; Cavalcanti 2014).

Traditions of violence are not restricted, however, to violence by the upper classes against the lower classes. Political violence in which local politicians contract killers to dispose of rivals is still not that uncommon in contemporary Brazil. More prosperous citizens also sometimes hire contract killers to provide solutions to personal disputes. Some of Brazil's more affluent citizens simply find association with the world of crime exciting. A colourful example from Bahia concerns two young women, aged nineteen and twenty-one, who were caught driving a stolen car in a military police 'blitz', an operation in which motorists are forced to pass through a checkpoint. Residents of an upscale condominium, one was the daughter of an official of the Federal Justice Ministry. They admitted to being friends with a woman who had been imprisoned for participating in the transport of cocaine from São Paulo to Salvador, partner of a member of the Comando da Paz crime faction who had been particularly noted for violence, and eventually killed by police. The women even said they had looked after her son while she was in prison (Meneses 2013). Civil police investigators told the press that they were suspected of being drug 'mules' and thoroughly involved in the world of crime. Yet they wept on the day of their arraignment before a judge, and their lawyers succeeded in securing their release on bail, arguing that they had money and no criminal records.[6] Members of the public commenting on the release of these '*patricinhas*'[7] on the *Correio da Bahia* newspaper website were indignant about this latest evidence of impunity for the privileged. One could not resist observing that their fate would have been very different had they been poor black women stealing milk for their babies. Two added that now that they were media celebrities, they would probably get invited to pose nude for *Playboy* magazine.

It is therefore important to remember that the powerful do not necessarily provide good role models when considering the supposed criminality and violence of the people of the urban periphery. With that idea in mind, I turn to São Paulo.

São Paulo: criminal power and state power

Given the death tolls and firepower involved, it has become commonplace, both in the mass media and among law enforcement agents, to compare the violence associated with drug trafficking in Brazil to a 'war', and even to talk about the need to combat 'insurgency' on the part of 'organized crime'. It is true that at certain moments violence perpetrated by criminals against the police does appear more aggressive than defensive, even amounting to a kind of 'terrorism', in the sense that it is intentionally spectacular and designed to provoke fear among the general public. This would provide a superficial reading of the violence perpetrated by the PCC in São Paulo in 2006. Yet it would not capture the underlying logic of what happened in 2006 or why history seemed to be repeating itself six years later.

The PCC was originally created in 1993, in the prison of Taubaté in the interior of São Paulo (Serapião 2014). Its original *raison d'être* was to organize the inmates so that they could cope better with the brutality of prison guards and the abysmal living conditions typical of Brazil's overcrowded prisons. This was in the immediate aftermath of the massacre of 111 prisoners that followed the military police's storming of the Carandiru penitentiary to suppress a protest riot in 1992, a tragedy that was not subject to a judicial process to examine the culpability of the police involved until twenty years after the event (Ferreira et al. 2012). Although seventy-three police were finally convicted of seventy-seven murders, the court allowed them to remain at liberty pending appeal, and survivors of the massacre felt that history could easily repeat itself in the future (Mendes Jr 2014). The PCC continues to draw strength from the defects of the Brazilian prison system. Its slogan, 'Peace, Justice, Liberty and Equality', reflects a second phase in its development that began in 2002, when discontent with the violence of its original leaders led to the assumption of command by Marcos Willians Herbas Camacho, aka 'Marcola', which produced a more predictable management of relations between prisoners (Serapião 2014). Indiscriminate violence ended, although violence might still be used where dialogue failed to resolve conflicts. Use of crack cocaine was prohibited, along with rapes, and only killings ordered by the PCC leadership were tolerated (Biondi 2010). Marcola's leadership brought two major changes to the character of the PCC.

The first was that in interviews given from his prison, statements issued through his lawyers, and messages diffused through the PCC's internal channels of communication, Marcola skilfully deployed a discourse focused on human rights and linkages between crime and social deprivation to project both himself and his organization in a sympathetic way (Holston 2009). Within this rhetorical frame, crime became the response of the poor to an unjust social order, and the PCC promoted 'war against the police and peace and equality amongst the thieves' (Biondi 2010). Originally incarcerated for robbing banks, Marcola had plenty of time on his hands in jail for reading philosophical classics, and his intellectual powers are not simply rhetorical. His second innovation was to reorganize the PCC into a vertically integrated crime organization based on an efficient division of specialized functions between sectors dedicated to drug trafficking, finances, and the management of operations in São Paulo, regional cities, and, as the organization extended its activity after 2006, other states of Brazil and other countries in which drugs marketed by the PCC were produced, such as Paraguay and Bolivia (Serapião 2014). These broad divisions are subdivided by responsibilities for different complementary activities. The sector responsible for managing trafficking operations, for example, has a 'discipline' division responsible for ensuring that the normative principles of the Marcola-era PCC are implemented in practice in the neighbourhoods and cities under its control. It supervises the administration of punishments, determines what kinds of punishments are appropriate, and regulates disputes between members. Another division organizes material and legal support for imprisoned members and their families.

The PCC has the capacity to respond to bad publicity. Serapião mentions two examples from messages informing the base of decisions made by the leadership (*salves*) intercepted by the Group for Special Actions to Combat Organized Crime (GAECO). One relates to burning buses: 'We are against the oppression of the community and it is the community that uses the buses.' The other related to the killing of the five-year-old child of a Bolivian immigrant who cried while his parents' house was being robbed. The message saying that it was prohibited to kill children during the commission of crimes was reinforced by the execution of two individuals accused of this infraction in São Paulo jails. Michel Misse (2007: 140–50) has cautioned against the unreflective use of the term 'organized crime' in the Brazilian context, arguing that 'such is the diversity of crimes and their contexts and the number of social organizations capable of committing them that sweeping them all under the same umbrella expression is bound to lead to considerable errors'. He is even more sceptical of the use of the term 'mafia', although, as we will see in the next chapter, ordinary people do sometimes refer to 'the mafia of crime', especially when thinking about the relationships between criminals and politicians. Nevertheless, Gabriel Feltran has argued that even though there are other criminal factions, independent gangs and unaffiliated individuals, including delinquent kids, committing illegal acts in the spaces in which the PCC has influence, so that this organization only controls part of the illicit markets even in its native São Paulo, the PCC does have special significance as an ordering force, as an organization that seeks to regulate the normative order of the entire 'world of crime' (Feltran 2010b: 123).

The PCC does have some practices that are reminiscent of the Italian mafia, which have aided the expansion of its networks. One is the custom of existing members 'baptizing' new 'brothers', which is based on a careful process of prior evaluation, implies a 'commitment to crime' on the part of those who accept the invitation, and requires them to pay monthly contributions to the organization, in and out of jail (Biondi 2010). In return, their families are guaranteed protection and support. Those who do not become 'brothers' can still be 'cousins' if they agree to abide by the PCC's ethnical code. Some 'brothers' become 'pilots', charged with guaranteeing order in sections of prisons or neighbourhoods.

Another development consistent with Serapião's hypothesis that the PCC is at least a 'pre-mafia' is the way that its increasing economic muscle, fortified by the addition of the proceeds of bank robberies, kidnapping and extortion to its drugs-based portfolio, allows it an increasing penetration of the legitimate economic sphere as well as the kinds of relationships with politicians that Brazilian traffickers have always tried to build to buy protection. In 2014, a PT deputy in the São Paulo state congress, Luiz Moura, was accused of having attended a meeting of a transport cooperative in which thirteen PCC members were also present. This case perhaps presents little that is surprising, given that Moura had been born in poverty, been imprisoned for armed robbery, and made himself a rich man by his entrepreneurship in the period in which clandestine transport services were being regularized into an alternative transport sector (Pagnan et al. 2014).

But it could be indicative of trends that may develop further if the PCC continues to expand its networks nationally.[8] Nevertheless, how far and in what directions the PCC will develop is as much a political question as a policing and judicial question, as the events of 2006 and 2012 demonstrate.

In 2006, a veritable war broke out between the PCC and the police of São Paulo. An in-depth investigation by the NGO *Justiça Global* and a team from Harvard Law School showed that the immediate cause of the outbreak of hostilities was extortion of the relatives of imprisoned PCC leaders by serving police officers (Ribeiro Delgado et al. 2011). Violence escalated because the police responded with a campaign of extrajudicial executions that left 120 dead (compared with forty-eight police). It ended after a military police helicopter took a senior functionary and Marcola's lawyer to the penitentiary in which the latter was incarcerated. Although the negotiation of a ceasefire deal is still officially denied, it appears that the state government agreed to allow the PCC to continue to run the jails. The renewal of violence in 2012 resulted from violation of the terms of this pact. The PCC began to launch new attacks on the police after two violent raids on PCC meetings in the urban periphery, one of them called to adjudicate a matter brought to the PCC's alternative justice system. In the first case six people, and in the second nine, were executed in clear violation of the understanding that the police would not harm any criminal who offered to surrender (Martins 2012). Worse, state governor Geraldo Alckmin initially appeared to endorse this change of policy, although he was subsequently obliged to make a strong condemnation of a police execution that a member of the public filmed from a house across the street. Another disturbing revelation was that it appeared that other police officers had sold the PCC computerized lists containing the full names, phone numbers and residential addresses of some of their colleagues (Caramante and Benites 2012). This not only increased the risks facing serving and retired members of the force and their families, but also revealed relationships between the guardians of public order and the criminal organization that talk of 'wars' on both sides served to obscure.

When police kill without attempting to capture delinquents or engage in revenge campaigns of extermination, it is difficult to make the distinction between aggressive and defensive action that the 'criminal insurgency' metaphor implies. What is clear, however, is the role of political considerations in the development of the PCC. The opposition Brazilian Social Democratic Party, PSDB, still controls São Paulo state, although the PT candidate won the 2012 municipal elections against former PSDB presidential candidate Jose Serra. More or less the same group of politicians and officials still running the state presided over the 2006 events and, according to the *Justiça Global* report, did nothing to discipline officials who were at fault on that occasion or attend to continuing causes of grievance such as conditions inside the prison system. Serapião argues that the state government might have strangled the PCC at birth at low political cost by pursuing a more civilized policy in its jails, although the prison problem is clearly wider than São Paulo and did indeed manifest itself in the form of similar violence in Santa Catarina in 2012. Yet now that it has endured two major confrontations and expanded its networks beyond São Paulo, eliminating the PCC by attempting to disarticulate its leadership simply by changing the conditions of their incarceration, or attacks on the PCC's brotherhood outside the prisons, is a task of a different order of magnitude. For São Paulo itself, the immediate political problem may be that the decline in homicide rates in the metropolis in recent years owes more to the rise of the PCC than to the actions of the government, something that Marcola himself has already claimed to be the case.

In making this claim, Marcola is supported by the ethnographic research of sociologists and anthropologists who have worked on the urban periphery of São Paulo, in particular Vera Telles (2010) and Gabriel Feltran (Feltran 2010a, b). Feltran points out that residents of the São Paulo periphery do have access to the official justice system, and the support of specialized government agencies in making use of that access. Yet there are three other normative apparatuses for regulating conduct and managing violence that coexist with the official judicial apparatus and do not always compete with it (Feltran 2010b: 111). These are the 'law of crime', administered by the PCC, another apparatus that creates rules and predictability through 'the de facto action of low-ranking police officers, who interact directly with the official law as well as with the members of the "crime world" and their modus operandi', and 'the law of God', associated with churches (ibid.). Throughout Brazil, church membership provides an important exit strategy from 'the world of crime' (Goldstein 2003). Evangelical churches in particular offer the kind of redemption and rehabilitation of former criminals that the prison system fails to provide. Although church affiliations can produce intra-community conflict, churches also mediate in disputes and can provide support to individuals with problems such as domestic violence and delinquent children.

The PCC apparatus provides residents with a kind of security, and in this it is at first sight similar to other drug trafficking gangs that establish control over a territory. Thieves who rob their neighbours, and rapists,[9] tend to be harshly treated. Yet 'the law of crime' administered by the PCC is not summary justice, since it is based on argument for and against the accused within deliberative procedures known as 'debates'. Feltran argues that 'debates' not only mimic the official justice system but have also 'occupied the legitimate space of the apparatus of violence previously regulated by practices of "popular justice" such as lynching and payments to assassins' (Feltran 2010b: 111). This is an important way in which PCC hegemony in the urban periphery may have contributed to São Paulo's declining homicide rates, but it is also important for understanding how the normative apparatus of the PCC can be situationally flexible, thereby increasing its legitimacy. Feltran recounts the case of a man on the run from prison who ran a drug-selling point. He was accused of being an informer after police who arrested him had allegedly persuaded him to cut a deal in order to avoid being returned to jail, and then subjected to a 'debate' by the main trafficker in his neighbourhood, who had been told of his treason by one of his own police contacts. Since the trafficker knew and respected the accused's mother, and the evidence was not conclusive, he decided to order him to 'disappear' from São Paulo before the 'brothers' got wind of the case. But the 'brothers' found out before the accused reached the bus station, and ordered a second 'debate' in which they would participate. Although some were in favour of immediate execution, there was no consensus since others remained uncertain and were reluctant to create 'bad feeling' by overturning the decision of an older and respected trafficker (ibid.: 125–6). Since decisions require a consensus, the 'brothers' ratified the decision to punish the accused by permanent exile. Although the accused was savagely beaten during his return journey to the bus station and could still be killed by PCC members in his eventual destination, his mother went to thank the 'brothers' for sparing his life (ibid.: 126).

The trafficker who made the original decision was an 'independent' rather than a PCC member, so this case illustrates the extent of the hegemony that the PCC normative apparatus has achieved over conduct in the entire 'world of crime', something that the crime networks of other states have not succeeded in replicating. Feltran also argues that the 'legal structure' of the PCC not only guides those involved in crime in their relations with both the criminal world and the police, but also orientates the entire community (ibid.: 125). If a person is robbed or killed by someone other than a police officer, the family would likely seek justice from the 'brothers', who would hold a 'debate' to adjudicate the complaint and determine the punishment of the perpetrator should it be upheld (ibid.: 127). If the police arrested someone without cause or gave someone a beating, going to the press or human rights defenders would be more appropriate (ibid.). Yet the 'ordering work' of the Paulista police themselves is also articulated to the PCC system. The police classify residents as either 'workers' (honest people) or 'bandits', and they learn about which families are most heavily involved in crime. Feltran recounts a case in which police arrested a young man whom they identified as a member of a 'bandit' family, and explicitly told him that they were going to talk to 'the Command' about 'solving his problem' (ibid.: 120). The case reveals a regular connection between the police and local members of the PCC who are known to them personally and with whom they maintain 'understandings' that are financial. The suspect was taken to the police station, but he was no longer there when his relatives arrived: the police received 15,000 *reais* for his release without charge and the lawyer, who was relieved of the necessity of making a legal argument, 1,000 (ibid.: 124).

This is another way in which the PCC contributes to the reduction of violence, in the sense that this kind of 'collaboration' reduces the potential incidence of shootouts between police and criminals. Nevertheless, it seems that extrajudicial killings by police in São Paulo, including actions carried out by extermination squads using motorbikes, continued beyond the 'state of exception' created in 2012, and unwritten pacts may reduce but do not eliminate shootouts (Salvadori and Cardoso 2014). Although the PCC itself carries out executions, it seems to have achieved a high level of legitimacy because of its willingness to hear both sides of the story in a formal way, 'make the punishment fit the crime' according to its own normative standards, and its interest in maintaining community sociability and the 'respect' due to criminals as well as honest citizens. The effectiveness of its regulation is measurable in terms of the elimination of 'self-help' justice and unauthorized revenge killings. This is an unintended consequence of the PSDB state government's allowing its enthusiasm for the penal state and electoral considerations to override its concern about the growing strength of the PCC, along with the pragmatic eagerness of some police officers to diminish the risks of their job and improve their earnings by accommodating themselves to the regulatory role of the PCC in the 'world of crime'.

Nevertheless, the possibility of another 'war' breaking out between the PCC and the police, and the continuity of this kind of violence at lower intensity, reflects the way that the culture of the security apparatus and police corporation in São Paulo continues to reflect the values of the era of military dictatorship, as well as efforts that are now being made to undermine the organization and finances of the PCC. In April 2014, the military police of São Paulo issued an official press release in response to an interview by a retired colonel who lamented the fact that the police still treated the population of the urban periphery as a potential enemy in the manner of the dictatorship. In its response, the police argued that they had been practising a style of 'community policing' appropriate for a modern democratic society since 1987, highlighted the good work the force was doing in schools, and defended its record on prosecuting officers guilty of corruption or illegal violence. But the statement also vigorously denounced academics and journalists who advocated the demilitarization of the police in the following terms:

> In what world do these 'specialists' ground their theories? Very probably the answer would be in another century and another continent, born in the head of someone who advocated the diffusion of a hegemonic model, which should be constructed by scattering intellectuals through parties, universities and the media. Consequently undermining the basic and solid structures of morality, such as family, school and religion. And in the end ruining state structures, the institutions of democracy. That's how the discourse of these 'organic intellectuals', as they are usually known, is in harmony with the revolutionary ideas of the Italian Antonio Gramsci, which echoed round the world from the decade of the 1930s onwards. (Lima 2014)

In other words, advocates of police reform are communist subversives, and the social role of the police is to defend the state and traditional bases of morality such as 'family, school and religion'. That kind of language suggests that the authors of this statement grounded their own theories in the period between 1964 and 1985.

Rio de Janeiro: the UPP experience

The organization of drug trafficking in Rio is very different from that in São Paulo. Michel Misse (1997) has emphasized that control of drug trafficking in Rio de Janeiro's *favelas* is highly fragmented. There was a stage, beginning at the end of the 1970s, when a single organization, the Red Command (*Comando Vermelho*), controlled the drugs trade throughout the city. But ten years later the panorama was one of violent competition between a series of organizations, with local gangs exercising precarious armed control over highly segmented territories. The level of police repression was increased after the populist Leonel Brizola ended his second period as Rio state governor in 1994. Brizola, looking to the urban poor as much as organized labour as a political base, had combined humane objectives with pragmatically clientelistic practices. He favoured provision of services and infrastructure over efforts to evict those whose occupation of land was illegal, and halted repressive police actions in *favelas*. Although the political right blame Brizola for surrendering the *favelas* to the control of drug traffickers, his successors' renewal of police repression did not provide a victory for 'law and order'. On the contrary, the change of policy increased the opportunities available to Rio's police to make money by selling the drugs they captured, and by selling firearms to the very criminals that they were supposed to persecute. Even when the police did actually persecute traffickers, they often simply extorted money from them in return for letting them go free. Nor was police corruption the only cause of a steady expansion of informal, illegal and criminal markets in which state agents participated: 'political commodities' were also transacted within this framework (ibid.). As Enrique Arias (2006a) also showed through his ethnographic research in three Rio *favelas*, local criminals not only forged backstage patron–client relations with 'legitimate' community leaders and organizations such as churches, NGOs and residents' associations, they also extended their networks beyond the community to include 'respectable' politicians who provided protection in return for the traffickers' services in mobilizing votes in elections (or impeding campaigning by rivals).

This prompted Arias to reject the contention that high levels of violence in *favelas* reflected 'the absence of the state' and the development of an independent 'parallel power' in the hands of traffickers. The problem was not the 'failure' of institutions but the way they worked, through networks that connected community leaders, politicians, police and criminals (Arias 2006b), something that is equally important for understanding the rise of the militias (Misse 2007).

As anthropologist Luiz Eduardo Soares (2006) pointed out, it was unlikely that public security policies would benefit the people who actually live in *favelas* while police and criminals blurred into one another as two sides of a single coin, which is exactly how poor citizens have long tended to view the matter, as Teresa Caldeira (2002) showed for São Paulo. Soares was briefly state secretary for public security in Rio de Janeiro until governor Anthony Garotinho dismissed him in 2000. He advocated a new model of community policing in *favelas* linked to social development projects. It seems to have been the very success of this early experiment with a 'proximity' policing model that aimed to build a relationship of trust between residents and police which led to Soares's removal, as a result of pressure from the police high command backed by politicians who had been benefiting from their manipulation of Misse's 'illegal and criminal informal political market' (Arias 2006a: 36). The withdrawal of the new police units not only allowed the traffickers to return, but also provoked 'settling of scores' with those who had welcomed the state's presence. This may be one reason why residents of communities in which UPPs were installed expressed anxiety about whether the units might be withdrawn after the World Cup and Olympics were over.

The present UPP programme was introduced under the state government headed by Sergio Cabral, of the PMDB, in partnership with Secretary of Public Security Jose Mariano Beltrame.[10] Re-elected for a second term in 2010, Cabral resigned on 3 April 2014, supposedly to allow his son to run for the state congress, turning over the governorship to vice-governor Luis Fernando Pezão. A less charitable interpretation, adopted by several quality newspapers, was that the flagship policy of his two mandates, the UPP, was now so discredited that it had become an electoral liability for his successor, although Pezão, with PT support, did in the end secure a second-round majority in the October elections.[11] Secretary Beltrame continued to enjoy public esteem for having refused invitations to run for political office when the UPP programme was generally getting an excellent press. Yet, as João H. Costa Vargas (Costa Vargas 2013: 288) points out, this positive mass media coverage also 'revealed core socially shared principles on which the new public security paradigm rested', principles that produced 'a telling conflation of the danger produced by the gangs and the alleged danger produced by and in *favelas*'. In other words, it reinforced a securitization of social disadvantage, with racialized undertones, that distorted understandings of social life in *favelas* by erasing positive aspects such as a sense of community and neighbourliness. It even distorted understanding of the deeper causes and empirical patterns of violence in Rio de Janeiro.

The partnership between Cabral and Beltrame in forging a new public security policy for Rio began on 7 May 2007, once again in the context of the city's hosting of a sporting mega-event, the Pan American Games. Rio's military police and 'elite squad' Special Police Operations Battalion (BOPE), supported by 1,280 troopers of the newly created federal National Security Force, laid siege to the sixteen communities of the Complexo do Alemão group of *favelas*, screening all those entering and leaving them to enter the 'asphalt' area of the city (Alves and Evanson 2011). Alves and Evanson found ample evidence from first-hand testimonies and photographs taken by residents that members of the federal force also entered the communities. They recorded the deaths of forty-three people during the siege, including children killed by 'stray bullets'. They also give a chilling account, based on the testimony of teachers in a *favela* outside the Alemão complex, of the dangers to staff and children and the disruption of schooling created by police habitually using a school as a firing base in operations against 'bandits' in nearby drug-selling points. On some occasions, the police drove their 'Big Skull' armoured vehicle right into the schoolyard. This, then, was public security as 'war' in a very direct way.

The UPP programme is, however, supposed to pursue a different logic. According to data compiled by the International Observatory of Violence and Drug-Trafficking (Observatório Internacional de Violência e Narcotráfico, Obivan), funded by the Soros Open Society Foundation, police raids were responsible for more than half the violent confrontations that occurred in Rio's *favelas* prior to the introduction of UPPs. In consequence the police were also responsible for most of the 'collateral damage' caused by firefights with traffickers or indiscriminate discharging of weapons by nervous police officers in public places. This led Benjamin Lessing, Obivan's coordinator, to argue, in an interview with BBC Brasil,[12] that the UPPs offer a more intelligent strategy of 'conditional repression'. Since the occupation of *favelas* is pre-announced, traffickers have an opportunity to flee, and even if they do not take it, they will not be harmed if they surrender without resorting to violence. The Rio UPP's official programme is based on the notion that the state is 'taking back' control of territories lost to armed non-state actors, but simultaneously reassuming responsibility not only for improving the welfare of the citizens it has abandoned but also for enhancing their ability to enjoy the full rights of citizenship. These include being able to vote for the candidate of one's choice in elections without coercion from armed actors and being guaranteed security by a police that will respect residents by adopting a community policing model.

The Cabral–Beltrame approach was inspired by methods used to reduce violence in the Colombian city of Medellín (Fleury 2012: 199). Although Medellín was still number 35 in the world ranking of violent cities in 2013 (Consejo Ciudadano para la Seguridad Pública y Justicia Penal, A.C. 2014), its homicide rates did fall substantially. Yet although the situation in Medellín today is different from the days when the cartel led by Pablo Escobar dominated the city, poor citizens do not necessarily view this as a change for the better, as the Brazilian newspaper *Folha de São Paulo* revealed in a report published in 2014 with an intentional sideways glance at Rio, which also copied Medellín's installation of a cable car to connect the upper parts of a *favela* to the city below in Complexo do Alemão (Colombo 2014). City budgets have been inadequate to maintain the improvements to urban infrastructure that accompanied Medellín's 'pacification', and small drug trafficking bands called *combos* have replaced Pablo Escobar's cartel. Whereas Escobar was lavish in his 'help' to the poor, in this more fragmented world of trafficking the *combos* expel families from neighbourhoods when one of their members crosses the 'invisible lines' traced by the rival groups and extort money from those that remain. The future that awaits Rio will also be influenced by the way that criminal groups reorganize in the face of *favela* pacification. That scenario will be further complicated by the presence of the militias, broader tendencies in development of 'protection rackets' linked to private security, and the particular dynamics of Rio's processes of urban restructuring.

The installation of a UPP is the second stage of the process that begins with the 'reconquest' of territory, normally undertaken by military police units, although federal armed forces have continued to participate in the occupations of large *favelas*, as they did in Vila Cruzeiro and Complexo do Alemão at the end of 2010. Despite anxieties on the part of commanders that troops would succumb to the same temptations to corruption as the police if they remained in the *favelas*, and some proven episodes of robbery from residents' houses by police during operations in which the officers were supposed to be hunting for traffickers, at first sight the pacification policy evolved relatively smoothly. When, in November 2011, security forces occupied Rocinha, one of Rio's largest and most visible *favelas*, its principal drug lord, Antonio Francisco Bonfim Lopes, aka 'Nem', was unable to escape imprisonment despite offering a gigantic bribe to the police who discovered him, hidden in the boot of a car that belonged to the Consulate of the Democratic Republic of Congo (Barón 2011). Federal police subsequently captured some of Nem's lieutenants who had paid civil and military police contacts to break through the cordon established around the community. A Residents' Association leader, linked to the traffickers and a councilwoman from the PSDB, was soon under arrest as well (Costa 2011). Thirty-five years old, Nem, linked to the Friends of Friends (*Amigos de Amigos*) criminal network, had murdered his way to the top in Rocinha. Yet he achieved a huge capacity to suborn public officials, and, in the aftermath of the pacification, at least some light was shed on the political and even diplomatic networks that had enabled him to conduct his business with impunity.

As the months went by, however, events diminished the initial euphoria. It became clear that even though the main drug processing operations might have been transferred elsewhere, drug trafficking had not been eliminated in Rocinha. Assaults and thefts were actually increasing: residents complained to the press that this kind of thing simply didn't happen when Rocinha was subject to the 'law of crime' (Gomide 2011). On 26 March 2012, a community leader was shot dead. Although the police presence was reinforced, and arrests made after information was received from residents,[13] the next month brought an exchange of fire between police and traffickers, who escaped, and complaints against the police began to increase.[14] On 21 April, a female resident accused three officers of torture and rape.[15] Three days after this incident, and additional reports of shooting, another 130 police were sent into the neighbourhood. These officers had been trained to patrol on foot and in techniques of 'proximity policing'.[16] But in September, a week before the permanent police base was due for inauguration, a policeman was killed. Governor Cabral put a brave face on the incident by declaring that the violence reflected the desperation of the traffickers. Before the pacification, he remarked, the police were the invaders; now it was the 'bandits' who were in that position (Costa et al. 2012). But Secretary Beltrame conceded that many months of occupation had not eliminated the 'parallel power' of the traffickers within the community and that 'pacification is a job that hasn't finished' (Martins and Brito 2012).

UPP community policing promised an everyday involvement of police in community development programmes designed to make residents feel that government cared about them and wanted to enhance their job prospects, educational opportunities and living standards. Some residents of the first *favela* to get a UPP, Santa Marta, located in the beachfront neighbourhood of Botafogo in the city's South Zone, initially complained that lack of consultation and community participation before the *favela* was occupied did nothing to enhance their sense of citizenship (Da Cunha 2012: 152). Nevertheless, violent confrontations between police and traffickers ceased to occur in Santa Marta after the UPP was installed. One factor that may be relevant to the apparent success of pacification in Santa Marta in terms of improving the everyday security of the residents and their relations with the police is simply this *favela*'s comparatively small population of 6,000 residents (ibid.: 145). Nevertheless, Sonia Fleury's fieldwork in Santa Marta confirmed that significant tensions persisted after pacification, and that many residents still did not feel that their citizenship was being fully recognized, let alone enhanced (Fleury 2012). The social projects dimension of pacification was much slower in arriving than the security dimension. It was only in October 2011, three years after the initial occupation, that the first assembly of the 'Social UPP' was convened, the delay being justified by the fact that Santa Marta already had more resources than some of the other pacified communities. So it did, but the public resources available to residents were located outside the *favela*, while those that existed within it were the fruits of the struggles of the residents themselves to gain public or NGO funding for their own projects, which included a crèche, a community radio, a cooperative, a cultural group, a community newspaper and a residents' association (ibid.: 211).

Fleury shows how recognition of these achievements was made difficult by the way that the state and the police understood the community that was being pacified. Although the first commander of the Santa Marta UPP was sympathetic enough to establish good relations with residents, the mission of the unit was 'disciplinary' in a sense that went beyond the 'ostensive' type of policing necessary to keep the traffickers out of the reclaimed territory. Despite its history of self-organization to secure services and build community projects, Santa Marta was seen as a 'disordered' place. Since any public social event was seen as a potential threat to order, permission had to be sought from the police. *Baile funk* music and dance were initially prohibited altogether, because of their association with drug traffickers in the minds of the authorities, although the ban proved somewhat contradictory because affluent young Brazilians and tourists also like *baile funk* (ibid.: 213). The disciplining of the *favela* population extended to the disposal of rubbish and prohibition of illegal connections to the electricity grid and cable TV network. The residents did not reject the principle that they should start paying for services, but since they did find the new costs difficult to meet, they sought, without any immediate success, to negotiate 'social tariffs' with the city government. They also complained that they still lacked the basic infrastructure that it was the responsibility of the state to provide, in particular good sanitation.

Fleury argues that pacification produces a strong subjection of 're-conquered' territories to the market which includes the establishment of new commercial businesses and formalization of existing ones, and a trend towards commodification that is reinforced by state-sponsored training courses on 'entrepreneurialism', which have been promoted in poor communities throughout Brazil. Other analysts of Rio de Janeiro, such as James Freeman (2012), have also explored this relationship between pacification and the deepening incorporation of *favelas* into neoliberal market society. Freeman points out that pacification is very big business. The privatized city electricity company Light, co-owned by Brazilian, French and US investors, reported that its receipts in

Santa Marta had increased 5,437 per cent; Light was expecting to increase its revenues in the vastly bigger Rocinha *favela* from 3.2 to 24 million *reais* annually (ibid.: 118). *Favelados* are not exactly outside neoliberal market society, as the invasions of upscale shopping centres by poor kids that are called *rolezinhos* ('little outings') demonstrate. Although some citizens, police and security guards assumed that the kids had come to rob, most had in fact come to spend money like anyone else, and simply wished to participate in consumer society in the same kind of 'safe space' as middle-class people. The problem the *favelados* face is the way that other classes' definitions of what enhances their own 'security' tends to exclude the residents of what Wacquant (2007) calls 'territorially stigmatized' areas from some spaces of market society while coercively including them in others.

Fleury records that Santa Marta residents still did not feel that they were being offered real participation in planning the development of their community three years after pacification, despite the fact that new commercial developments within it threatened the removal of some families (Fleury 2012: 215). The growing intrusiveness of tourists was another bone of contention. Yet the community was not homogeneous, and some residents were not opposed to those kinds of changes. The police viewed 'autochthonous' cultural activities with suspicion, as potential vehicles for resistance, but appeared to have secured the compliance of the Residents' Association by means that those less happy about the coercive nature of the regime could only speculate about (ibid.: 217). An attempt by one group of residents to start a human rights initiative in response to 'truculent' police behaviour in stop and search operations was also viewed as a manifestation of 'resistance' to the UPP that could indicate the continuing influence of the traffickers (ibid.: 218). Although the neighbourhood had become more secure in the sense that shooting had stopped, dissatisfaction about the continuation of other sources of insecurity, such as the slowness of land titling, was compounded by a stronger regulation of domestic construction work that prevented residents from improving their self-built homes (ibid.: 217).

As we will see in the next chapter, a large part of Fleury's observations and analysis would apply equally well to the very much bigger neighbourhood in which I have done my own fieldwork in Salvador, Bahia. But it was not simmering resentment which provoked growing public disenchantment with the Rio de Janeiro UPP programme and turned it into a wasting political asset for Sergio Cabral, whose popularity was also diminished by the disproportionately violent response of the military police to the 2013 World Cup protests, which shocked parents of middle-class students who were beaten, and repeated violence in police repression of protests against forced removals of population and of homeless people trying to occupy empty buildings.

First, ending confrontations between police and drug traffickers in the larger *favela* complexes proved far more difficult than in Santa Marta. By 2014 violence had even returned to Cidade de Deus, the second *favela* to be pacified, previously hailed as another success story to be shown to visiting foreign leaders, including Barack Obama (Silva 2014). Secondly, it became increasingly apparent that even some police in the UPPs had not left behind the vices of the past, provoking protests that it became increasingly difficult to dismiss as the result of traffickers manipulating residents who continued to feel more affinity to the world of crime than the new forms of 'order and progress' that pacification was aiming to create. The former commander of the UPP of Morro São Carlos was arrested in February 2012, accused of receiving weekly payments of 15,000 *reais* (6,600 euros) from traffickers, after federal police investigations had revealed the existence of such payments in several UPPs (Torres and Werneck 2012). In September 2014, Colonel Alexandre Fontenelle, third-ranked in the hierarchy of Rio's military police and head of its Special Operations unit, was arrested, along with twenty-two other officers, for running a major extortion racket.[17] But continuing corruption was not the issue which did most to change public sentiment.

The tipping point was the disappearance of a 'worker', the stonemason Amarildo de Souza, in Rocinha *favela* in July 2013. Mr de Souza had last been seen being detained by the police of the UPP, and his wife accused the police of torturing and murdering her husband. The protest that she and her friends and relatives mounted rapidly became viral, receiving the support of Amnesty International and Maria do Rosário, minister of the National Human Rights Secretariat. Governor Cabral's initial response was to argue that it was 'premature' to accuse the police, but this proved a serious political error as the facts of the case began to emerge (Alencastro and Ramalho 2013). It transpired that the UPP's security cameras had been deliberately turned off at the time of the incident. The soldier of the military police who had detained Mr de Souza had been accused three months earlier of menacing two other residents and fabricating evidence against them. Mr de Souza's sixteen-year-old cousin Luiz testified that he had been beaten and suffocated with a plastic bag by the same group of police (Bottari and Ramalho 2013). In October, the major who was the ex-commander of the Rocinha UPP, a lieutenant, sergeant and ten soldiers, surrendered themselves to the justice system after arrest warrants were issued, following an investigation in which twenty-two people had given depositions accusing the UPP police of torturing them.[18] Secretary Beltrame put a brave face on the crisis, arguing that the prompt investigation and prosecution of the police deemed to have been involved showed that there was no justification for impugning the UPP project in general (Elencar 2013). But new accusations against the police were made later in the year in Rocinha, despite the removal from the UPP of the officers accused of killing Mr de Souza.

Protests against UPP police for killing innocent people increased in 2014. The context was a resumption of 'war' between traffickers and the police. This was not simply the result of shootouts that resulted from police operations to root out traffickers, but of a counter-offensive by the traffickers themselves that resulted in the killing or wounding of a growing number of police and direct attacks on UPP bases. Responding to an attack on the UPP base in Cidade de Deus on 25 May 2014, newly installed governor Fernando Pezão admitted that attacks on the UPPs were 'preoccupying' given the imminent start of the World Cup (Paiva 2014). But like his predecessor, he tried to put a positive construction on the situation by observing that the UPP had broken the territorial control of the traffickers and that they were now obliged to come in, shoot and withdraw. When the administration entered office, the governor remarked, there were 21,000 people imprisoned for trafficking. Now there were 37,000. School attendance was up 70 per cent in communities with UPPs, homicides were reduced, and there had now been important economic growth in the pacified areas. Governor Pezão also suggested that, in an election year, his political opponents were trying to score cheap electoral advantages by attacking the administration's public security policy. That latter claim was probably justified, but the other elements of this defence of the policy deserve more critical scrutiny.

One problem is that of explaining persistent police violence, abuse of human rights, and the difficulties which seem to stand in the way of consolidating a 'proximity policing' model. This is an issue to which I will return in depth in the next chapter using my own ethnographic data on Bahia, but in the case of Rio de Janeiro, renewed trafficker aggression is a significant part of the scenario. There was possibly a conjunctural relationship between trafficker aggression and the enhanced business opportunities for drug sales offered by the influx of tourists for the Cup. One group of traffickers who did not need to take a course on becoming 'entrepreneurs' (or perhaps they took one?) even put the World Cup logo and mascot on the plastic pots in which they sold their marijuana and cocaine.[19] Yet not only money but also hyper-masculinity is at stake in the suppression of trafficking. Violence continued after the World Cup: 'conditional repression' has lost ground to more traditional approaches to suppressing crime, and violence may be exacerbated by the way that the UPPs heighten the fragmentation of trafficking in the city.

Medellín's *combos* provide one example of where the policy may lead, but Medellín, with a population of less than two and a half million, is a much smaller city than Rio. The UPP programme is continuing to expand gradually, but it still only covers a relatively small proportion of Rio's *favelas*, selected principally in terms of improving the image of the city as a secure one during sporting mega-events and calming the anxieties of the city's more affluent residents. It is not a cheap programme. The state government spent 6.8 billion *reais* on security in 2012, rising to nearly 8.6 billion in 2013, a rising share of the total budget, while the share of spending on public health remained flat and at a much lower level at 4.28 and 5.3 billion *reais* respectively (Dias 2014). The difference was set to widen in 2014 because of the additional security spending needed on the World Cup. Incarcerating growing numbers of criminals is also a costly business, although it may become an increasingly profitable business for private capital in Brazil, as São Paulo is already showing. Yet despite expenditure on UPPs, residents have been protesting about increases in crime and violence in neighbouring municipalities such as Niterói. At least some of this increase reflects the migration to those other areas of crime suppressed in its original location by the UPPs, and perhaps also by the militias.[20] Bringing the militias into the picture as the other main armed actor operating in Rio's *favelas* also raises further questions about the future trajectory of Rio's 'protection rackets'. There have been reports of *milicianos* in other cities charging for providing 'security' in the new popular housing developments created under the federal government's *Minha Casa Minha Vida* (My House, My Life) programme (Thomé 2014). Although the federal government's response to this was to look to Rio de Janeiro for lessons about 'retaking territory', the proliferation of armed actors produces new insecurities that open up further spaces for practices of extortion.

A major cause of that proliferation is the growth of private security companies, legal and clandestine. At one level, the growth of private security is a defensive reaction by better-off citizens to their lack of confidence in the ability of the state to protect them from crime. But at another level, which I will illustrate with a concrete example in the next chapter, private security can become a means of aggressive action against poor people in pursuit of class interest, when private security guards are used to 'persuade' families to abandon land that is of interest to property developers, for example. In general, when it is a matter of evicting people from their homes when a court order has declared their occupation of a site a violation of the legal rights of its owner, it is the police who will do the evicting in their official capacity. The violence with which police habitually perform this task was illustrated once again in Rio in March 2014 with the beating and teargassing of squatters who had made their homes in an abandoned factory owned by the Oi telephone company.[21] But police are also armed actors in a private capacity in the private sector.

Brazilian police do not consider themselves well paid, and there is no legal prohibition on them taking on other jobs in their off-duty hours. Although these second jobs (called *bicos* in Portuguese) may be something as innocent as running a shop, they are quite often jobs working for private security companies, since the officer comes complete with an authorized weapon.[22] Private security itself may be perfectly legitimate work, such as looking after security at a big party or concert, or doing extra work during Carnival in off-duty hours. Yet it may not be, and when off-duty police participate in privately hired extermination squads or do the dirty work of property developers, what is taking place is the private appropriation of public power. Police who commit illegal acts in their off-duty hours, as *milicianos* or private security agents, may, of course, be arrested and punished. Yet they may also be able to commit a crime with impunity because friends and colleagues in the police and justice systems protect them.

Favela pacification as accumulation by dispossession

This brings me, in concluding this chapter, to return to the question of what consequences Rio's UPP programme might have other than its ostensible purpose of making poor communities more secure and reducing homicide rates. James Freeman (2012) has argued that the UPP is an integral part of a neoliberal urban development strategy that conforms to David Harvey's model of 'accumulation by dispossession' (Harvey 2007). I have already mentioned the part of Freeman's argument that deals with the way the 'reconquest' of *favela* territories enables Light and other companies to increase their revenues, and in general peaceful communities offer improved opportunities for all kinds of different suppliers of legal goods and services. Yet to the extent that pacification does create greater security, it also increases the value of *favela* land and property, and it will also increase the real estate values of homes located on the frontiers of *favelas* whose values were previously depressed by anxieties about 'stray bullets' (Cavalcanti 2014).

Hernando de Soto (2000) argued that those who live in self-built homes actually possess a substantial capital asset, but cannot realize its real value (for credit purposes, for example) if it remains in a situation of juridical irregularity as a result of the dead hand of state regulation. In his view this made the granting of full private property titles an essential step towards emancipating the poor. Yet there has long been a lively informal land market in many of Rio's 'consolidated' *favelas*, where a combination of state investment in infrastructure and family investments in housing has created an environment that would be extremely 'liveable' were it not for the violence, and even the problem of violence could, to some extent, be mitigated by converting the house into a 'fortress' (Cavalcanti 2009). As Kenan Handzic (2010) has shown, 'notorious' Rocinha had one of the most active real estate markets in the city *before* it was pacified. This observation leads him, however, to reject De Soto's emphasis on the virtues of full private property titles. Handzic argues that this would reinforce processes that were already making *favelas* like Rocinha too expensive for existing residents on lower incomes who had to rent, a process that has continued after pacification and has also occurred in Complexo do Alemão, despite the continuing presence of traffickers in both areas. Indeed, a large number of the squatters evicted from the factory owned by Oi were previous residents of Alemão who could no longer afford the rents there (Watts 2014). Although many middle-class Brazilians find the idea of living in a *favela* unattractive, this was not true of younger foreigners, and pre-pacification Rocinha was experiencing a significant degree of 'gentrification'. Some houses even remained unoccupied for part of the year because their owners were satisfied with the high rents paid by tourists coming to the city for Carnival (Handzic 2010: 5). Handzic therefore advocates a 'social interest' type of state-regulated property regime that concedes 'right to use' rather than full private title to land, as a measure to prevent market forces producing the kind of differentiation that would displace poor families. Such families would often be obliged to move to more insecure and environmentally risky settlements that would also greatly increase their transport costs if they remained in their current jobs. This, in turn, would likely create new 'states of insecurity' on the urban periphery. The social and economic problems associated with spatially peripheral locations tend to occur even when government itself relocates *favelados* to newly constructed housing projects in such areas, and may be compounded by poor-quality construction and loss of a sense of community.

In practice, the Rio state government has displayed little interest in interfering with market forces, formal or informal, and pacification has not simply been raising the value of properties in the more peaceful *favelas*, but has also been making the other costs of living in a consolidated, pacified, *favela* much higher. Even restricting titling to the 'concession of right to use' may not, as we will see in the next chapter, guarantee the security of tenure of all families currently living in a *favela*, since they can be removed within the terms of the social interest land regularization process for a variety of other reasons, including environmental risk and competing public interest land uses. In the case of Rio de Janeiro and other cities, *favelados* have been relocated to make way for the improved transport systems, car parks and other facilities required for the World Cup and Olympics. The *favela* of Mangueira, pacified in 2011 and in plain sight of the Maracanã stadium, was graced with a cable car and improved public spaces so that it would create the right visual image for a global television audience. But its transformation from a place that might seem dangerous and threatening into a picture postcard is, as Freeman points out, at the cost of some residents losing their homes (Freeman 2012: 108–9). In De Soto's terms, they are dispossessed of their capital, in return for compensation far lower than the gains that capitalist interests make as a result of the commercial revalorization of the space from which they have been removed.

Another of Freeman's case studies is the redevelopment of the old port area. This transformed the original *'favela* hill', the *favela* of Providência, in which a UPP was installed in 2010. Residents came home from work to find eight hundred of their homes marked for demolition by the Municipal Housing Agency. After this peremptory action, repeated in other Rio *favelas,* they were left to try to make their own way through the labyrinth of bureaucracy in order to find out 'if and when they will actually be removed, and where they will be relocated to if at all' (ibid.: 111–12). Far from providing these residents with greater security, the authorities had injected a profoundly deepened sense of insecurity into their lives. Redevelopment of Rio's port area is designed to create a waterfront complex similar to those of London's Docklands or Barcelona. The building of yet another cable car, financed by money from the federal Programme for Acceleration of Growth (PAC), displaced more residents. Community activists began a protest against this project under the slogan 'cable car for whom?' This made the presence of the UPP useful beyond its original remit of clearing the area of traffickers, since the soldiers could protect workers surveying the soon-to-be-transformed central plaza of Providência (ibid.: 112). In Cruzeiro, the highest part of the community, which offers spectacular views of the city, all houses were scheduled for demolition (ibid.). The answer to the 'for whom?' question is clearly 'for visitors from different social classes and other countries', which includes passengers from cruise ships.

This kind of dispossession of poor working-class people is the basis for a process of capital accumulation of spectacular scale by another social class. The first beneficiaries are the construction companies contracted to build the new facilities, but once the facilities are there, the value of the site where the evicted originally lived becomes incomparably higher and the income streams generated from this transformed urban space vastly greater. Although there was public money in the projects, administration and service provision in this transformed and revalorized space was privatized, right down to the garbage collection (ibid.: 110). By revitalizing 'run-down' areas and not simply 'pacifying' strategically located *favelas* but transforming their social character through a kind of gentrification, Rio aspires to create a neoliberal city that will thrive in the longer term beyond the World Cup and Olympics. In the light of the way that the *favelas* are incorporated into the logic of urban renewal, it is not surprising that promised improvements to infrastructure and services for existing residents, and better public schools and healthcare, supposedly key components of the social dimension of the UPP project, have been slow in materializing and have only materialized in limited ways. It is not simply that the public money has been spent on football stadiums and improving roads that principally benefit the middle and upper classes. A combination of forced removals and market forces should promote differentiation, gentrification and a lowering of population density, provided, that is, these areas can be made safe, not simply for those who might want to live, work and play in them in the future, but also for capital in its eternal quest to expand the field of accumulation.

Accumulation by dispossession based on the class violence of what Neil Smith (2002) termed the 'revanchist' neoliberal city is a Brazil-wide phenomenon that transcends the hosting of sporting mega-events. It is indicative of the close relations that exist between municipal and state governments and real estate development interests. But there could be another way. As Raquel Rolnik, Brazilian urban planner and former UN Special Rapporteur for the Right to Adequate Housing, summed up the general situation with regard to the 'right to the city' of people who live in *favelas*:

> At the very moment when ample public resources are available for investments in the urbanization of the country's *favelas* – with the PAC of the *favelas* – what we observe is the de-constitution of participatory forums and processes, geographical selectivity in the *favelas* to be urbanized and massive processes of eviction in the course of implementing projects and works, frequently with the use of violence. Still graver is the lack of recognition, on the part of municipal authorities, of regularization of tenure as a 'right' of the residents, the theme being treated as a 'social question' and, con-sequently, subject to their discretion, and, in the majority of cases, a lack of balanced consideration of this right through implementa-tion of sustainable alternatives to eviction. (Rolnik 2012)

In the next chapter I explore how this and other problems discussed in this chapter manifest themselves in Salvador, Bahia.

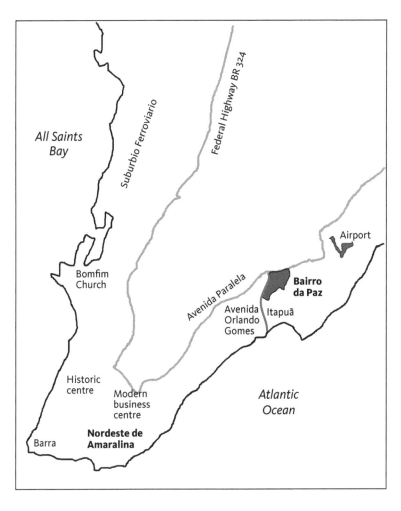

Map 2.1 Salvador, Bahia, showing the location of Bairro da Paz

3 | PACIFYING THE URBAN PERIPHERY: A CASE STUDY OF THE BAHIAN UPP

My research in Bahia focuses on a neighbourhood with around sixty thousand residents formed by a land invasion of a spatially peripheral area of the city during the 1980s, when the country was still ruled by the military (Hita and Gledhill 2010). Originally known as the 'Malvinas Invasion' because of its residents' dogged resistance to attempts to expel them from the land that they had occupied, Bairro da Paz, as it came to be called after the state government called a halt to the policy of forced removal, is particularly sensitive to the issues highlighted in Raquel Rolnik's analysis. Its residents do not possess strong land rights. Located at the intersection of the Avenida Paralela, the major traffic artery linking the international airport to the city centre, and Avenida Orlando Gomes, which connects the Paralela to the attractive beach area of Itapuã and the coastal road into the centre, parts of this settlement will be expropriated to make way for new transport systems planned to smooth the movement of visitors coming to the city and alleviate general problems of congestion. By 2014, the state government's Urban Development Company (CONDER) was embarking on the removal of family homes to make way for expansion of the Orlando Gomes intersection and construction of a metro station on a new line that will follow the route of the Paralela from the airport.

Fear of removal is central to residents' own definitions of the kinds of insecurity that matter most in their lives. This is a community of poor people whose previously empty surroundings have been invaded by middle- and upper-class people. New condominiums are pushing up against the borders of a neighbourhood that now seems out of place in terms of the lifestyle that the development of this area of the twenty-first-century city is supposed to offer. The municipal administration of João Henrique Carneiro, which governed the city for two terms until the end of 2012,[1] had been notoriously helpful to property developers, waiving environmental regulations and turning a blind eye to dubious land transactions. But in truth the

PT administration ruling the state under two-term governor Jacques Wagner was as beholden to property and construction companies for campaign funding as any of its opponents. This increased the anxiety of Bairro da Paz residents about the security of the investments they had made in houses and small businesses, often directly associated with the living space occupied by the families that owned them.

The state government installed the Bahian equivalent of a UPP, a Community Security Base (*Base Comunitária de Segurança*, BCS), in Bairro da Paz in September 2012, on the eve of city government elections won by the candidate of the right-wing Democrats, Antônio Carlos Magalhães Neto, despite these efforts by the PT to be seen to be addressing the city's problems of crime and violence with a firm hand. In May 2013, the new municipal administration announced that Bairro da Paz would be the first neighbourhood in the city to participate in a new project of land regularization named *Casa Legal* (Legal Home), which ultimately aimed to benefit 6,500 families in the community with a title of 'concession of rights of use'.[2] Although 500 titles were distributed by the mayor in July that year, the coordinator of the most inclusive of the neighbourhood's community organizations, the Permanent Forum of Entities of Bairro da Paz (FPEBP), expressed widespread concern among residents about the implications of the project in an area of intense property speculation.[3]

The number of families included in the official estimate of those to benefit from regularization was considerably less than the number resident in the neighbourhood in 2013. Residents feared that regularization would lead to removal of some families on grounds of environmental risk or hitherto unresolved questions about which parts of the total area presently occupied were public lands or not. Community representatives argued that the municipality was failing to carry out stipulations in federal laws that local authorities should make improvements to a settlement's urban infrastructure before proceeding to titling. Such improvements would include road paving and sanitation, but could also include civil engineering works that would eliminate some of the environmental risks to existing self-constructed homes. Some took the view that the real objective of the titling process, and the new surveys on which it would be based, was precisely to reduce the number of residents in the community by declaring their homes unsafe and to free up other areas of the community for redevelopment by the construction companies already working in the surrounding area. At a mass meeting held to consult the residents, the parish priest of the neighbourhood supported the contention that the regularization process might represent the most delicate moment yet in the long history of threats to the community's integrity. None of those present found it easy to forget that it was the grandfather of the new mayor, Antônio Carlos Magalhães, normally known simply as ACM, who had ordered the police to remove the original Malvinas Invasion.

Appointed mayor under the dictatorship, three times state governor, federal cabinet minister and state senator, ACM had commanded a powerful political machine that appeared to be in decline by the time of his death in 2007, but has now revived under the leadership of his equally politically astute grandson. It is therefore reasonable for the residents to be anxious about the implications of the *choque de ordem* (shock of order) that ACM Neto, following the lead of the city government of Rio de Janeiro in 2009, proposed to administer to Salvador. It has involved restrictions on street traders, pedestrianization of roads along the seafront, and other measures that principally benefit tourists and the city's more affluent citizens. His grandfather's programme for modernizing Salvador involved a strong element of 'social cleansing', the forced dispossession of poor black families from areas where their presence impeded the construction of new roads and colonization of space by middle- and upper-class families (Dantas Neto 2006). Yet since public security is principally the responsibility of the state government, which controls the military and civil police, any link that the residents of Bairro da Paz make between 'pacification' and threats of dispossession cannot be laid at the door of the political right alone. Indeed, this is already obvious from the case of Rio de Janeiro, where, in contrast to Bahia, PMDB-dominated state and city governments established cordial relationships with the PT federal administration and have been able to call on federal military forces to support the *favela* pacification programme.

In this chapter I explore the experience of pacification principally from the point of view of Bairro da Paz residents, relating it not only to their previous experiences of the police and justice systems, but also to experiences of domination by a militia, and then by drug traffickers who sought to implement an 'order of crime'. But I will also try to tell the story from the side of the police, not directly from the side of the police posted to Bairro da Paz, since interviewing police stationed there could have provoked ethical problems because of my relationship with the FPEBP and its leadership, but through interviews conducted with police working in other community security bases. Bahia is an appropriate setting in which to consider the police point of view, given that military police went on strike for twelve days in February 2012, just before Carnival, and for forty-three hours, just before the Easter holiday, in April 2014. The first strike provided an opportunity for police to vent what many would consider legitimate grievances, but both episodes also highlighted ways in which deeper reform of policing remains a condition for achieving a public security regime in which all citizens, irrespective of colour or class, can have equal confidence.

The order of the state and the order of crime

Bairro da Paz, as the Malvinas Invasion, was born in violence. Dogged resistance did enable the community to survive until 1987, when Waldir Pires, then a member of the PMDB, formed a broad front of political forces united by their opposition to ACM's political machine and captured the governorship. Although this interruption of Carlista hegemony lasted for only two years, it proved sufficient to end the threat of eviction and over the next two decades the neighbourhood slowly began to accumulate infrastructure and services, many provided by NGOs. In 1992, however, the owners of various businesses that had developed to cater for the consumption needs of the community hired a militia to 'cleanse' the neighbourhood of 'undesirables'. As Nunes and Paím (2005) have shown, this became commonplace throughout the Salvador metropolitan region. In poor and territorially stigmatized communities, the cleansing of 'bandits' by extermination squads (generally made up of off-duty or retired police) could evoke ambiguous feelings on the part of residents when it came to the deaths of specific individuals, but lynching and other 'self-defence' practices were generally accepted in a context in which little was expected from the state except ill-treatment and authoritarianism. In the case these authors studied, homicide rates declined after the initial 'cleansing', but when they began to increase again in the second half of the 1990s, the residents did not appear to register this change subjectively. Nunes and Paím suggest two, not mutually exclusive, explanations: first, that certain types of violence, including police violence against young people considered 'marginals' because of their involvement in crime, had now become accepted as 'normal', and secondly, that the stronger control now exercised over the neighbourhood by the local drug lord was inhibiting expressions of dissatisfaction with an 'order of crime' that he had imposed on the community. My own ethnographic material leads me towards a somewhat more complicated account, however.

Following the pattern of Rio de Janeiro, the militia soon escaped the control of the people who brought it to the neighbourhood and began to extort protection money from everyone. Being a community that had been obliged to organize itself better than most simply in order to avoid being evicted, Bairro da Paz's leaders managed to create enough political and press turbulence to get the militia disbanded and some of its members imprisoned. The authorities responded to community demands for better security by installing a police post, but it proved a devastating failure. I found an impressive consensus that the officers in the post were unacceptably authoritarian and racist among residents of both sexes, and different ages, educational levels, occupations, creeds and political persuasions. Younger people recounted endless stories of being stopped and searched without reason, talking of physical assaults as well as verbal abuse. Such abuse, which has proved a continuing problem, was often explicitly racist, despite the fact that the military police themselves are often dark Afro-descendants who live in similar kinds of peripheral neighbourhoods. There are various ways of looking at this apparent paradox. The dominant culture of the military police (often criticized by new entrants) is authoritarian, and the policed communities were stigmatized as nests of violent criminals. Police intelligence did not generally permit officers to identify who might be dangerous or not. This problem is aggravated when police are based outside the communities and simply enter them to engage in 'ostensive' policing or hunt for 'suspects': best to treat everyone as a 'suspect'. But residents themselves sometimes identify neighbours or their children as 'marginals', following the logic of an unequal society that obliges all 'those below' to engage in a daily struggle to assert their claims to 'personhood' and 'respect', even if it is at the expense of others (Linger 1992). Members of the military police are entangled in the same logic.

Their profession does not enjoy a high level of esteem among members of any social class, a problem that is, as we will see later, a cause of resentment in the ranks. Police reactions to any situation that they view as a challenge are heightened by the real dangers of death or injury that they face in their work, on or off duty,[4] as well as by their internalization of discourses that exaggerate the criminality of all poor people (and may thus help to convince some officers that their extermination is legitimate). Yet when a police officer who also lives in a poor community stops a young black man something further is at stake. The officer's dignity and claims to respect depend on his (or her) recognition by the citizen as a legitimate representative of the state. When the 'other' manifests any sign of disrespect, even if the 'reaction' is simply verbal, this becomes a challenge to a claim to authority that validates the officer's own claims to be more than just another poor person from the urban periphery. Even respected (and verbally articulate) community leaders who step into such situations to try to rescue some young man from a beating may receive verbal abuse themselves, or subsequent anonymous threats. In one case that I recorded, the police charged one of the community's most important leaders with manifesting 'disobedience' against legitimate authority.

Two unfortunate consequences follow from this paradoxical expression of authoritarianism as racism. In the first place, it reproduces the 'blackening' of poverty so characteristic of Brazil in general, and a long-standing tendency for phenotypically black people to be subject to disproportionate victimization by police in Bahia (Paes Machado and Noronha 2002). In the second place, since power relations based on class and racial hierarchies continue to dominate, police officers from poor communities often end up acting as instruments for the defence and reproduction of those hierarchies in their everyday practice. This is particularly ironic since at another level most police who come from the 'periphery' identify with the 'periphery', stressing that most people who live there are, like themselves, 'good people' (*pessoas de bem*) who deserve to be treated with respect and enjoy a public security system that defends their interests and not simply those of property owners and other social classes. But they may also believe that the poor are often not as 'well brought up' or as 'self-controlled' as their social superiors, and therefore need to be treated in a different manner.

The paternalistic and authoritarian ethos that the police corporations instil results in a style of policing that offends almost everyone. Nevertheless, there are some older residents, especially women, who express discomfort when younger community leaders attack public officials of any kind verbally in public meetings. They think that what they read as 'rudeness' is disrespectful. These residents are, however, also those most likely to blame the state, or more precisely the liberal politicians and middle-class do-gooders who shape the policies of the democratic state, for the problem of young people being attracted to 'the world of crime', a world that they would strongly like to see eradicated from their neighbourhood. The problem as they see it is that parents have lost their ability to discipline their children properly as a result of child protection laws, while legislation against child labour leaves young people lounging about in the street and getting into bad company rather than gaining an early experience of the discipline that comes with work, a discipline that would make them more likely to opt for the identity of 'worker' rather than 'bandit'. Questionable though these arguments may be, they do confirm the existence of some support for a police that 'disciplines' in poor communities, although it is not support for a police that expresses its ordering authority in a racist or arbitrary manner or prejudice against morally upstanding citizens.

The Bairro da Paz police post was eventually replaced by mobile patrols whose visits were infrequent and generally focused on hunts for known drug traffickers. When I first started visiting the neighbourhood in 2006, the post was still in operation and residents grumbled about the need to train more 'civilized', and less corrupt, guardians of public order. Yet after the post was withdrawn, some people began to say they were now happier about their security and would tell me that it was much safer to walk around the streets of Bairro da Paz in the early hours of the morning, as young middle-class people would do when they came to buy drugs, than in the upscale neighbourhoods, where middle- and upper-class Bahians live defensively inside closed condominiums and hardly anyone ventures on to the streets after ten o'clock at night. This tranquillity reflected the fact that the leader of the drug traffic in Bairro da Paz had instituted 'a law of crime' in the community consciously modelled on the practices of the PCC in São Paulo. The group's services included mediation of personal and inter-family disputes, and although those who persistently broke the new rules against robbing other members of the community might expect harsh punishment, the community did became a more 'tranquil' place and drug trafficking operations became discreet, without public ostentation of arms. Nevertheless, my interviews with residents did not reveal a uniform pattern of positive enthusiasm for this 'order of crime'.

Some made positive comments about the way the traffickers had suppressed thefts and assaults inside the community. 'Marginals' from outside the community could no longer come there to rob either. Some also felt that the traffic was now run in a more 'businesslike' way and preferred to go to the drug lord to resolve a problem than to a police force that was prejudiced against the residents and had principally been experienced as a violent, repressive force. Although young men showed the greatest positive enthusiasm for the 'rule of crime', given their greater likelihood of being victimized by the police, one housewife expressed considerable satisfaction with the way in which the traffickers had dealt with the drug-addicted son of a neighbour who had stolen from her husband and finally been executed after attempting to rob a pharmacy in the community. The traffickers had managed to create a sense of social proximity with some honest residents. One of them remarked that 'it was better now because the criminal groups which are operating today are on the side of the community and offer protection, and it wasn't like that before because they were different groups acting in the neighbourhood'. Others pointed out that the advantage of going to the traffickers for help was that they were inside the community, whereas the police were outside it and had neither the ability to provide effective assistance to residents nor great interest in doing so.

Others, however, especially but not exclusively older people, saw the official police and justice system as the only legitimate authority. Even some who were highly critical of the police were not enthusiastic about the rule of crime either. One young woman described the drug lord as 'a boss of nothing'. Another resident felt less rather than more secure now that the traffickers were operating in the shadows, and a few continued to insist that the streets of the neighbourhood were not really safe. Nevertheless, even some of those who would have preferred to live without the presence of criminals in their community did feel that the neighbourhood was more secure relative to the past as a result of the changes that had taken place in the organization and role of the traffickers, and better in comparison with other more violent neighbourhoods in the city where traffickers were more abusive.

Yet that view became less prevalent when signs of a new conflict for control of the traffic began to emerge. Even before the situation destabilized, a significant number of residents interviewed did see the restoration of a permanent police presence as desirable, and were positively disposed towards the possibility of a BCS being installed in the future, although many remained sceptical about whether any new police presence would treat residents with greater respect, and about whether trafficking could ever be eliminated from their lives. Since not everyone felt more secure, there were also some who felt another 'cleansing' of the neighbourhood would be desirable, although there was no unanimity on whether this would best be done by the police or the criminal *comando*. Yet many more did not see the role of 'ordering agents' as the central issue. They argued that if priority were to be given to removing the community's deficits in health and educational services, improving its infrastructure, leisure and sporting facilities, and creating jobs and offering training that would give everyone better opportunities in the labour market, that would be the best way of reducing indices of criminality within the local population itself and reducing the domestic violence and drug abuse associated with a continuing situation of poverty. Although most people felt that things had improved a little in recent years, even those who had achieved some kind of 'decent work' outside the neighbourhood still tended to see their home as a *comunidade carente* (deprived community) that was stigmatized by outsiders.

Another regular theme in my interviews with residents was fear. Although there was also fear of the police, not simply because of police violence, but also because some residents worried about police corruption and possible complicity with criminals, many people referred to their fear of the traffickers. It seems almost self-evident that drug trafficking gangs that enjoy armed control of territories must have the ability to impose a 'law of silence' on the population by threatening to eliminate informers or anyone who opposes them. There were many occasions during my fieldwork when individuals manifested tangible fear of talking about traffickers, referring to the phenomenon obliquely in a way that fits a broader pattern, as we will see in a moment. But people could be persuaded to talk about the traffickers when they felt themselves free of a surveillance that was often tangible, given that the criminals paid children to act as their eyes and ears. As we have just seen, some individuals were prepared to express their repudiation of the criminals and the 'system' that they represented in a private interview. But others saw themselves in a dilemma because of corrupt relations between traffickers and those who represented the state, as well as because of the state's incapacity to guarantee their security. As one resident put it:

I find myself between a rock and a hard place. I don't know whether to go to the police or not because of these things. Today the police are infiltrated by the mafia of drug trafficking, the mafia of crime. So, the fact is that people don't know whom to turn to. To be honest, I find myself in two minds, I don't know the position of others, but I think that it's best not to go to the police, because the police want to interview people, want you to go to the station. Who's going to protect our security? They won't, so it gets complicated and I prefer to let it go.

Fear is not the only means by which the traffickers can build relations with communities. If neither the police nor the justice system attend to poor people's needs or provide security, then this enhances the value of whatever 'protection' criminals can provide. Traffickers can also supply aid to individuals and families in moments of emergency and support for community activities (Goldstein 2003). Yet as Ben Penglase (2009) has pointed out, the patronage networks of drug traffickers are often selective, targeted towards families with which they enjoy stronger social ties, or influential individuals in the community. Relations are negotiated and renegotiated on a basis of 'asymmetric reciprocity' in which the threat of violence and forms of material support are usually co-present.

A key point in Penglase's analysis with which I wholeheartedly concur, and will pursue again in my analysis of Mexico in the chapters that follow, is that residents' relations with traffickers can be understood only in relation to the role of other ordering and threatening entities, which 'co-participate' in the production of the 'states of security and insecurity' that generate the 'protection rackets' in which all these entities are implicated (ibid.: 52). The *Comando Vermelho* traffickers that Penglase studied in Rio de Janeiro exploited the opportunities to present themselves as 'protectors' on the side of the community provided both by the violent nature of police incursions into poor communities and also by the threat to residents posed by rival gangs seeking to invade their territories. He argues that the maintenance of a regular 'state of insecurity' was helpful for maintaining the hegemony of the local drug gang in the neighbourhood and the residents' acceptance of the 'law of silence'. Fear of being identified as an informer was only one of the mechanisms that maintained the power of these traffickers. Penglase observed that although traffickers distinguished themselves from the police by insisting that they abided by rules that respected the residents in a way that the police failed to do, in practice they did not always behave fairly or in accordance with the moral principles that they claimed to be upholding. Traffickers sometimes forced residents to let them use their houses for storing arms and drugs and sometimes even evicted people from their homes. They put people at risk of being caught in crossfire during police raids by setting up drug sales points close to their houses. Although they claimed to 'respect' local women, when traffickers were rejected by local girls, both the girls themselves and their families might suffer. Penglase contends that this apparent arbitrariness creates a sense of anxiety that is part and parcel of trafficker power. Traffickers' sovereignty over the *favela* rests on their ability to break the rules, to 'decide the exception' (ibid.: 59; Agamben 1998).

Penglase concludes that the effect of the arbitrary and ambiguous nature of trafficker power can best be understood in terms of the idea of a 'public secret', as defined by Michael Taussig (1999). There is a strong incentive for people never to name names – in Bairro da Paz, the drug lord is always referred to as *o cara* (slang for a person of importance, 'the man') – and for residents to voice concerns about trafficker violence as concerns about 'stray bullets' that leave the question of whether a death was caused by police or trafficker fire indeterminate (Penglase 2009: 58). Residents mutter about problems with the traffickers among themselves, and look for oblique ways of negotiating with them about problems, through the leadership of residents' councils, for example. But what they do publicly is maintain the fiction that the normative order of crime is as predictable and community-oriented as the traffickers claim that it is, since individuals hope that this will keep them safe and convince the traffickers to rule in their favour should an issue arise (ibid.: 59).

Given that insecurity is co-produced by both criminals and state agents, it is not surprising that people find themselves 'between a rock and a hard place'. Yet in the case of Bairro da Paz, it seemed clear that any 'sovereignty' that traffickers could achieve was limited and likely to be unstable. Elements of the 'public secret' model do apply to Bairro da Paz. People spoke in very indirect terms and usually tried to get off the subject as quickly as possible when the question of the traffickers threatened to intrude into public discussions, in meetings of the FPEBP, for example. Yet there were not only many expressions of outright rejection of the 'rule of crime' in safer spaces, but also avoidance of entanglements with it in practice on the part of many individuals. This was perhaps predictable in a community that was not only socially heterogeneous but also remained organized, with leaders who were not co-opted by the traffickers but linked into wider religious, NGO and political networks. Most residents wished to be, and be seen to be, 'honest citizens'. They saw themselves as struggling against prejudice, but were seldom interested in embracing an identity that might reinforce their separation from the rest of society, despite the differences of orientation that existed between, for example, evangelicals and those for whom hip-hop was a vehicle for expressing militant opposition to racism. Violence between traffickers that was seen as putting residents' lives at risk made even the flawed policing and justice offered by a state that is far from being entirely absent from Bairro da Paz seem like the preferable option to many of those interviewed.[5] As we saw in the previous chapter, Feltran (2010b) shows that residents of poor neighbourhoods might use the official justice system or other mediating organizations for some purposes, and turn to the normative apparatus controlled by criminals to solve other kinds of problems. Yet although Bahia's Comando da Paz crime network resembles the PCC in the sense that it developed in the state penitentiaries, it does not enjoy the kind of hegemony over the regional 'world of crime' that the PCC has achieved in São Paulo. Infighting and conflicts between different local groups for control are as typical of Bahia as they are of Rio de Janeiro.

The interviews suggested that people felt more positive about the situation when the gang dominating the community was rooted within it, as this was associated with a greater probability that community members really would be respected most of the time. If the traffickers are born and bred in the community, then they will also have friends who are not involved in crime but will be less likely to denounce them. Fear and lack of confidence in the police were important for the degree of acceptance that the Bairro da Paz traffickers achieved in the period when there was no permanent police presence in the neighbourhood, and the 'rule of crime' was accompanied by little violence that seemed threatening to ordinary residents. Yet in this case the threat of invasion of the neighbourhood by other gangs did not strengthen that hegemony. Nor did it reinforce solidarity within the gang, since disputes over leadership emerged. Once new struggles for control of the traffic broke out, and an invasion eventually took place, escalating fears of violence rapidly increased levels of repudiation by the rest of the community, although fear kept it tacit.

It follows that a 'rule of crime' will be more difficult to implement when communities are taken over by gangs from other places that do not embed themselves in any positive way in community life, either because their only interest is in securing a place to stash their supplies, or simply because police pressure denies them the time or scope to build relations with any significant number of community members and construct claims to the moral high ground. It also follows that if the state can improve the relations between its agents and the residents, instilling greater trust, offer residents effective protection from violence and access to justice, and simultaneously provide services of social protection that make 'help' from criminals unnecessary, the state can win the battle for community hegemony. Traffickers do prosper by making good the state's deficiencies, not simply by offering material patronage, but also by offering an alternative justice system that 'works' for people. The recent history of Bairro da Paz confirms that poor Brazilians may accept violent retributive forms of justice (even at the hands of police who victimize them) when the targets seem appropriate, do not think that appropriate targets (such as rapists) should enjoy human rights, may not protest much at 'cleansing' of their neighbourhoods by a variety of violent actors, and may consider lynching an appropriate community response to certain kinds of crimes. But it also highlights that if the worst continues to happen, this is because the state is not doing what it needs to do to win the battle for hegemony, even when, as in this particular case, circumstances were quite propitious for a breakthrough.

Securitization as a reproducer of insecurity

Bahia's new public security policy is strongly framed in terms of the relationship between homicide and drug trafficking in poorer neighbourhoods of the city. The state government's 'Pact for Life' (*Pacto Pela Vida*) programme seeks to dissuade young people from taking drugs and getting involved in trafficking, but its primary emphasis is on measures designed to 'reduce crimes against life and against property' through implanting police bases inside poor communities considered to manifest high levels of violence and criminality. The concept of 'approximation' between police and residents that comes across in much of the official discourse of the *Pacto Pela Vida* programme is one that focuses on making residents more willing to denounce the criminals in their midst. Such framing marks out particular communities as the source of crime and violence in other parts of the city, transforming their social problems of poverty, lack of clear titles to land and property, and substandard infrastructure and living conditions, into problems that threaten the security of all the city's other residents. Securitization of these social problems is in danger of exacerbating the territorial stigmatization of poor communities, something that many Bairro da Paz residents had already experienced as a practical difficulty in relation to competing for jobs and other aspects of their lives.

Although by the start of 2011 a few residents and community leaders knew that something like Rio's UPP model was planned for Bahia, and that Bairro da Paz was on the list of communities scheduled to receive a BCS, the idea initially provoked little enthusiasm. This reflected scepticism about the possibility of creating a more 'civilized' type of police, even more scepticism about whether the promised new infrastructure investments and social development programmes would actually be delivered, and anxieties about whether intensified policing of the community might actually be part of a strategy to reduce its capacity to resist displacement, or at the very least simply a means of keeping the surrounding middle-class condominium residents happier about their security at the cost of further humiliation and inconvenience for residents. One of the things people noticed about the BCSs was their use of surveillance technologies based on CCTV systems. Given that the streets were not actually dangerous at that time, this seemed provocative as well as intrusive. The traffickers no doubt also inhibited public expressions of support for the return of a permanent police presence.

But 2011 was to bring momentous changes. In April, the company building condominiums next to Bairro da Paz sent its private security agents to evict a group of families who had built shacks on the frontier, arguing that they were on the company's property. In September another conflict broke out over a piece of land on which Bairro da Paz residents had hoped to build a sports centre using funding from the PAC. Ownership of this terrain was disputed between two speculators. Armed guards came to protect workers clearing the land and there was a confrontation with residents who objected that environmental laws were being breached. Further violent confrontation occurred in January 2012, but shortly after that incident, one of the two entrepreneurs to claim title to the land, Mr Cintra, was lured into a trap and shot dead in his car in front of the disputed terrain, together with his son, a student who played no part in his business affairs. Cintra had agreed in a meeting with residents the previous year to donate the land to the community for the sports centre. The crime was laid at the door of the head of the security guards who had been menacing the residents, whom the victim had earlier denounced for making death threats. It subsequently emerged that Cintra had been giving information to the public prosecutor's office about illegalities in the titling of the lands on which his rivals were building (Meneses et al. 2012). Here, then, the residents of Bairro da Paz and their leaders had a frightening demonstration of the lengths to which property developers might go to defend their interests. But since off-duty and retired police were implicated in the violence, this was also a paradigmatic case of public power being appropriated by private interests. The incident heightened feelings of insecurity, but not in a way that increased confidence in the state. The dead entrepreneur was lured to his death by the erection of what appeared to be an official municipal billboard on the disputed land, subsequently declared a forgery by the prefecture.

Yet developments were simultaneously undermining the 'order of crime' in Bairro da Paz. The trafficker who had set up the PCC model in Bairro da Paz was now in prison, although this did not, for the moment, constitute an impediment to his continuing to command the community. But in September 2011 a woman friend who had visited him in jail, and worked as a cleaner in a nearby shopping centre, was savagely executed with thirty bullets pumped into her body, ten of which were directed, in a self-evidently symbolic way, at her mouth. A struggle for control of the traffic in Bairro da Paz had developed that eventually resulted in an armed invasion attributed by the media to rival traffickers from the nearby Alto de Coqueirinho settlement, the burning of some houses, and looting of stores. The next day an uncanny silence still hung over the normally bustling main streets even in the early evening. Bairro da Paz had ceased to be a tranquil place. But the state's security performance was abysmal. The police and fire brigade took forty minutes to respond to emergency calls from residents.

A year later Bairro da Paz finally received its BCS, but few community leaders showed up for the opening ceremony in which governor Jacques Wagner and Public Security Secretary Mauricio Barbosa were treated to Afro music and a *capoeira* display. The building for the base was still not ready, so it was located in a temporary structure on the periphery of the community, and the young male commander did not have any female officers under his command, in striking contradiction to the best-practice model of the BCSs, which recognized the importance of men and women working together when trying to build more constructive relationships with the population on the streets, and in particular when entering homes in which women and children might be unaccompanied by men. The aggressive manner in which police invaded homes searching for drugs, guns and suspects in the original occupation provoked complaints that continued into the first months of the base's existence, accompanied by accusations of damage to property and intimidation of minor children in intelligence-gathering operations. Although there appeared to be plenty of residents who welcomed the police presence because it promised to end the drug wars, the police did not undertake the regular foot patrols in the streets that were essential for building positive relations with residents through regular interaction and overcoming their scepticism about the possibility of new styles of policing. Even the base's motorized patrols rarely ventured into the upper half of the community. All this might simply reflect the way in which implementation of the Bahian programme, already running behind schedule, was being driven by political expediency without a sufficiently solid investment in training and preparation, but it could also reflect that making life safer for residents is not a priority in Bahia's public security policy.

Although military police officials spoke with some Bairro da Paz community leaders prior to establishing the base, no attempt was made to involve the community as a whole in the project. Consultation had been more noticeable in the case of the large *favela* complex in Nordeste de Amaralina the previous year, and perhaps the fact that traffickers assassinated a Candomblé[6] priest who spoke in favour of the base in the preparatory public meetings there encouraged a different approach elsewhere. But the subsequent experience of pacification in

Nordeste de Amaralina remained troubled. Despite the installation of three separate bases, drug trafficking did not end in the complex. Working with the new local drug lords that emerged remained a source of prestige for those who chose that option. During the year after the installation of its BCS, trafficking in the Boqueirão area was taken over by a faction that had broken away from the Comando da Paz network. The police did achieve some successes against the existing Nordeste drug lords. Leandro Marques Cerqueira, aged thirty-two, was detained towards the end of November 2012, while preparing to leave for São Paulo with 39,500 *reais* in cash, following the arrest a few days earlier of Marcelo Henrique (aka 'Elias'), another alleged leader who was distinguished by being the 'Ace of Diamonds' in the 'deck of crime', playing cards featuring the faces of traffickers that the Bahian public security secretariat used as a 'most wanted' list on its website to encourage denunciations (Borges 2012). Leandro, who was in prison in 2006 for involvement in a homicide, claimed that he had long since put drug trafficking behind him and that he had since engaged in solid work as a taxi driver. This was perhaps not the ideal cover story to choose at that moment, since the police had just arrested another thirty-two-year-old taxi driver from another part of the city, Elio de Jesus Matos, together with his girlfriend, for leading a gang of cocaine wholesalers. Through a network of contacts, they bought drugs arriving from São Paulo by road, hidden on regular cargo trucks, for resale to community drug lords.[7] Although Elio allegedly threw lavish parties for his friends, many of them traffickers, and also liked to take schooner trips with them around All Saints Bay, providing prostitutes for their entertainment, the other drivers at his taxi stand expressed amazement on hearing of his arrest, since he continued to spend long hours driving his taxi (Ribeiro 2012).

Such arrests gain ample publicity and allow the authorities to project the image of a successful campaign against crime. Yet what they are actually doing is removing from circulation small elements of complex and fragmented networks, principally at the local distribution end. Progress in Nordeste proved difficult to achieve. Violence even occurred in the immediate vicinity of one of the community security bases: a school caretaker was murdered. Residents reported that the police did not leave the base regularly to patrol, thereby minimizing their possible contribution to ensuring the safety of ordinary people.

It is possible that the following comment published on a newspaper website reflects a propagandistic counter-attack by the traffickers, since very similar statements and metaphors appeared in both Nordeste de Amaralina and Bairro da Paz: 'The police of the UPP [sic] are only good for beating up family men and calling respectable mothers tramps ... what we need here is more security but the police just hang around the entrance of their base to put it about with the young girls instead of seeing to the security of the people.' Nevertheless, even if the denunciations were orchestrated, there was ample evidence that they corresponded to real situations and incidents in both communities. It proved difficult to control trafficking in Nordeste de Amaralina because surrounding high-income residential areas provide an important market for drugs. Police not attached to the BCSs mounted a series of 'mega-operations' against the Nordeste traffickers. These caused significant amounts of collateral damage. In one such raid, a forty-two-year-old domestic servant was shot through the door of her house while watching the television on her sofa, and a forty-nine-year-old car park attendant received a bullet in the abdomen while walking back to his house from work. Neighbours and family members insisted that 'the police arrived shooting', and the police that the shots had come from the criminals, but no resident wanted to be identified by the press 'for fear of reprisals' (Alban 2013).

As 2013 advanced, arrests continued, but so did the collateral damage, provoking protests by residents. The most notorious case was the death of a twenty-two-year-old hotel worker, who was the cousin of a ten-year-old boy, son of a much-loved *capoeirista*, who had indisputably been killed by a police bullet in an incursion prior to the installation of the BCSs. The bullet passed through the wall of the child's bedroom and hit him in the face while he was sleeping. In that case the responsible officers were held to account. Yet in the case of the cousin, the official claim was that he had been armed, and was carrying drugs, while friends insisted that it had been an execution and a gun had been placed in his hand after his death (Wendel 2013). Whatever the truth of these incidents, protests over the 'truculence' displayed by base police in stop and search operations and forced entry into homes showed that it was difficult to establish a successful 'proximity policing model' in the context of a continuing 'war against drugs'.

Nordeste residents also complained that nothing was being done to improve their access to services, including medical services. As protesting residents summed up the situation in a statement to the press: 'We want more security. Not this badly trained police that shoots without knowing who the target is or arrives in a truculent way for yet another stop and search operation ... The only state presence here is the police ... They forget that we need basic services' (Villarpando 2013). At the time of those protests in 2013, despite the installation of the BCSs and a claimed reduction in homicide rates in most of the rest of the city, crime and violence had actually shown a significant increase in Nordeste de Amaralina, prompting Public Security Secretary Mauricio Barbosa to observe that Nordeste was the Bahian capital's equivalent of Rio's Rocinha or Complexo do Alemão (Valporto 2013).

In the case of Bairro da Paz, some people did say that the police from the base treated them 'correctly'. Yet there were many complaints of continuing 'truculence' in stop and search operations and damage to property by police invading houses which mirrored those that were denounced in public protests in Nordeste de Amarilina. It was not long before developments took a yet more sinister turn.

In April 2013, residents blocked the Avenida Paralela and Orlando Gomes in protest at the rape and murder of a thirty-four-year-old mother of two and member of an evangelical church who was abducted by a man as she crossed the walkway that gives pedestrian access to the neighbourhood over the busy main road. It seemed incredible to the residents that such a crime could occur close to a police base that was supposed to improve their security. The alleged culprit was subsequently lynched. The police allowed this act of community justice to take place without consequences. Some months later a brother of the victim was stopped and searched by the police in the street, 'reacted', and was taken inside the base for a beating. He made a complaint to the Public Attorney's office, which was upheld. On 14 September 2013, another young man was shot dead while drinking with friends in a bar, by masked assassins who, according to residents, arrived in an unmarked car that had previously stopped for a few minutes in front of the BCS building. It is alleged that when the shooting started calls for help to the base by residents went unanswered, and that when a patrol from the Rondas Especiais (Special Patrols) division arrived on the scene from outside the neighbourhood, the police simply collected spent cartridge cases and refused attention to the victim. This is the normal pattern of events associated with police covering up a deliberate act of extrajudicial execution by their colleagues. It also appears that the security cameras of the base were switched off during this incident, just as they were when police from the Rocinha UPP killed Arnildo de Souza.

The young man who was killed was the brother of an employee of a Catholic charity in the community that offers training courses to young people. The opinion of the brother and other residents is that he was killed because he was mistaken for the brother of the murdered woman, to whom he bore a strong physical resemblance. The case was taken to the Public Attorney's office, along with a further denunciation of police from the Bairro da Paz BCS by the families of four young men who were allegedly taken to a secluded place and not simply tortured but obliged to have sex with each other to increase their experience of humiliation. In August 2014, those responsible for the killing remained unidentified, a fact publicly protested in Salvador's contribution to the National March Against the Genocide of Black People. But that month did produce a publicly acknowledged equivalent in another part of Salvador of the Amarildo de Souza case. Twenty-two-year-old Geovane Mascarenhas Santana disappeared after being placed in the back of a Special Patrol vehicle. His dismembered, decapitated and burnt remains were scattered, but thanks to his father's insistence that the authorities pursue the matter, were found and identified two weeks after the disappearance. The officers who had taken him were identified from a video surveillance camera in this case, and arrested (Wendel 2014).

Although police–community relations had not been as good as they might have been even before these incidents, the commander of the BCS did make a significant effort to reach out to the community leadership by attending meetings of the FPEBP, and listening to what from the beginning tended to be a litany of complaint, urging residents to make formal denunciations of any episode of misconduct by the officers under his command. He accepted, for example, that one of his officers had a personal drug use problem. But he responded to complaints about 'truculence' in stop and search operations by suggesting that residents should take classes in how (not) to 'react'. This suggests that paternalistic and authoritarian attitudes are still common even among younger officers who have received special training in community policing methods. Complaints against the base also include the way that community social life has been diminished by restrictions on bars and music. There have also been complaints that street parties were closed down after police permission had been given for them (with the suggestion that money might have changed hands for deals that were not honoured). None of this aided the transformation of the image of the police in the eyes of residents from that of an invasive occupying force to that of an institution meriting trust and mutual respect. Community leaders in Bairro da Paz have also complained of having been threatened by the police commander for not being willing to declare publicly that the BCS is a resounding success, and even more worrying, for having offered support to the family of a young man that the police killed as a drug trafficker. In this case, there is no dispute over the young man's involvement in the traffic, but there is a humanitarian issue, unless one takes the view that parents should be considered morally responsible for what their children do. The problem may well be that many police do take precisely that view, so that the world becomes neatly divided into *pessoas de bem* and the criminal element, but the entire scenario that I have just recounted is strongly suggestive that priority number one for the BCS is arresting traffickers.

Arresting traffickers makes good headlines, but this may not bring a good deal of change to the lives of the residents of the communities, if new traffickers take over. In June 2012, months before 'pacification', the police had arrested three members of one of the factions whose struggle for control of the traffic in Bairro da Paz had provoked the invasion in the previous year, and its principal leader, aka 'Flor' (Flower), fled. Yet, according to my informants, traffickers from other places entered the community even after the BCS was installed. In January 2014, a 'stray bullet' killed a six-year-old girl in what the newspapers termed 'an assumed exchange of fire between traffickers'.[8] This provoked a blocking of the Avenida Paralela by residents protesting about the failure of the base to guarantee their security. The base commander responded by arguing that from the beginning of the police occupation, some traffickers remaining in the community had been attempting to regain control, while others that had 'migrated' were trying to return, provoking this scenario of violence. He promised that police actions would be intensified to ensure that violence did not return to its previous levels, and emphasized that 'internal inquiries' indicated that there were no longer leaders of drug trafficking emerging within the community itself (Mendes 2014).

Yet the initial reaction of the police to a tragedy that they had done nothing to prevent provoked another protest.

Friends and family waiting for the hearse to arrive to take the child's body to be buried in the interior city of Santa Barbara complained that a group of police from the base had suddenly appeared dragging a man into an alley. After a time two shots rang out and the police reappeared with the now wounded man, screaming at the mourners to keep their distance and claiming that the victim had fired on the base. Other witnesses claimed that the man had been unarmed when he was seized, and the verbal aggression of the officers towards residents, which took place in the presence of a TV crew, left the atmosphere extremely tense.[9] A few days after this incident, a resident sent a critique of the BCS to the Bairro da Paz News Facebook page. I will quote directly from this text, because it shows how the community's intellectuals can present their own analyses by exploiting the democratizing potential of social media, analyses that nevertheless continue to be ignored by officialdom:

Empathy! This is the word that became the banner of whatever police force seeks a positive relation with a community. The Community Security Bases should be based on the principle of a peaceful relationship between police and residents. It was necessary that the police understood that their actions should be based on the force of words and not so much on physical force. To achieve this good relationship, the bet was on recently trained soldiers commanded by sergeants with years of experience. It was thought that recently trained soldiers would not yet have acquired the vices of the police corporation. The police that are serving in the BCS had only 40 to 60 hours training as community police operators. Many police understood being sent to the bases as a 'punishment' for having committed some wrong act.

The reduction of violent crimes was one of the biggest justifications for implanting a BCS in Bairro da Paz. But did this really happen? According to the Secretariat of Public Security, in 2011, without the BCS there were 15 homicides, and then in 2013, with the base, there were at least 17 homicides that were committed in the neighbourhood or in its immediate vicinity. Does that sound like a reduction?

Once the base was established in the neighbourhood, with

a temporary infrastructure, the interaction between police and residents began. There was no delay in the beginning of reports of abuse. Probably if you are a resident reading this text, you must know of some case of police abuse. The most common are: entry into houses without a warrant, bad language and aggression in stop and search, illegal detention, not to mention fabrication of evidence for guilt. Where is the empathy in that?

If we ask any resident the name of any policeman serving in the neighbourhood, it is probable that he won't be able to name one, and that's because there isn't any real interaction. Patrol cars passing on the streets that are asphalted is patrolling, not community policing.

In a meeting with representatives of the state government ministries, as the result of a courageous act on the part of a community leader, diverse situations of total disrespect of the laws and their own military code were recounted. Yet nothing was done about it and we continue living together with these individuals. The cases of abuse reached the ears of the Public Attorney in another meeting, recounted by the victims themselves, but once again we don't see any change. We are obliged to live together with a police force that does not know us or respect us.[10]

Bairro da Paz remains an organized community that is capable of expressing demands. Yet as this 'venting' of frustration shows, dialogues with public authorities all too often turn out to be dialogues with the deaf. The 'left hand of the state' did organize an event to present the social development actions that would follow pacification to the community in December 2012, and the BCS has spawned a number of new educational and training projects. Yet associations of neighbourhood residents financed by government (directly, or indirectly through Petrobras), and in some cases by private companies, together with NGOs linked to the Catholic Santa Casa de Misericórdia and other external entities, had long been pursuing a wide variety of work training and self-esteem building programmes, cooperative production projects and cultural activities based on the community residents' impressive talents in the fields of music, dance and the creative arts. None of this was really dependent on 'pacification'. Regulating the 'conduct' of residents might be considered a secondary priority when it came to spending public money, leaving aside the costs of maintaining a BCS itself. It was not until July 2014, with elections approaching, that Mayor ACM Neto finally began to take action on the decrepit physical state and inadequate staffing of the community health clinic, in partnership with the Santa Casa, promising future attention to a host of infrastructural problems with drainage and street maintenance, and absence of spaces for sport and other leisure activities, all problems on which the FPEBP had been campaigning since its foundation in 2006. The fact that the base was given a permanent home but continued to be seen as a hostile and incapable presence by many residents reinforces their argument that the money invested in 'securing' Bairro da Paz might have been better spent on these other urgent needs. Yet the most obvious question of all is why the Bahia state government pressed ahead with a pacification programme that was so ill prepared and under-resourced. The answer appears to be that it became politically imperative to be seen to be 'doing something' about Salvador's continuing ascent in the national statistics on crime and violence, whatever the cost in the communities of the urban periphery themselves.

The next question must therefore be whether that strategy is not proving contradictory in its own terms. A consequence of fragmentation in the organization of drug trafficking is violence related to attempts to take over distribution of drugs in a particular locality, producing cycles in which phases of tranquillity and stability, during which a particular local gang may achieve a *modus vivendi* with residents, and also with corruptible police, may turn overnight into scenes of violence and chaos before the conflict is resolved by the victory of the defenders or invaders. Yet on the basis of the evidence already presented on Bairro da Paz, it seems necessary to ask whether violence may not sometimes be exacerbated by migration of traffickers resulting from the installation of UPPs/BCSs.

Bahian Public Security Secretary Barbosa accepted that migration of crime would be a normal consequence of pacification in an interview with *Correio da Bahia* newspaper, given at the moment when the Bairro da Paz base was being installed (Wendel 2012). My own interviews with serving police confirmed that this was taken as read throughout the force. Secretary Barbosa argued that the migration of traffickers was taken into account in strategic planning of where to locate BCSs, which was based on 'intelligence', although he also said that it was too early to say where 'Flor', the leading protagonist in the 2011 violence in Bairro da Paz, might have sought refuge. For the Secretary and the police chief coordinating the BCS programme, Colonel Zeliomar Almeida, the installation of UPPs inevitably produces an increase in violence in the areas to which the traffickers migrate. The alternative of traffickers simply finding a safe haven elsewhere with kin or friendly members of the same faction was not considered in this analysis. Its unspoken premise was that traffickers will generally have established a social base in the communities that they dominated before they fled, if not through successful administration of the 'law of crime', then at least by various kinds of patronage, such as buying medicines for the sick, sponsoring community events, or handing out gifts to children at Christmas. Constructing a clientele by peaceful means takes time, so once displaced they will be seriously weakened, the Secretary concludes, even though they have money. Reduced to desperation, traffickers expelled from their territories will use as much violence as they can muster to establish control over a new one, and since local traffickers will normally resist, the implicit logic of this analysis is that the bandits will make the job of the police easier by killing each other.

Bahia's public security apparatus should be given credit for making such thinking relatively explicit. Yet since it is seldom just the 'bandits' who die as stray bullets fly around in violent struggles to control drug distribution territories, this transparency only increases the suspicion that the security of community residents is a secondary priority, and possibly not a priority at all, in a policy driven by the desire to score 'victories' in combating drug trafficking. We already know, on the basis of decades of experience, that imprisoning or even killing entire generations of community-level drug lords has not had the slightest effect on the continuing growth of drug trafficking and addiction in Brazil, which now offers the world's biggest market for crack cocaine and is the second biggest for overall cocaine use, according to a Federal University of São Paulo study (Pearson 2012). From this perspective, there might be better prospects of reducing crack consumption if supply was reduced as a result of the need of traffickers who remain 'embedded' in their communities to negotiate their relationships with residents and manifest some sort of social conscience. In mid-2012 the drug lords of Mandela and Jacarezinho *favelas* in Rio de Janeiro made a decision to prohibit the sale of crack in their communities. The official reading was that this was a defensive move in response to the public security offensive, which also involved actions against *cracolândias* in which city authorities sought ways of legalizing the compulsory internment of addicts. These *favelas* were already slated for pacification (Ahmed 2012). But the traffickers insisted that the decision was theirs, a reflection of their concern for the way crack was accelerating the social disintegration of the communities in which they had been born and raised (Barbassa 2012). As I noted earlier in speculating about the 'orchestration' of some community protests, Brazilian drug lords are just as capable of being 'political' as policemen and career politicians. Yet since it seems unlikely that rounding up addicts and locking them up in a clinic against their will can solve the public health problems that crack cocaine causes, this is another reason for thinking about the unintended consequences of policies that foster the migration of violent criminals to zones where they do not have social ties with the local population.

Given that, with existing budgets, 'pacification', whether in Rio de Janeiro or Bahia, can be extended, even in the medium term, only to a limited number of communities, migration is a serious issue. Many of the other aspects of programmes such as Bahia's *Pacto Pela Vida* do not depend on police occupation of communities. As some of my police interviewees explained, reform-minded police battalion commanders had long been encouraging their officers to participate in community education programmes. This is an area in which schools, NGOs and community organizations were already carrying out good work against both violent behaviour and drug addiction which could be strengthened further with greater public investment. If police bases within communities do not succeed in providing real security for residents and retain a strongly repressive policing style because of the continuing presence of traffickers, they can even serve to transmit the wrong message, especially when residents believe that innocent young people have been killed or framed by the police. If the policing introduced by the UPPs and BCSs does not break with past patterns, it is unlikely that the state will succeed in breaking the power of traffickers, since they will benefit from community resentment. Even if aggressive or corrupt policing that alienates residents from the state is more strongly sanctioned, taking out existing leaders or even whole gangs will not prevent others wishing to take over these lucrative illegal markets, and if these others only have the resources of violence to depend on, the fact that the permanent police presence obliges them to conduct their business and launch their attacks from backstreets and alleyways in the margins of the settlement will make them more rather than less deadly.

For pacification to realize its potential it is necessary to have real community policing and to change the social and physical environment in which drug trafficking and consumption are taking place. This means carrying out the promised improvements to infrastructure and providing and improving the public schools and health services that deprived communities are demanding. It also means recognizing that the middle and upper classes provide an important part of the market for drugs, but have not traditionally had to worry about the conditions under which people live in the supply zones, although that, ironically, is changing as street crimes and apartment robberies increase in the 'noble' districts of the city as another result of the repression of trafficking as a mode of livelihood in occupied neighbourhoods. These are all good reasons for concluding that 'pacification' cannot be a cup that is half full, based on the false premise of a securitization of social deprivation that paints tens of thousands of decent, hard-working, church-going citizens, fully committed to their own self-improvement, as 'enemies' who threaten the rest of society.

This is not to say that socially stigmatized communities are devoid of their own social problems or united through unshakeable bonds of social solidarity. In Bairro da Paz, there are tensions that reflect socio-economic and educational differences, and differences that arise from religious cleavages, such as those between Catholics and followers of Candomblé, on the one hand, and some of the congregation of the Neo-Pentecostal Universal Church of the Kingdom of God, on the other. The community is not immunized against the often divisive, and sometimes co-opting and corrupting, effects of the patronage network of political parties. Yet most people who live in Bairro da Paz do actually like living in their community and deeply resent its stigmatization by others. Although poor Brazilians do not necessarily get on with all their neighbours, they are aware that neighbourliness and a sense of community in which 'everyone knows each other' are factors that better-off citizens living in closed condominiums cannot easily enjoy. It is ironic that the better off live in such fear of them, since many people from poor neighbourhoods throughout urban Brazil are nervous about entering spaces dominated by middle-class people – at Carnival time, for example – for fear of suffering discrimination and police harassment (Sheriff 1999: 8). Bairro da Paz provides an example of a peripheral community that continues to organize itself, an asset on which government needs to build. Although the BCS commander clearly appreciated that, to some extent, in trying to build a relationship with the FPEBP, he seems to have found it difficult to make the leap from being an authority to becoming a partner. This is not, however, a problem of individuals. It is a problem of structural constraints that are also a burden on the police themselves. Before reaching a final conclusion on the Bahian UPP, I will now attempt to offer the police side of the story.

The Bahian police: another deficit of respect?

In an effort to be as fair as possible to both the military police and to the Bahian UPP project, I decided to canvass the views of police working in the first, and to date most successful, BCS project in Salvador. This was installed in the Calabar neighbourhood, a relatively small area of irregular settlement that extends down towards the coast from just below the site of the Federal University of Bahia's social science department in the Federação neighbourhood, on a ridge occupied by the great house of a plantation. This choice also made it possible to explore the question of the role of female police in the new public security strategy, since this prototype project had fully complied with the mixed-sex policing model that was not implemented in Bairro da Paz because of lack of trained officers. The women interviewed were between twenty-five and thirty-five years of age and mostly relatively recent entrants: only one, still in the rank of soldier, had served in the force for more than ten years. These women were not from socially advantaged backgrounds, and tended to use expressions that demonstrated their sense of social distance from the established upper and middle classes. One of them remarked that she wished they would instal a base in the neighbourhood where she lived. They were, however, also young women with strong aspirations to social mobility through continuing education that would enhance their opportunities as professionals. Entry into the military police provided financial stability, despite what they all saw as low pay, as well as the status and security of becoming a public servant. The job's working hours left time for study. Working in the military police also provided the satisfaction of providing an essential service to society, the selflessness of which was enhanced by the risks that came with the job, even if society itself did not appreciate police work as it should. Several, but not all, of the interviewees came from families in which parents or other relatives had been military police or firemen. Yet these highly motivated women who had volunteered to serve in Bahia's first experiment in a new approach to policing poor communities also expressed frustrations about the career structure on offer in the force, arguing that it did not provide adequate opportunities for access to the higher ranks to those who began their career at the bottom as soldiers, especially if they were women.[11]

A member of my research team also obtained data, using the same questions, from male police in another BCS established in the working-class *subúrbio ferroviário* district of the city. The *subúrbio ferroviário* runs from the Calçada neighbourhood of the old lower city, the port area in which Geovane Mascarenhas was seized by Special Patrol officers, through twenty other poor neighbourhoods connected by a suburban railway line up to Paripe, to the north-east. Originally a zone of textile production and light industries, the now deindustrialized *subúrbio* is a series of low-income neighbourhoods with high crime and homicide rates. The location of BCSs here cannot be explained as a measure to reassure neighbouring middle- and upper-class residents of the area since there are none, although the neighbourhood that the interviewees police is urbanized and relatively well provided with services.

A common theme throughout all these interviews was the low public esteem that police enjoy today. The oldest interviewee, Carlos, lamented the change that had taken place during twenty-four years of service that had brought him to the rank of corporal. He said that he had been proud to wear his uniform in the days when it brought him respect in his neighbourhood, and being a policeman was to have a profession, 'like a mechanic or stonemason'. He felt that he served the people and young people then respected the police. What was prestigious these days was to be a bandit or a football player, 'the easy life', and the young now had no respect for anyone. The idea that young people had no respect for the police was also echoed by the youngest of the women police interviewed, who joked that the generalization applied even to small children. Among the men, Gustavo, slightly younger than Carlos but still in his forties, was disturbed that his own son, an 'innocent worker', ran away when the police approached, complaining that 'the people' wanted the police to exercise control but didn't accept how they acted, calling them 'brutes', 'ignorant' or 'other nice adjectives'. This was a game that it was simply impossible for the force to win. The longest serving of the women police, Jussara, was especially disillusioned. She hoped to leave the force, because she felt it was impossible for a woman soldier working the streets to achieve promotion in internal competition with officers 'who work without losing nights of sleep and running the risk of being victim of some bum [*vagabundo*]'. Her sense of not being valued by the police corporation itself was echoed by the younger Eliene, and not one of the subjects interviewed had a good word for politicians, hardly surprising in a year in which the state government's failure to implement improvements in pay and career structure had led to a bitter twelve-day strike. Jussara referred to her own experience of the strike in making the case that nobody valued the police, saying how sad it made her when members of the public, who seemed to expect their police to work miracles, called the strikers themselves lazy bums. This was just another demonstration of how the police were the 'arse end' of public service, she complained. The theme that the public demanded much but understood and sympathized little ran through the entire set of interviews.

Various interviewees criticized media representations of policing. Eliene grumbled that the most-watched national television news programme, *Jornal Nacional*, just fuelled public prejudice by mainly reporting on Rio de Janeiro and 'their corrupt police' (something that, by implication, she seemed to accept as a reality). Kátia remarked that all these things came together to foster demoralization:

> Brazilian society is very prejudiced, ignorant even. It sits looking at this crap that's shown on TV, which demoralizes the male and female warriors [*guerreiros*] of the corporation, makes the public think that every PM [military policeman] is a thief, is corrupt, but that's a consequence of the lack of dignity that the government transmits to its police, with miserable salaries. Except the government and public forget something important. We're not academics, we don't live stuck in our books, but we know the reality of the streets, which no higher education course can teach. On the day that that class organizes itself and stops work, Bahia, Brazil, comes to an end.

All the women interviewed saw the BCS project as something that had the potential to transform the public image of the police for the better. They emphasized that they were all volunteers, attracted to the programme because they saw it as a way of proving themselves able to make a real difference to the public order situation, as police, and as women police determined to show themselves worthy of professional respect on the part of their male colleagues and the public. I have no doubt that they have carried out their work effectively, establishing a true 'proximity policing' practice whose appreciation by the residents is demonstrated not simply by a lack of violence in this neighbourhood today but by the everyday gestures of hospitality, affection and gratitude that all the interviewees recounted. The only thing that most residents of Calabar seem to be worried about is that the base might be withdrawn in the future and that they would lose the kind of twenty-four-hour security whose absence Jussara lamented in her own place of residence. Yet the officers themselves were as realistic about the programme as a whole as they were proud of their own achievements. Clara summed up the balance sheet as follows:

I can say that the experience of Calabar is super-successful, and I don't really need to say it because the media has taken that on. In other communities where bases have been installed, the experiences haven't been very good, and there we can cite various factors. Is Calabar small? Yes it is. Was it easier? No, because we were the first, and if this one had gone wrong it would have been very bad for the next experiences, I can say a calamity for the Public Security Secretariat's project. Like I said, it's successful, but it's restricted to Calabar. On the other side we have communities like Roça da Sabina and Alto das Pombas, hostages of the traffic that served as the escape route for the traffickers that operated in Calabar. Do the police know this? They know, but they don't have enough personnel to control it. There we've got a problem, if we can't operate on the surrounding area, what's going to happen? If the traffic gets stronger in the surrounding areas, what isn't dealt with in time could become a problem for the Calabar base itself. So I think the project has to be control Calabar, which has now happened, and preoccupy ourselves with the neighbouring conspiracies [laughs].

I think that the problem of trafficking remaining in places where the base has been installed results from the simple fact of not having studied and not knowing the slightest thing about the type of people with whom the base was going to have to deal. For me what is happening in Nordeste [de Amaralina], I could call it 'Operation Suicide' – I'm going to speak very quietly now! The police were just thrown in there, many of them against their wishes, different from us who came of our own free will, and then what happens is what we're seeing, police risking their lives, the community against them, etc.

Once again dropping her voice so that her commander in the next room could not overhear her, Clara confided that she regarded her police training as 'dreadful', outmoded, and too much theory and too little practice. She complained, in particular, that developing the necessary practical skills was inhibited by the current practice of not allowing trainees to learn how to perform ostensive policing on the street in the company of more experienced officers. This latter practice was, she concluded, part of a general effort to prevent novice police becoming 'contaminated' by the bad attitudes of more experienced colleagues, 'all those ideas that we earn little for the risks we take and so on'. What is obvious from her perceptive remarks on the pacification policy is that Clara is the kind of highly intelligent young woman that any police force in the world would like to recruit. It is therefore worrying that not only Clara but the rest of her equally capable and professional colleagues in Calabar were critical of the quality and resourcing of police training and many other aspects of the military police corporation, including its career structure. Although Clara herself was hoping that the university course that she was taking in her spare time would enable her to compete successfully in the competition to enter the officer corps, she was not sanguine about the prospects of moving from soldier to officer, and said that her fall-back plan if she failed to achieve her ambition was to get a postgraduate qualification and go into teaching, which would be less advantageous economically but involve less risk. Her colleague Eliene had already decided that, once she completed her own university course, she would try to enter another career.

The youngest of the men working in the other base, Henrique, was much more confident about his ability to become an officer. He had used the argument that his time as a soldier would only be temporary to convince his mother that his career choice was not a bad one. His older colleague Gustavo was content that he would eventually achieve the rank of corporal, noting that he was 'well connected' and had no blots on his record. Carlos, who reached the rank of corporal after seventeen years of service, did not feel it was 'correct' to talk about any criticisms that he might have of the promotion system, and pointed to the advantages of having a job that provided himself and his mother with a health plan that freed them from the need to wait in the queues at public hospitals. Both he and Gustavo supplemented their police salaries by running successful small businesses that had a loyal clientele. All the interviewees were asked about off-duty second and casual jobs (*bicos*). Eliene worked in her off-duty hours providing security at events and especially during Carnival, remarking that six days' extra work brought the equivalent of a month's salary. But this was simply extra money to do her nails and hair, and what she could undertake was limited by the need to study. Claudia, who had a child to support, was very interested in earning extra money at the beginning, and mentioned the possibility of working in a private security operation run by a police colleague. But she argued that it was easier for men than women to get extra work 'just by winking their eyes'. She found working during Carnival tiring, as well as disagreeable for religious reasons since she is an evangelical, and the extra money didn't compensate for losing time with her son. Jussara had also received invitations from a sergeant to work in private security operations, but declined, once again because she wanted the time to attend to her family, and her husband disapproved of her working extra hours. Given their higher levels of professional aspiration, it is clear that it will be much harder for the police corporation to 'retain and motivate' officers such as the young women working in the Calabar base because the problem is not simply one of base salary but of satisfying their desire to secure professional recognition in a less stressful occupation.

In relation to the way in which the training for service in the BCS was supposedly based on the *Kōban* community policing model,[12] Jussara remarked that the Japanese would be shocked by the absurd way in which their ideas were being applied in Bahia. All the women complained about the inadequacy of the training in the use of firearms that they had received at the police academy. Claudia had joined a gun club to which her father belonged, which she both enjoyed as a leisure activity and felt helped her in her job, although she had never actually had to fire a shot while on duty. She had, however, experienced the dangers of her professional role when travelling on a bus with her son that was subjected to an armed assault in the early hours of the morning. Claudia was certain that she would be killed in front of her child if the bandits looked inside her handbag and saw the documents she was carrying that would identify her as a policewoman. Fortunately, despite having had the time to be more thorough, they were satisfied with the small amount of cash she was carrying and her cheap cell phone. Other off-duty officers using the city's public transport have sadly been less lucky, and this risk was a preoccupation of several other interviewees.

In speaking about the role of female police, Kátia and Jussara referred to *machista* culture within the corporation, and there was general dissatisfaction with the still-limited number of places available to women relative to men, as well as with the number of women occupying senior posts, although Eliene felt that the situation was improving, noting that the number of women police chiefs in the civil police had increased, and that there were now more female commanders in the military police itself. Even Jussara, who argued that many women were disillusioned by the present structure of command, looked forward to a day when a woman would be general commander of the military police in Bahia. For Jussara, there were plenty of women who did the job better than men, even if they were still obliged to prove their competence to some of their male colleagues, and there were lazy women in the police just as there were lazy men. Like the other women interviewed, Jussara did argue that women were different from men in their more 'sensitive and delicate' nature, which gave them advantages when a situation called for an ability to communicate rather than use of physical force. These women saw feminine qualities as opening up new spaces for women in the future development of police work, as the community policing model with which they all identified became increasingly important. Clara remarked that the high command had perceived the importance of women in the project of 'pacifying' Calabar, but insisted that women could do everything a man could do 'without loosing her gentleness and sensibility'. Claudia argued that only the oldest officers, or those who were a pain in the neck whatever their age, now argued that 'ostensive' policing on the street was only for men: 'I always say that what makes a good police officer is not the sex, nor the sexual preference, but level of preparation or lack of it. There are men in the corporation whose bellies are dragging on the ground who couldn't manage to run five hundred metres, so it's not a matter of being a man or a woman, it's a matter of being competent.' Marcia, who insisted she could do anything as well as a man, summed up her view of the special advantages of women in community policing as follows:

> Women always try to bring in a more human logic, closer to the community, and today we are at the height of the recognition of the woman's role, because two things came together at the right moment. Women are more attentive to the necessities of the population and, as a result, we are better received. A police officer who is a mother, for example, succeeds in entering into the universe of these women of the periphery with greater ease, the conversations sometimes take off from vaccination for the child, the diet and education of children. It is easier for us to understand the anxieties and necessities of these women and, in some way, to try to help them.

Eliene also elaborated on the theme of why the 'proximity policing' model would enhance the role of female police:

> You won't easily see a woman starting off by slapping people about, calling them bums, and all those things that generally happen with male units. Men use more brutality, the physical force that they have, don't they, and we go about it with more skill. Our physique is part of it, but I think it's a question of good manners as well. Our society says that women are better mannered, while men are brutal. Here in the base the police are organized in pairs to pay visits to homes, you don't arrive just demanding information, you have a conversation, you ask about day-to-day things, household activities, how are the kids doing in school, health. Men generally don't have the capacity for this type of conversation. I think that in the relationship with the public we women come out much better, and with the tendency to have more community security bases, there'll be more places for women in the police recruitment competitions as well.

All the female police interviewed shared these ideas about the differences between male and female 'natures', which are also embedded in official public security policy.

At first sight, they may seem alarmingly essentialist ideas, especially in a city in which some women participate in criminal activities such as drug trafficking and kidnapping, school kids sometimes stab each other in quarrels over boyfriends, and female police have shown themselves capable of the same kind of violence as men. In her analysis of the workings of Salvador's system of Women's Police Stations (*Delegacias de Policia dos Direitos da Mulher*) during the 1990s, anthropologist Sarah Hautzinger (2007) has shown how the expectations of the feminists who were the intellectual authors of this system were confounded in practice. Created specifically to address the endemic problem of domestic violence by men against women, these units of the civil police, staffed entirely by female officers, were expected to provide battered women from the lower classes with a sympathetic hearing. Hautzinger found that female officers used violence towards accused men as part of their effort to convince male colleagues that they were 'real police' doing 'real police work' (a problem that might have been less acute if the programme had not opted for single-sex units). This tended to increase rather than diminish the likelihood that perpetrators would reoffend. Hautzinger also found that the women police were often very unsympathetic towards the victims, seeing them as weak women who had failed to stand up for themselves.

In this case, there was a substantial social class distance between the predominantly white officers of the *Delegacias* and the poorer black women from the urban periphery who formed the majority of complainants. This is not so much the case with the military police officers discussed here. Nevertheless, Hautzinger's community ethnography revealed that 'blaming the victim' also occurred within the poor communities themselves, when women who had managed to achieve a significant degree of economic independence from men spoke about other women who stayed with partners who repeatedly beat them, often because they lacked not simply the economic means to maintain themselves and their children independently, but also support networks in the form of kin living locally, or the moral and material support of members of a religious community sympathetic to their plight.[13] How individual women officers might react to a given situation is conditioned by social relations as well as by personal experiences. It certainly cannot be taken for granted that women will inevitably be more 'gentle' than men. Hautzinger's work on Salvador aside, there has been a recent case of a female police officer beating a detained man in the testicles in Acapulco, Mexico (Michel 2014b). The well-documented participation of female US soldiers in the torture of Iraqi men detained in the Abu Ghraib complex in 2003 indicates that the way a situation is constructed within the group exercising power and authority is crucially important for understanding human rights violations.

Yet the fact that the women police under discussion here saw behaving in a more sympathetic, communicative and less violent way than men as crucial to their own empowerment seems to be the crucial point. Although they remained eager to prove they could 'do the job' as well as men when it came to walking the mean streets and dealing with 'bandits', they also saw the advantages of an intelligence-based approach to policing that would be built on establishing good relations with the population by means of 'proximity policing'. Their enthusiasm for adopting this approach was based on their firm conviction that this was a type of policing for which women were better suited 'by nature', and that it would lead to a significant enhancement of the career prospects of women in the police corporation in the longer term. Their propensity to think in this way no doubt reflects their social profiles as younger women who were seeking their own social mobility. Yet they did display a genuine 'empathy' for the poor citizens of the periphery throughout the interviews, and were critical of the 'outmoded' military culture of the corporation, and of middle classes, media and politicians that were largely unappreciative of their contribution.

It was interesting that some who had experience of policing in the more 'noble' areas of the city did not feel that this fitted their notion of what was important in *public* service. Clara, for example, recalled that her experience of carrying out ostensive policing in the upscale Camino das Árvores district was not positive: 'the residents, principally the store owners, provided food, mineral water, a nice kind of support, but nothing comes free, either the bread or the *cachaça*,[14] so the quid pro quo was to take care of their establishments, guard their homes, just like a private security guard'. Moving to Calabar was a shock, since if in Camino das Árvores the problem was 'arrogance', in Calabar it was 'lack of trust and good manners'. But treating the residents with extreme good manners and respect had paid dividends, and Clara saw the problem as one of deprivation. Once the state started providing 'the minimum in a decent way', she was confident that many social problems would be resolved. Claudia agreed with this diagnosis, pointing out that she told residents: 'look, I'm not an extra-terrestrial, I live in the periphery like you do and I know what your problems are'. Yet in discussing the question of 'policing the periphery' these women were also strongly conscious that priority had been given to poor communities that were close to upscale neighbourhoods, even if there were some bases in other areas. They saw it as essential that all the poor neighbourhoods in the city receive the kind of policing that they were providing in Calabar because they insisted that the security they were providing was principally for the residents themselves and that it was their *right* as citizens to enjoy this new kind of respectful and humane policing.

Eliene explicitly took the view that future policy should make a priority of the security of poor communities in their own right. Like the other women, she tended to see the BCS project as a social project, to which the police could contribute in important ways beyond simply guaranteeing security, but whose potential could not be fully realized without actions by other sectors of government, and investments in infrastructure and public services including transport. Gustavo, in contrast, explicitly rejected the idea that the BCS was a social project. He saw it as part of a 'public order' strategy that should focus on areas with high indices of crime and violence, which would in itself benefit the poor neighbourhoods in which crime and violence were reduced. His younger colleague Henrique, who liked to identify himself as 'a resident of the ghetto', was, however, more insistent on the need to treat the population with respect and invest in public services and tackle the problems of the periphery, from potable water to the 'law of silence', in a holistic manner. He blamed 'the middle and rich class' for its 'abandonment of honest citizens to their fate' and hoped that the BCS programme was a sign that things would change.

Carlos, the oldest officer interviewed, as we might expect, took a 'traditional' view of policing. He accepted that his unit's orders were to achieve greater 'proximity' to the population, taking 'drastic measures' (shooting) only as a last resort. But although he mentioned the need for dialogue, he responded to questions about relationships with the community by saying that the residents 'don't interfere with our work', while the shop owners 'help a lot' by supplying coffee, water and biscuits. For Carlos, what was needed was change in society, especially for parents to bring up their children better, and for the federal government to deliver on its promises to create more drug rehabilitation centres. Police work was, however, impeded because it was only the human rights of bandits which were taken into consideration, and he had heard that police who caused deaths could lose their bonuses. It would be easy to mock Carlos for being an 'old-fashioned' exemplar of a military police culture harking back to the years of dictatorship. Yet he was not wrong in seeing violence as a social problem, even if blaming the parents is inadequate both as a diagnosis and a guide to possible solutions, or in criticizing the government's inadequate response to its own diagnosis of drug addiction as a public health, rather than police, problem. Although it is hardly possible to draw sweeping conclusions on the basis of such a small sample, there is evidence here that attitudes are different between generations. The idea that a new generation of police could form the basis for reform of policing style is therefore not utopian, although it clearly depends on improved resourcing and a political commitment to creating the wider conditions under which community policing can work.

As the commentaries of the police interviewed demonstrate, the limitations of the existing policy were only too apparent to those charged with implementing it on the streets. Everyone took it as read that crime would migrate, not only within Salvador and its Metropolitan Region, but also from Salvador to the cities of the interior. The installation of bases in some 'hot spots' could not resolve the larger problem of drug trafficking and violence in the state. It was clear to the serving police that action against trafficking needed to take the form of disarticulating wider supply networks of both arms and drugs as well as persecuting local dealers. There was also a consensus that it was often difficult to understand why some areas had received bases and others had not in the light of their crime and violence indices, although Carlos and some of the female officers suggested that answers to that question should be sought in the sphere of politics. Existing resources were clearly inadequate to resolve the public security problems of Bahia, and it was unfair for the public to blame the police for a situation that was the responsibility of politicians.

There was little satisfaction with pay and career prospects among the younger soldiers, but dissatisfaction with the state government and the high command of the police corporation extended beyond

resentment about how under-resourcing and lack of adequate preparation were making the BCS programme deliver very uneven results,
with the blame for problems likely, as usual, to be laid at the door of
the people who put their lives on the line. The interviewees recognized
the existence of problems of corruption within the ranks, and made
direct reference to the relationships between serving police and private
security operations. The importance of the latter problem will be
illustrated in my analysis of the police strikes in the next and final
section of this chapter. These interviews also showed, however, that
young officers can survive economically without being involved in
those kinds of activities, that they are willing to embrace new ideas
about policing, and that they can possess a strong ethic of public
service that is to a considerable extent a manifestation of class consciousness. The conclusion to be drawn must be that it is possible
to develop a public security policy for the urban periphery that is
principally for the people who live in the urban periphery, and to
find police who will be strongly motivated to participate in building
such a community-security-oriented model, although retaining the best
educated of them may prove difficult. The problem is the politics that
drive the implementation of the current policy, driven by a securitization of poverty that responds to the fears, aspirations and interests
of the more privileged sectors of the population, and fails to support
the capacity of poor communities to produce leaderships that could
become effective partners of the right kind of police.

Lessons from Bahia

The wrong kind of policing easily undermines possibilities for
winning community support for the bases. In the case of Bairro da
Paz, fear of the traffickers inhibited public expressions of support for
the project among residents and community leaders alike, although
many people were privately willing to admit that they thought that
a 'UPP' was now the best option, given the number of killings that
disintegration of the 'order of crime' was provoking. Unfortunately,
the first months of 'pacification' did not build on that potential basis
for winning hearts and minds as successfully as they might have done
because too many people felt they were being treated as 'suspects'
by a force that was criminalizing the entire population. Although
the base organized a Christmas party for children and handed out
presents, bringing in the press and television to bear witness to the

'success' of the new order, other children received Christmas presents from the hands of traffickers. The subsequent story so far and its consequences have already been related.

The performance of the Bairro da Paz base in terms of reduction of homicide rates has thus far been less than satisfactory. Even if pacification cannot eliminate drug trafficking entirely, it has been expected to promote changes in the way drugs are distributed, away from models based on armed control of a territory, and perhaps even reduce the supply of the drugs that cause most damage to health and ability to function in society. Yet the traffickers have not only maintained a place in the *becos* (back alleys) of the community, but have continued to compete for control from this marginal space, not much of an improvement over a prior situation in which the traffickers were already operating in a relatively discreet way. Opinions of the base in Bairro da Paz could become more positive, and the prospects for expelling the traffickers improved, if much-needed improvements in infrastructure and services are implemented alongside a security regime that becomes more focused on the needs of residents. Yet that would require more personnel than the base currently has, and police with a stronger dedication to a community-policing model of 'approximation' to the residents. Attitudes may also be changed if more residents can be given security of tenure and guarantees that they will not be displaced for reasons of class-biased 'public interest' without consideration of Raquel Rolnik's 'sustainable alternatives' to eviction. At the very least they will need a rehousing offer that would represent a move forward, rather than backwards, in their individual lives, but there is a broader issue of the desirability of allowing more residents from higher social classes to colonize urban spaces that could easily be transformed into safe and pleasant working-class neighbourhoods that will promote the upward mobility of their residents and their families.

It remains unclear whether there is a political will to think about such alternatives. Yet it is crystal clear that public security policies need to be democratized, so that the people to whom they may be applied in their more repressive forms feel that they have participated in the setting of priorities, priorities that are meaningful to them in terms of their particular experiences of economic, social and physical insecurities. They also need to feel that the authorities understand their immediate everyday problems and longer-term aspirations and desires. Institutional mechanisms for this exist, such as the Audiências

Publicas that community organizations in Bairro da Paz have convened to dialogue with public authorities, and the Community Security Councils (Conselhos Comunitários de Segurança, CONSEGs), which are supposed to bring together police and representatives of the different kinds of residents inhabiting a region (Galdeano 2010). But although representatives of Bairro da Paz have participated in the local CONSEG, it has always been difficult to transcend the barriers of suspicion that divide Bairro da Paz from the middle-class residents of the surrounding condominiums, particularly given the tendency of senior police officers to identify Bairro da Paz as the home of the area's armed robbers and burglars as well as its drug traffickers.

We have also seen, however, that even the most limited aspirations for the BCSs will not be fulfilled unless the nature of policing changes. Doing that will not depend simply on better training and firm application of sanctions to reduce authoritarianism, failure to respect human rights, and corruption. It will also require improvements to pay and career structures that will diminish the present 'capture' of the agents of public power by private interests. The difficulties of securing a radical reform of the police were brought home by the strike, in February 2012, of Bahian military police affiliated to the ASPRA (Association of Police, Fireman and their Families of the State of Bahia, *Associação dos Policiais, Bombeiros e dos seus Familiares do Estado da Bahia*). The strikers adopted tactics that were very similar to those adopted by crime organizations: they burned buses and patrol cars, and created a 'rumour central' that spread misinformation and fear all over the city. Wire taps revealed joint planning with colleagues in Rio de Janeiro, and political agendas. Among them was a recording of a female officer trying to organize the armed invasion of a police post occupied by officers who were not striking.[15] Since many other actions taken during the strike were illegal (and military police strikes are technically mutinies), when it ended the state government sent some of its ringleaders to jail. Yet the principal leader re-emerged to stand as candidate for councillor in the municipal elections for the PSDB, and as 'Soldado Prisco' achieved the fourth-highest vote of the sixty-nine candidates elected. Although federal troops were sent in to secure the city and protect the state parliament building, which the strikers occupied and trashed, imitating the striking firemen of Rio de Janeiro, both they and non-striking colleagues in the military and civil police made little effort to disguise their sympathy for the strikers.

At one level, this seemed reasonable, since Governor Wagner had followed a nationwide pattern in not fully implementing agreed pay rises and improvements in career structure, and was fulminating about the illegality of the 'mutiny' despite having supported an earlier strike by the police before his career path shifted from trade unionism to electoral politics. But the governor was not entirely wrong in focusing on illegalities. During the twelve days of the strike, 135 murders were committed. Of these the Department of Homicides and Protection of the Person detected forty-five cases that manifested 'characteristics of extermination'. Among those, the department's director suspected that between twenty-five and thirty killings were probably committed by police acting as militias or clandestine private security agents paid by storekeepers in poor communities, since while the perpetrators were masked they had used arms restricted to military use (Brito and Cirino 2012). This is not the only evidence available of the long-standing significance of death squads in Bahia. Faced with frequent public protests by victims' relatives, the state government had set up a special police department to deal with the problem, although it succeeded only in achieving the conviction of three of the more than three hundred persons against which it issued indictments between 2004 and 2007, when it underwent a severe cutback of personnel (Noronha 2008).

The ASPRA declared a new strike on the evening of 15 April 2014, although the union had put its rumour mill into operation earlier in the day. Although the strike lasted only for forty-three hours, fifty-three persons lost their lives in the course of the action, public transport was shut down, and supermarkets were looted in various parts of the city, despite the arrival of 5,000 federal troops, principally deployed in the 'noble' neighbourhoods and tourist zones (Rodrigues and Longo 2014). Nine months earlier a working group had been formed to discuss the 'modernization' of the Bahian military police, and the state government argued that this was not the moment to discuss salaries again, since the payments agreed after the 2012 strike would not be fully implemented until 2015.[16] Nevertheless, Public Security Secretary Barbosa stated that new concessions that would cost an extra 50 million *reais*, including retirement for female police officers after twenty-five years' service, had been made in response to demands from the ASPRA representatives before the strike, and that the union had broken an undertaking not to strike again.[17]

In the end, and following the intercession of Archbishop of Salvador and Primate of Brazil Dom Murilo Krieger, the strikers returned to work without apparently having secured significant advances over what had already been in the modernization plan, beyond a marginal improvement in bonus payments and an agreement to delay revision of the corporation's ethical code pending further discussion (Dourado 2014). Many members of the public as well as the government viewed the strike as political in motivation, given the forthcoming elections for state governor and the ASPRA leader's militancy in the PSDB. The high cost in terms of life and damage to property demonstrated how dependent the city was on the order that its police maintained, yet it hardly improved the force's public image. Shortly after the strike ended, the ASPRA leader was arrested on a federal warrant for crimes against the Law of National Security allegedly committed during the 2012 strike, while relaxing in an upscale resort on the northern coast of Bahia.[18] On arrival in Brasilia, he was incarcerated in a cell with common criminals, which evidently presented a serious threat to his personal safety. By this act, the state sent a powerful message, although it did not inhibit civil and military police in other states from striking in the hope of gaining further concessions in the year of the World Cup and presidential elections. 'Soldier Prisco' himself emerged from jail to be elected a member of the state congress, receiving the third-highest vote on this occasion.

As officers frequently remarked in the interviews discussed in this chapter, police are human beings, and like other human beings 'liable to make mistakes'. As I stressed earlier, working-class Brazilians are not necessarily opposed to the extermination of 'marginals' and 'bandits' (Caldeira 2002), while the 'law of crime' itself is not noted for its willingness to grant human rights to rapists. It is important not to romanticize any of the actors in the complicated scenarios in which public security policy is entangled, but it is also vital not to demonize them unreflectively, not least since the biggest crooks of all do not live in *favelas*. In exploring the contradictions, unintended consequences and possible hidden agendas of public security policies, we need to peer through the smoke created by the securitization of poverty to grasp the social realities and power relations that shape the way such policies are implemented and enacted in practice, realities and relations that it is still possible to transform through democratic public action in a country like Brazil.

4 | STATE TRANSFORMATIONS, ILLEGAL ECONOMIES AND COUNTER-INSURGENCY IN MEXICO

In contrast to Brazil, no military coup interrupted the civilian rule established in Mexico after the twenty years of instability that followed the 1910 revolution. The architect of long-term stabilization was a former general greatly respected by his peers, President Lázaro Cárdenas (1934–40). Cárdenas was also responsible for the radical phase of Mexico's agrarian reform and the nationalization of foreign oil companies that gave the state company, PEMEX, a monopoly over the production of oil and sale of petrol. What came to be called the Institutional Revolutionary Party (PRI) was the political instrument that the *caudillos* (military strongmen) that won the Mexican revolution created to stabilize their rule. Mexico had elections in which different parties, some satellites of the PRI, others truly independent, put up rival candidates. But until the year 2000, the Mexican president was always the candidate of the PRI, enjoying six-year terms of almost untrammelled executive power but without the right to re-election. The Peruvian novelist Mario Vargas Llosa described Mexico as 'the perfect dictatorship' because of the apparently limited amount of repression that was needed to maintain the system.

In reality, the state ruled by the PRI was never truly a Leviathan, or as Mexicans liked to say, using the image of the pre-colonial Aztec empire and its monarch, a 'pyramid' lorded over by a '*tlatoani*' (Pansters 1997). Anthropologists and political scientists devoted considerable energy to 'decentring the regime', showing how rule was negotiated between the political centre and both elite and popular actors in the different regions of a very diverse country (Lomnitz-Adler 1992; Joseph and Nugent 1994; Rubin 1996). Attention has also been paid to reproduction of the PRI apparatus itself, through enduring clique structures that contributed to the regime's stability by being relatively inclusive in their incorporation of new members (Camp 2013). The PRI regime created a system of state clientelism and practices for co-opting and controlling dissident peasant and workers' movements.

Yet despite the effectiveness of its more pacific hegemonic practices, PRI hegemony was always, in Gramsci's famous phrase, 'protected by the armour of coercion' (Pansters 2012).

In this chapter I discuss two historical moments in which this became particularly visible, although violence has always been a regular facet of the everyday 'negotiation' of rule in Mexico in localized forms. The first is the counter-insurgency war carried out during the presidencies of Gustavo Díaz Ordaz and Luis Echeverría in the state of Guerrero in the 1960s and 1970s. This was Mexico's equivalent of the 'dirty wars' carried out in other Latin American countries by military dictatorships against what they presented as 'communist subversion'. The second is the counter-insurgency operation against communities that supported the rebellion of the Zapatista Army of National Liberation (EZLN) in 1994. In the next chapter I will examine a third historical moment and its consequences in the state of Michoacán, the 'war against drugs' conducted by the second administration of the National Action Party (PAN) under President Felipe Calderón (2006–12) during the period of alternation of power after the PRI's candidate lost the 2000 elections to Vicente Fox. Although the PRI itself was not in power nationally, the political alternation that took place did not change much that was not changing for other reasons at the structural level. Many citizens felt that the shallowness of Mexico's 'transition to democracy' was confirmed by the manner in which the PRI itself returned to power in the 2012 elections, which provoked the student protest movement *YoSoy132*, subject to prompt repression once Enrique Peña Nieto assumed power.

My interests in this chapter are in both continuity and change. The 'authoritarian' regime of the PRI in the 1960s and 1970s tended to be seen as stable and effective despite its need to resort to repression, which included killing students in the centre of Mexico City at the time of the 1968 Olympic Games, the Tlatelolco massacre, followed by a sustained persecution of activists that linked mobilization in the cities to the 'dirty war' in Guerrero. But if we look at Guerrero itself, it becomes apparent that the superficial 'success' of the repression simply removed the incentives to seek solutions to long-term problems that are still relevant to understanding conflict and violence in the twenty-first century. The Guerrero counter-insurgency war and later operations in Chiapas exemplify elements of continuity in the 'development–security nexus' discussed in the first chapter. Yet change is important as well. One key element of change was the unravelling of the established bases of PRI hegemony as the import-substituting industrialization model of the Mexican developmentalist state became exhausted under the pressures of globalization. The response of the apparatus to this structural crisis, and the conjunctural need to resort to electoral fraud to secure the election of the PRI's candidate, Carlos Salinas de Gortari, in the strongly disputed election of 1988, was an attempt to remodel the economy on neoliberal lines. The political methods used to secure the transition included the more selective use of traditional means of securing consent, state clientelism to co-opt some social movements, and repression to deal with others. But the Salinas administration also embraced new neoliberal techniques of rule, including neoliberal multiculturalism (Overmyer-Velázquez 2011). Mexico was the second country after Norway to ratify the International Labour Organization's Resolution 169, the Indigenous and Tribal Peoples Convention, and Salinas subsequently changed the Constitution to declare Mexico 'a nation that has a pluricultural composition originally founded in its indigenous peoples' (De la Peña 2006). Yet the same administration grasped the politically sensitive nettle of making changes to Article 27 of the Constitution, which declared an end to the land redistribution policies of the post-revolutionary state, and opened a legal door to the privatization of lands granted by the state to the agrarian reform communities called *ejidos* under a social property regime that conceded only inalienable rights of use.[1]

A second, more subterranean, series of changes took place during this neoliberal transition in the networks of power lying behind the public façade of the state and its dignified institutions, which I have analysed in earlier publications as the formation of a 'shadow state' in which illicit economic activities played an increasingly important role in constructing political relations (Gledhill 1999). These included backstage transactions related to the privatization of public assets, along with dubious kinds of financial speculation, asset stripping and investments in property and tourism development. The state continued, however, to play its long-established, and in the context of a neoliberal transition, apparently perverse, role of featherbedding private capital. To ensure that investment deals that went sour did not redound on the investors but rather on the taxpayer, in 1990 the Salinas government created the Banking Fund for the Protection of Savings (FOBAPROA). This used public money to cover the losses of private investors, under the pretext of solving the liquidity problems of a privatized banking system that had provided ample scope for dubious transactions involving politicians and their entrepreneurial protégés. Although long-established forms of corruption involving both the workers' union and management continued to be the order of the day in the state-owned oil company PEMEX, important consequences did flow from the way that politically assisted manipulation of market relationships increased in importance as a source of elite wealth accumulation relative to traditional forms of corruption based on looting state-owned enterprises. These consequences were extended by the increasing interest of political figures in sharing in the profits of drug trafficking and money laundering. Individuals cultivated different relationships in the sphere of illicit wealth accumulation and provided political protection to different players. The shadow networks of power therefore became more fragmented and disarticulated. The effect of these changes within the shadow state sometimes became visible at the level of the official state in incidents in which different elements of the security forces worked at cross-purposes, and on occasion exchanged shots with each other.

The changing articulation of political and criminal networks is related to changes in the organization of Mexican drug trafficking and the increasing importance of Mexican cartels in the supply of drugs to the United States during the 1980s (Campbell 2009; Grillo 2012). As time went by, consumption of drugs increased within Mexico itself. Levels of violence increased as rival cartels competed for control of trans-shipment routes, marijuana and opium poppy production zones, and facilities for processing cocaine and manufacturing methamphetamines. Smaller cartels broke away from the original parent organizations. The growth of the drugs economy, accompanied by less threatening kinds of illegal economic activities, was, as Salvador Maldonado (2013) has shown for the Hot Country region of Michoacán, a consequence of the meltdown of the agrarian economy provoked by Salinas de Gortari's neoliberal 'shock therapy' and the disadvantageous terms that his administration accepted in negotiating the North American Trade Agreement. But it was the growing violence of the competition between the cartels which provided the pretext for Felipe Calderón's 'war' and talk of Mexico being a 'failed state' in some quarters.

Although the concept of 'failed states' has become a commonplace of North Atlantic security discourses, I do not find it a helpful concept for understanding the relationships between political and criminal violence in Mexico, not least because not only drug traffickers but also other kinds of economic interests can benefit from the violence perpetrated by paramilitary groups, always a 'deniable violence' from which the state can readily dissociate itself. The PRI's return to power was marked by an apparent restoration of order to the house, represented by the new federal operations to 'pacify' the Michoacán state discussed in the next chapter, and high-profile arrests of cartel chiefs, including Joaquín Guzmán Loera, *El Chapo* ('Shorty'), boss of the Sinaloa cartel and still ranked 67 in the *Forbes* list of the world's most powerful people in mid-2014.[2] That there has been some change under the Peña Nieto government seems clear, for the reasons that I have already mentioned in discussing Ciudad Juárez in Chapter 2. As in Brazil, criminal organizations have reacted to a changing situation, but in Mexico it seems that the two biggest organizations, the Sinaloa and Gulf cartels, have begun to collaborate against a third network, the Zetas, in the interests of ensuring that their core businesses are not disrupted. Journalist Jesús Esquivel has suggested that the motive of the two big cartels for putting the criminal house in order is to maintain the flow of profit not simply from trafficking drugs, but also from the illegal mining that has become an increasingly strategic sector of the illicit economy in Mexico (Esquivel 2014a).

Yet, as we will see, the idea that the PRI government itself was succeeding in 'putting the house in order' was profoundly questionable even before the forced disappearance of forty-three students training to be rural teachers in Guerrero in September 2014 provoked a national and international crisis of credibility. Asking the questions that need to be asked about that may shed light on the issue of what is happening with the shadow state structures that developed in the previous period. Another series of questions about the new PRI government relate to its commitment to completing the neo-liberal capitalist project on which the Salinas government embarked, particularly, though not exclusively, by changing the Constitution to permit private and foreign capital to share in the profits of exploiting Mexico's hydrocarbon resources. These issues are all interrelated and linked to the way in which Mexico's elite is seeking to reimpose state authority by incorporating some armed actors that have their origins in the world of crime into new structures of governance, seeking to co-opt others that may also do little to enhance the rule of law in the longer term, and criminalizing social movements that constitute potential impediments to the onward march of capital accumulation in Mexico's rural areas.

Taking a historical perspective is always helpful for gaining a perspective on the present. It is difficult, for example, to give much credibility to a discourse that focuses on 'the need to restore the rule of law' if the rule of law has in fact never existed in the place to which it is supposedly being restored, and the underlying conditions that created that situation have not been changed. It is also important to follow Arias and Goldstein's observations about the 'violent pluralism' of Latin America's 'violent democracies': violence is no novelty in Latin American history, but historical comparison can tell us something about truly significant changes and variations between countries in the region (Arias and Goldstein 2010). What is disturbing about recent developments, especially in Mexico, is not simply the proliferation of different types of violent organizations, but the ever more shadowy and ambiguous relationships between these organizations, the state and capital, in a formally democratic society. To begin to construct a historical perspective on these issues, I turn to the 'dirty war' in Guerrero.

Establishing 'truths' about state terror and insurgency

In 2002, President Fox appointed Ignacio Carrillo Prieto, a law professor at the National Autonomous University, as Special Prosecutor for Social and Political Movements of the Past (*Fiscalía Especial para Movimientos Sociales y Políticos del Pasado*, FEMOSPP). The Prosecutor's task was to investigate human rights crimes committed during a period in which the state seemed unambiguously authoritarian, under presidents Gustavo Díaz Ordaz (1964–70), Luis Echeverría (1970–76) and José López Portillo (1976–82). This period began with the repression of the student movement after the Tlatelolco massacre in 1968, and continued with counter-insurgency operations against insurgent movements that not only involved the torture, murder and forced disappearance of armed and unarmed left-wing activists, but also harassment, mistreatment, and in some cases mass killings, of members of civilian populations seen as actual or potential supporters of insurgent movements. The epicentre of state terror was in Guerrero, where an armed insurgency established itself in the mountains, financing its operations by kidnapping landowners, businessmen and politicians, and by robbing banks.

The report, compiled by a group of academics and activists, found evidence for the commission of crimes against humanity by the Mexican army and security services. A version that its authors regarded as definitive, entitled *¡Que no vuelva a suceder!* (That it may not happen again!), was delivered to the Special Prosecutor in December 2005, but not made public. An incomplete earlier draft of this text, already circulating among some Mexican intellectuals and journalists, was, however, made public through the Internet in February 2006, by Kate Doyle, director of the Mexico Project of the National Security Archive, a foundation-funded non-profit organization based at George Washington University in the United States.[3] In the discussion that follows I make extensive use of Chapter 6 of the original draft of the report (FEMOSPP 2005).

On 21 November 2006, the Fox government released what it declared was the definitive version of the report (FEMOSPP 2006). Three weeks later the team responsible for the original version accused the Special Prosecutor of having censored their text, noting that the published version completely eliminated the final chapter of conclusions and recommendations and cut parts of others.[4] Words and phrases were changed systematically so as to avoid classifying acts as crimes against humanity in terms of international law, and to minimize the responsibility of the army. The published report did conserve the testimony and documentary evidence that enabled its authors to name 645 persons who disappeared, although the revised text eliminated the adjective 'forced' from references to disappearance. Since Mexican authorities largely remained in denial about more recent forced disappearances eight years later, this was a significant form of censorship.[5] The report also identified ninety-nine cases of extrajudicial execution and more than two thousand cases of torture. But the changes to the text not only impeded the possibility of those responsible for these crimes being brought to account and the relatives of their victims compensated, but also eliminated the original report's diagnosis of what needed to be done institutionally to prevent the future involvement of the state and the army in crimes against humanity.

The Special Prosecutor's office was, as expected, closed immediately after the official version of its report was published, a month before Fox

STATE TRANSFORMATIONS | 115

handed over the presidency to Felipe Calderón. Carillo Prieto himself was accused of judicial incompetence and, subsequently, financial impropriety. Calderón was soon to embark on his 'war' against the drug cartels, which put the army at the forefront of domestic policing operations yet again. This hardly provided a favourable environment for revisiting the original FEMOSPP report's conclusions and recommendations, one of which was that the military should not be used in this way. The Special Prosecutor's only gesture towards bringing those responsible for past crimes to account was an attempt to prosecute the now very elderly former president Echeverría for acts of repression against the student movement. One was the original killing of student protesters in Tlatelolco's Plaza of the Three Cultures on 2 October 1968, when Echeverría was interior minister under Díaz Ordaz. The other, during Echeverría's own term as president, was the 'Corpus Christi massacre' of 10 June 1971. This is also known as the *halconazo*, since students on a protest march were killed by members of an extra-official paramilitary corps known as the Falcons, while riot police stood idly by.

The resurgence of student militancy during Echeverría's presidency was, ironically, a reflection of his government's more populist and anti-imperialist tone, release of some imprisoned leftist leaders, and promises of democratization (Camacho de Schmidt and Schmidt 2007). Echeverría had even called for a minute of silence during his election campaign in memory of the victims of Tlatelolco. But although Echeverría promised a thorough investigation into the 1971 killings, his failure to bring any of those involved to justice made this event a catalyst of new recruitment to revolutionary groups as young activists concluded that peaceful, democratic means of securing change continued to be impossible. The Special Prosecutor's attempt to bring genocide charges, not subject to the Statute of Limitations, against the former president provoked plenty of legal and, in an election year, political controversy, but did not provide the basis for a prosecution, and this sideshow served to further deflect attention from the systematic role of the military in past state repression.

As the FEMOSPP report's authors noted, the language of 'national security' explains the appearance of armed insurgencies as the result of the subversive actions of a handful of politically motivated leaders. The suggestion was that such actors exploited the widespread poverty of peasant farmers who lacked organization of their own. Peasants tended to be portrayed as ignorant and gullible, especially if they were also indigenous people who still spoke indigenous languages and maintained cultural practices that differentiated them from other rural people whose identities rested on the mestizo cultures that the post-revolutionary state sought to promote through public education and the media, as the basis for constructing a 'modern' national society.

Yet, as the draft report showed, the 'subversives' were quite diverse and rather fractious. The guerrilla episodes of the 1970s and 1980s involved some external actors from outside the insurgent regions who belonged to more privileged strata of society, including 'radicalized' students attracted by the Maoist model of taking themselves off to the countryside to 'learn from' the peasants, as well as pro-Soviet Communist Party militants attached to the Revolutionary Action Movement (MAR, *Movimiento de Acción Revolucionaria*). The Maoist outsiders tended to be critical of local insurgent leaders, such as Guerrero's Lucio Cabañas. Cabañas became politically active as a student in the rural teacher-training college (*normal*) at Ayotzinapa, built relations with militants in other regions as secretary general of the National Union of Socialist Peasant Students, and became directly involved in legal peasant struggles from the start of his career as a rural schoolteacher before launching his guerrilla movement in 1967 (Bartra 1996). For Alberto Ulloa Bornemann, one of the militants from an elite family who had regular contact with Cabañas, this charismatic womanizer who seemed little preoccupied about safeguarding his own security was a bit too close to being the 'bandit' that the government accused him of being, in his careless management of the money that the insurgents robbed from banks (Ulloa Bornemann 2007). Discomfort in the relationship was reciprocal. As Gerardo Tort's 2005 documentary film on Cabañas, *La guerrilla y la esperanza*, shows, although Cabañas was familiar with the ideas of Lenin and other Marxists as well as the anarchist tradition of the Mexican Flores Magón brothers, he did not really share the ideologies of his new allies, preferring to emphasize the Christian basis of his commitment to taking from the rich to give to the poor.

There was therefore a major bone of ideological contention between the orthodox communist urban radicals and Cabañas as a leader socially embedded in rural society, which led to an unsuccessful attempt to remove him from leadership of the fighting force that he had created in early 1973, while he was away receiving medical treatment in Mexico City (ibid.; FEMOSPP 2005: 62). Cabañas regarded peasants as protagonists of revolution in their own right, and for that reason saw it as crucial to build support bases in rural communities whatever risks operating in the open in this way created. Marxist-Leninists, in contrast, viewed peasants with suspicion as a 'class' incapable of socialist revolutionary consciousness that could at best only function as a subordinate ally of the 'proletariat'. Maoist activists from the metropolis such as Ulloa Bornemann criticized other urban comrades for trying to impose ideas on peasants that went against the grain of their current cultural and social sensibilities (on gender equality, for example). They wanted to invest resources in rural development projects and to pursue more patient work in rural communities which would produce a better understanding of people whose ideas and attitudes they frequently found perplexing, albeit with a view to 'guiding them' towards socialism. In practice, however, all factions of the left dissipated much of their energy in sectarian squabbling. The communist groups splintered, with 'vanguardists' accusing former comrades of 'populism' and 'reformism'. Proposals to unify insurgent groups foundered not only because of ideological differences and disagreements over tactics and strategy but also because of local rivalries that linked politics to personal ties and family and clan affiliations.

The differences between locals and outsiders were, however, particularly striking, despite the fact that local leaders in Guerrero participated in wider inter-regional and national networks. Even Maoist attitudes frequently betrayed racism as well as paternalism. Their scepticism about the wisdom of armed struggle, however rational it may seem with hindsight, must sometimes have sat uncomfortably with peasant interlocutors who may have lacked access to the weapons needed to confront the army effectively but did not lack their own insurgent traditions, albeit traditions that had little to do with building a Soviet, Cuban or Chinese-style socialist society. After he was finally released from incarceration, Ulloa Bornemann came to change his view of a regime that, in keeping with the other side of its hegemonic strategy, proved willing to reincorporate a reformed citizen from a respectable family. Some of the other Maoists who survived the repression of the 1970s and 1980s were to continue their commitment to grassroots work in the social development programmes promoted by the neoliberal administration of Carlos Salinas in the 1990s (Moguel 1994).

Yet although the divisions and weaknesses of the insurgent movements of the 1970s are important for understanding their defeat, it seems far more important to follow the FEMOSPP report's suggestion to look beyond the discourse of national security to grasp the true nature of the environment of discontent into which these insurgent actors stepped. This is the key to understanding why the systematic annihilation of both armed groups and significant numbers of civilians did not lead to the long-term pacification of Guerrero. A generation of insurgents died or disappeared, but the problems that provoked insurgency did not.

Guerrero: a war that did not pacify

Guerrero's mountains provided an ideal setting for guerrilla warfare, and the state certainly did not lack zones of poverty, marginality and strongly oppressive inter-ethnic relations, although peasant rather than ethnic identities dominated rural mobilization until the 1990s. As Armando Bartra (1996) shows in his study of the political and agrarian conflicts of the 1960s and 1970s, the epicentre of peasant discontent was the Atoyac region of the Costa Grande. The Costa Grande was a region so potentially prosperous that migrant workers from more marginal areas called it their 'North' – that is, a domestic alternative to the United States (FEMOSPP 2005: 6). The government of Lázaro Cárdenas promoted agrarian reform here, one of whose leaders was the great-uncle of Lucio Cabañas, a Zapatista revolutionary general who had fought in Michoacán. Cárdenas armed local *Defensas Rurales* (rural self-defence forces) or 'Red Guards' to fight the 'White Guards' that the landlord class employed to defend a monopoly over land that became even more valuable as coffee and copra production became increasingly important. The organized and armed peasant agrarian movement that developed on the Costa Grande faced considerable resistance from local elites, but it did succeed in achieving a considerable amount of land redistribution. The new landholders' problem then became that of securing real improvements in living standards and access to services such as healthcare and education, for local elites reconfigured their domination by taking control of the commercialization of products, exploiting their continuing ability to control access to political offices and suborn or kill peasant leaders.

Elites used their extra-economic power as local and regional political bosses (*caciques*) to rob ordinary peasant producers of the profits that they should have gained from the buoyant demand for their coffee and copra by paying low prices and charging usurious real interest rates on credit, imposing additional local taxes, and co-opting and corrupting the authorities of the *ejidos* (ibid.: 11–12). With the collaboration of the military forces stationed in the sierras, they also guaranteed impunity to the private interests that used logging concessions granted by the state to extract far more than the legally permitted quantity of timber from community forests without mak-ing even the minimum payments due to the *ejido* communities that remained the legal owners of these resources (ibid.: 10; Bartra 1996: 120). The peasants continued to organize politically to demand an end to this plundering, and more serious steps towards provision of the public services to which they saw themselves entitled. Yet they faced higher authorities that governed in a despotic manner, readily able to call on the police and military and their own gunmen to repress dissenters when co-optation failed, and using ballot fraud to prevent any kind of democratic opening. Leaders who had initially sought to work for peaceful change through peasant unions and civic movements were therefore drawn towards insurrection. Nevertheless, it is interesting, in the light of the more recent history of Guerrero and its neighbour Michoacán, that the original local movements formed in the 1960s to contest this system of 'accumulation by dispossession' backed by armed repression called themselves *Consejos de Autodefensa* (Self-Defence Councils) (FEMOSPP 2005: 12).

The appearance in 1967/68 of two separate guerrilla movements in the sierras of Guerrero, commanded by Lucio Cabañas and another former schoolteacher, Genaro Vázquez, set in train a series of develop-ments in which the FEMOSPP report sought to establish that the Mexican army was the central actor. Cabañas began his clandestine campaign with an intense process of consciousness-raising that aimed to build a rural social base for his revolutionary movement by ex-ploiting existing forms of community self-government, calling village assemblies in which he not only addressed the peasants' principal economic grievances but also called on the communities to form self-defence forces and collect arms and volunteers for the coming guerrilla struggle. Although initial reactions to the guerrilla project were sceptical, Cabañas formed 'study circles' that he insisted were about 'learning from the people' and building on their existing sense of injustice in order to convince the sceptics that armed struggle was the only way forward (ibid.: 29–30). The politico-military organization that Cabañas built was based on the creation of a Party of the Poor (PdlP). This had a pyramidal structure whose base was community-level 'clandestine committees'. Its military arm, the Peasant Execution Brigade (*Brigada Campesina de Ajusticiamiento*, BCA), consisted of trained volunteer fighters (ibid.: 30–1). Some of the fighters would be active full-time, others temporary members of the military column who would return to their communities after three months or so in the field to continue their militancy through the PdlP cells in their home communities.

Although there were also some cells in urban areas, the principal actions of the BCA took place in the sierra, its core of permanent loyalists drawing in additional numbers of fighters for specific operations. These initially focused on extortion of wealthier 'class enemies', followed by a mounting campaign of robberies and kidnappings for ransom. Such revolutionary 'expropriations' not only served to maintain the guerrilla forces, but also enabled the movement to build further support by redistributing some of the captured resources within the peasant communities that provided it with moral and logistical support. The FEMOSPP report observes that although the state's security forces detected the movement's construction from the outset, they initially underestimated the amount of support that it was building. An initial campaign of sweeps of the countryside in pursuit of the leaders and members of the armed groups failed to yield results. But in mid-1969 the military strategy changed to one of arresting and torturing relatives of the insurgents and other suspected supporters, a move justified as a necessary campaign against 'subversion', accompanied by forced relocation of peasants to more controllable 'strategic villages' modelled on US practice in Vietnam (ibid.: 38).

The FEMOSPP team found considerable evidence of extrajudicial executions as this counter-insurgency experiment, codenamed 'Operation Friendship', developed in the sierras where the forces of Genaro Vázquez and Luis Cabañas were operating in 1970 (ibid.: 36). The following year, a number of communities were subjected to aerial bombardment, and detained persons began to 'disappear' in increasing numbers, generally after having been shipped off to the notorious Military Camp Number One in Mexico City. Ulloa Bornemann (2007), who was subsequently detained there after being arrested in Cuernavaca, Morelos, has provided a graphic account of the torture routinely meted out to inmates guarded by persons that he identifies as members of the paramilitary 'Falcons' group responsible for the killing of students in 1971.

The repression, along with the divisions between the insurgent groups mentioned earlier, proved sufficient to disarticulate the guerrilla movement of Genaro Vázquez, whose final attempt to return to the mountains of Guerrero in 1972 ended in disaster after his car crashed in Michoacán. Whether Vázquez died of his injuries or was killed by the soldiers who took control of the hospital to which he was taken remains in dispute (FEMOSPP 2005: 47). What is a matter of public record is that developments after Echeverría became president in December 1970 reflected an official endorsement by the Secretary of National Defence of 'irregular operations' by the military as a necessary part of counter-insurgency operations (ibid.: 48). By 1971, a third of the Mexican army was stationed in Guerrero, undertaking actions against the non-combatant civilian population that the original FEMOSPP report defined as 'genocidal'. Another interesting detail, which differs between earlier and later versions of the report, is passing reference to the drug traffickers operating in the sierras. Whereas the original refers to an 'alliance' between the army and the *narcos* against the guerrilla dating back to 1969 (ibid.: 50), the final version retained only a reference to a 1974 incident in which traffickers passed information to the army about the whereabouts of a camp established by a minor insurgent leader. Although Ulloa Bornemann recalled that Cabañas allowed his men to smoke marijuana in the guerrilla camps, it seems that the insurgents were uninterested in establishing a *modus vivendi* with drug trafficking organizations and that no *narco-guerrilla* tendencies of the kind that developed in Colombia or Peru emerged at that time in Guerrero. It was the guerrillas' continuing campaign of robbery, extortion and kidnapping against 'the class enemy' and powerful political figures which provided them with resources to continue the redistributive policies that gained them popular support despite growing military aggression. This strategy also kept their own relations with the peasantry free of the violence and coercion that sometimes entered into the traffickers' relations with the farming communities of the sierras. State repression against the armed movement's support bases did, however, escalate to a new stage after Lucio Cabañas decided, in mid-1972, to enter into open confrontation with the army.

Although Cabañas's fighters managed, to the last, to inflict significant casualties on the military columns that they ambushed, the army, convinced that the guerrilla now enjoyed either the active or passive support of the entire rural population, responded by descending on villages and rounding up large numbers of people who were not released into the custody of the civil authorities. Old men and adolescents were taken as well as adult men, some died under torture, and some were secretly shipped off to Military Camp Number One, never to be heard from again. Villages were burned and populations displaced. Yet such atrocities increased rather than diminished support for the guerrilla, as some military documents from 1972 recognized in recommending that search procedures be modified to reduce the civilian population's rejection of the army.

The year 1973 was to see an escalation of disputes between insurgent groups that reduced their collective military effectiveness. Betrayals of their fighters also became more likely after a further escalation of army massacres (described as 'homicides' in the final report) and forced disappearances (reduced in the final version to 'disappearances' without the adjective), the process that the original report described as 'a policy of genocide' (ibid.: 69). The military force responsible for killing unarmed civilians in the village of Los Piloncillos, near Atoyac, in April 1973 included fifteen individuals not wearing uniforms (ibid.: 70). The report sent to President Echeverría by the defence secretary fabricated an imaginary firefight with Lucio Cabañas as its explanation for the deaths. Six months later, a group of fishermen on the coast reported to the army that men and women's clothing was being washed ashore, along with human bones (ibid.: 73). They were ordered to keep silent about clear evidence that detained persons were being thrown into the sea from helicopters, sometimes already dead, sometimes still alive. That this became common practice was confirmed by the testimony of a detainee who was fortunate enough to be released that other detainees who subsequently 'disappeared' had recounted how soldiers had told them that they were going to make good shark bait (ibid.). In this as in other areas, the Mexican military committed acts during the 'dirty war' of the 1970s that eventually resulted in successful prosecutions for crimes against humanity in other countries, notably Argentina, despite earlier legislation designed to secure impunity for the perpetrators.

Military documents now began to refer to persons illegally detained by the army as 'packets', not simply to cover up the identity of individuals who were not being handed over to the civil authorities for due process, but to mark the fact that their detention was the result of their membership of, or support for, a 'subversive' group, which was what now constituted their crime, rather than any individual act (ibid.). 'Packets' could serve as sources of intelligence but despite the application of the harshest tactics by the military, Cabañas managed to continue his war with the army into 1974 by a combination of rewarding friends, punishing collaborators and a tactical agility that sometimes led government troops to kill each other in the confusion created by sudden movements of the guerrilla column (ibid.: 79). At the end of 1973 a new opportunity for building the movement seemed to present itself when Cabañas received an offer of talks, supposedly approved by Echeverría, from Rubén Figueroa Figueroa, then a senator and PRI candidate for governor in the 1974 elections.

The talks did not prosper and Cabañas decided to take Figueroa hostage, demanding a very large ransom that appears to have been paid before his final liberation from his captors by the army (ibid.: 98). The army response was a wave of new detentions and disappearances. The victims included a hairdresser whose only crime appears to have been distant kinship with Lucio Cabañas (ibid.: 85). Dead bodies marked by torture started turning up in urban neighbourhoods, at least some of them seemingly guerrilla supporters coming down from the *sierras* for supplies (ibid.: 86). Blockading the access of rural communities to supplies became part of an intensifying counter-insurgency campaign. Recognizing that past strategy had created a deep fear and loathing of the army in the *sierra*, the military now had little option but to pursue ruthless tactics. Hungry peasants would find that they could get food from the military if they turned informant, and the guerrillas were obliged to split their forces as provisioning became increasingly difficult (ibid.: 90). In July 1974, Cabañas decided to take a small group to create a diversion while a larger force maintained guard over Figueroa. Two months later the latter was discovered by the army, which was receiving information from deserters, who may have been killed after they ceased to be useful (ibid.: 102). The rebels failed to change location after the army detained one of the members of the group sent out to make arrangements for the ransoming of the prisoner or secure provisions. No attempt was made to kill governor-to-be Figueroa after the army attack began. This, as Lucio Cabañas explained to an assembly in October 1974, was a matter of policy, since 25 million pesos of ransom had been paid to the benefit of the movement (ibid.: 108).

By this stage, Cabañas, who had reached the village of Los Corrales walking barefoot with only four surviving comrades, knew that his ability to break out of the circle of troops closing in around him was diminishing fast. His mother, wife and daughter were now detained (to be held, along with his siblings and their spouses and children, for three years) (ibid.: 112). Although the remaining fragments of the guerrilla movement fought on, Cabañas and three companions were betrayed by a peasant guide and trapped by the army (ibid.: 114). Cabañas and two of his men died fighting. The other was taken alive but apparently executed later. The FEMOSPP team concluded, on the basis of forensic evidence on his exhumed remains, that the guerrilla commander had likely reserved his last bullet for himself (ibid.: 117).

After the death of Cabañas, the police became the main visible agents of repression, torture and forced disappearances (ibid.: 120). Governor Figueroa had, however, chosen military men with proven records in the 'dirty war' to lead the state police. That force continued to hand over prisoners for detention in regional military facilities or Military Camp Number One. Bodies continued to fall into the sea (ibid.: 131). Figueroa did, however, also employ more subtle means to further the disarticulation of dissident forces by offering amnesties to some of those who were detained in return for public undertakings to abandon the armed struggle. In 1978, the state congress passed a general amnesty law, after which Figueroa declared, in a press interview, that the entire question of the 'disappeared, as they call the communists' was closed, since there were no longer any 'disappeared or political prisoners left in Guerrero'. Those who hadn't been amnestied were dead, the governor assured his interviewer (ibid.: 140). As the threat of further guerrilla insurgency receded, the military returned to traditional kinds of armed interventions to protect the interests of *caciques*, loggers, landlords and merchants against the less revolutionary kinds of local challenges offered by a still-disgruntled peasantry.

The fact that Guerrero's peasantry was cowed but not truly pacified maintained a pattern of periodic repression that brought back memories of the past. In June 1995, with Figueroa Figueroa's son Rubén Figueroa Alcocer now occupying the governor's chair, a group of members of the Peasant Organization of the Southern Sierra (OCSS) set off for a march in Atoyac to demand that the state present the disappeared activist Gilberto Romero Vázquez alive, and to protest about their still-unsatisfied needs for schools, hospitals, paved roads and drinkable water (Gledhill 2003). The police who intercepted them en route, at the river crossing of Aguas Blancas, in the municipality of Coyuca de Benítez, placed weapons in the hands of their victims in order to justify the killing of seventeen farmers as self-defence, but the video that they made of the scene was leaked and broadcast on national television, adding shocking collaboration of the testimony of survivors that unarmed people had been shot at close range in a massacre whose pre-planned nature seemed to be confirmed by the presence of a helicopter containing the head of the state police, as well as by some incautious remarks on the part of the governor himself before and after the event.

In the face of a national public outcry, Figueroa Alcocer was obliged to resign, to be replaced by Ángel Heladio Aguirre Rivero, then a member of the PRI, although he returned to the governorship in 2011 as candidate of the Party of the Democratic Revolution (PRD). As interim governor, Aguirre used the language of a reformer. Yet like his predecessor, he was a major regional boss (*cacique*), whose networks extended throughout the Costa Chica region of Guerrero; a native of Ometepec, the political and commercial centre of a region with high poverty indices among its indigenous population, Aguirre not only enjoyed the friendship of local *caciques*, but also commanded his personal force of gunmen (ibid.: 52).

Yet although many of the methods used by the regional elites to maintain their political and economic dominance over the local population remained 'traditional', the generation to which Aguirre belonged had 'modernized' in other respects, like its equivalent in other parts of country, including Chiapas (Ascencio Franco 1998). Its leaders were university educated, generally in the National Autonomous University in Mexico City. They tended to study economics, and promoted new forms of investment, particularly in tourism and upmarket real estate projects in the resort areas. One of the advantages of these kinds of projects was the opportunity that they offered for laundering money produced by illegal activities. Some of the upscale real estate developments were, however, extremely disadvantageous for residents of more modest neighbourhoods. In Acapulco, the developers of the Zona Diamante residential complex, in which national as well as regional political interests had a stake, was built on former *ejido* farmland despite warnings from engineers about the environmental problems that this would create. The decision by the municipal authorities to modify the city development plan to permit the project to go ahead proved catastrophic when Guerrero was devastated by tropical storm Manuel in September 2013. Since the development blocked the channels through which floodwater had previously been able to flow into the sea, Zona Diamante not only suffered flooding itself, but also affected less affluent neighbourhoods (J. Sánchez 2013).

The transfer of power from Figueroa to Aguirre in 1996 did not go entirely smoothly. At a commemoration ceremony held a year later for the victims of the massacre, addressed by Cuauhtémoc Cárdenas, the PRD's founder and the candidate denied the presidency of Mexico by Salinas de Gortari in the disputed 1988 election, a large contingent of armed fighters appeared on the scene to announce the birth of a new guerrilla movement, read their manifesto, and set off for the mountains (Weinberg 2000). Seen by many as the successor movement to Cabañas's Party of the Poor, the Popular Revolutionary Army (EPR) had a somewhat uncomfortable relationship with the Zapatista Army of National Liberation in Chiapas, since the latter had embraced negotiation, and then autonomy based on self-defence, rather than active guerrilla warfare. Although the EPR claimed responsibility for various armed actions against the army in Michoacán, Oaxaca and Chiapas as well as in Guerrero in the second half of the 1990s, and was clearly trying to recruit new followers, it adopted a lower profile after the PRI lost the presidency in the 2000 elections. Both the PAN governments attributed various bomb attacks on PEMEX gas ducts and other acts of 'terrorism' to this organization and a breakaway group that named itself the Insurgent Revolutionary Army of the People (EPRI). Military intelligence claimed that they had acquired grenade launchers (Alejandro 2012). Yet whatever the truth of these claims, small and apparently socially isolated revolutionary cells were no longer at the forefront of public concern by 2006. The spectre of guerrilla insurgency 1970s-style had been relegated to a distinctly marginal position in public security discourse by the threats posed by what some analysts had now started to call the 'criminal insurgency' of drug cartels (Grillo 2012).

Yet it is difficult to see the drug cartels as engaged in any kind of systematic 'insurgency' against the state or powerful economic interests. The principal victims of the violence of drug traffickers in Guerrero are the same mestizo and indigenous peasants who have long been victimized by these other powerful actors. Violent conflicts between different cartels in Mexico cause displacement of population simply because people flee the violence, although the threat of kidnapping and extortion also forces individuals to move, especially when they have no confidence in the ability of the official security forces to protect them or, usually with good reason, consider those forces to be in league with the criminals. The consulting group Parametría estimated that 700,000 persons were displaced in the country as a whole between 2010 and 2011 alone, indicating Guerrero, which has a relatively small population of less than 3.5 million, as one of the 'hot spots'.[6] But residents of rural communities in Guerrero that are disputed between different cartels have often had to flee their communities and abandon their farms because the *narcos* burned their houses and threatened to kill them if they tried to stay in the area (Ocampo Arista 2013b). Governor Aguirre admitted publicly that there was a problem, although the authorities downplayed reports of villagers actually being killed (Covarrubias 2013).

There has been a continuing persecution of peasant activists in Guerrero by official security forces, although their campaigns against illegal logging have been increasingly accompanied by complaints against the impunity enjoyed by drug traffickers. What has changed since the end of the redistributive land reform is that many such activists now seek to build wider support networks as environmental rather than agrarian militants, and often substitute indigenous identities for the *campesino* (peasant) identities that they adopted in the land reform era in an effort to take advantage of the new sensibilities produced by neoliberal multiculturalism (Overmyer-Velázquez 2011). The *normal* students of Ayotzinapa have also continued to be militant, and persecuted: two died during a combined federal and state police operation against a highway blockade protest at the end of 2011. Two years later their relatives were still demanding justice (Covarrubias and Cervantes 2013). Further violent confrontation occurred after a militant teachers' movement mobilized in 2013 to oppose the implementation of the federal government's educational reform package, which is particularly unpopular with teachers of indigenous origin (Poy Solano 2013). The military and police are not, however, the only actors in violence that has a political character, and there have been ever more frequent claims that organized crime acts in collusion with the political interests ruling the state. At the end of May 2013, eight members of the Popular Union of Iguala (UP), six of them militants of the PRD, were kidnapped and killed. At the burial of the UP's leader, Arturo Hernández Cardona, his widow declared: 'Organized crime, and I am going to say this with all the risks that it implies, acted on political orders' (Ocampo Arista 2013a). The risks are real, as demonstrated by the deaths of Isabel Ayala Nava, Lucio Cabañas's still politically active widow, and her sister Reyna. They were shot dead from a car as they left church in November 2011, after two of their brothers had been killed earlier in the year. The assassins took Isabel Ayala's cell phone, using it four hours later to send a death threat to her daughter Micaela (Lucero Estrada 2011). Isabel Ayala had been campaigning not only for justice for the victims of the 'dirty war' that had taken her husband, but also for an end to contemporary impunity.

In late September 2014, both Ayotzinapa and Iguala returned to the news. Municipal police in Iguala killed six people, including three Ayotzinapa students, and forty-three more students were taken from buses and delivered into the hands of gunmen of the Guerreros Unidos drug cartel (Turati 2014). In the weeks of protests and searching for the missing students that followed, it was almost forgotten that one of the students who had been killed on the first day, twenty-two-year-old Julio César Mondragón, from the State of Mexico and father of a newborn baby, had been tortured to death by being skinned alive (Petrich 2014). The PRD mayor of Iguala, José Luis Abarca, and his wife Maria de los Ángeles Pineda fled, but were eventually arrested. By this stage the couple's long-standing and intimate links with Guerreros Unidos had been amply exposed by the press. The Attorney General's office also now belatedly discovered that it had evidence of Abarca's responsibility for the killing of Arturo Hernández Cardona and his comrades (Garduño 2014).

The Iguala case created an outcry because it laid bare the emptiness of the federal government's claims to have got a grip on the security situation. At the state level it revealed the extent to which organized crime had captured local government, and showed that this was not simply a problem for the PRI. The PRD national leadership initially tried to absolve governor Aguirre of responsibility, but soon found his resignation unavoidable. For weeks the federal government failed to produce either the missing students or a convincing official account of what had happened. Questions continued to be asked about why federal troops stationed in the area had not intervened, about what the state and federal governments had already known, and about other kinds of connections with politicians and security forces the cartel might have enjoyed (Turati 2014). Ayotzinapa was still seen by state elites as a hotbed of 'subversion', albeit, like the other rural teacher-training colleges, something of an anachronism that belonged to the state-building projects of a different era. Federal security forces had been involved in the 2011 violence against Ayotzinapa students, and there were known official concerns about the possibility of a resurgence of guerrilla activity. The 2014 attack on the students continued long-standing patterns of political violence in Guerrero. Although cartel killers were held responsible for dispatching the victims on this occasion, it proved difficult to sell to the thinking public an 'official version' that postulated criminal motives and sought to evade interpretation of the incident as a 'crime of the state'. It also proved impossible for the federal government to keep what happened contained within discussions of the particular circumstances of Guerrero. Many citizens rightly saw the forced disappearance of the students as exemplifying a much bigger national problem that it was no longer possible to cover up.

Despite the continuing political violence of recent years, impunity had not gone unchallenged in Guerrero itself. Indigenous communities in the state revived the 'self-defence' traditions of an earlier era by forming a regional coordinating organization of communal police units in the mid-1990s in the Costa Chica and Montaña regions, the Regional Coordinator of Communal Authorities (CRAC), which strongly subscribes to the principle of indigenous autonomy. A former CRAC leader created a new *autodefensa* in Ayutla in 2013, setting up another organization that subsequently established itself in some urban neighbourhoods as well as other rural communities, the Union of Peoples and Organizations of Guerrero (UPOEG). Although there have been moments of dialogue, relations between the CRAC and UPOEG have been strained, since the latter appeared more willing to collaborate with the state government. The CRAC leadership accused it of being less democratic in organization, less interested in working according to community justice principles that would guarantee the rights of persons accused of crimes, and more like a paramilitary vigilante group (Castellanos 2013a; Conn 2013). The CRAC, which had supported the militant teachers against the state government and accused the Aguirre administration and federal security forces of harassment, itself suffered internal conflicts in 2014. A CRAC leader who had advocated closer collaboration with the UPOEG was removed (Rojas 2014). Civil society groups in Guerrero therefore remain as fractious as ever, but there are good reasons why these kinds of conflicts break out when the state is playing a backstage role in the process. Governor Aguirre was accused of being responsible for the continuing detention in a high-security prison in Nayarit of Nestora Salgado, female coordinator of the Olinalá Communal Police, arrested in 2013 for alleged involvement in kidnappings (Muñoz Ramírez 2014). It has been widely argued that Aguirre sought to undermine the autonomous communal police movement organized by the CRAC, and promoted other *autodefensas*, because he wanted to use these armed groups to break popular resistance to the extension of mining operations in Guerrero (Hernández Navarro 2014).

Although the horror of Iguala may eventually help the country to move on, events in twenty-first-century Mexico have shown how difficult it has become to establish the ultimate intellectual authorship of disappearances and political murder, and especially to demonstrate the complicity of government in these acts. The country lives in an era of 'deniable violence'. To pursue this question further, I now turn to the other major counter-insurgency theatre in recent Mexican history, Chiapas.

Paramilitarism and the state in Chiapas

For the past twenty years, Chiapas has become synonymous for many with the rebel movement created by the Zapatista Army of Liberation (EZLN). Yet although the rebellion did win widespread support at the outset, the EZLN never established Gramscian hegemony as 'intellectual and moral leadership' over the entire peasantry of Chiapas. Its initial support was rapidly reduced by a government strategy that combined offering social development aid to those willing to defect with the application of violence, initially by the army alone, but in short order supplemented by the 'deniable violence' of paramilitary groups. Some of these groups secured official registration as non-governmental rural development organizations. For example, an independent British delegation to Chiapas was able to photocopy a contract that the state government had signed that granted half a million dollars for 'rural development work' to the paramilitary organization *Paz y Justicia*, based in the northern zone of the state and led by a PRI member of the state congress, Samuel Sánchez Sánchez (Craske et al. 1998: 9).

The most notorious episode of paramilitary violence, which caused the PRI federal administration headed by Ernesto Zedillo considerable international embarrassment, took place in the hamlet of Acteal in the municipality of Chenalhó in 1997. Gunmen invaded the chapel used by a Catholic group, *Las Abejas* (the Bees), which was sympathetic to the social and political demands of the Zapatistas but opposed to the use of violence in pursuit of those goals (Moksnes 2012). Forewarned of the paramilitaries' intention to attack, the direct adherents of the Zapatista movement had already left the village, but the members of *Las Abejas* decided not to allow themselves to be driven out and were killed as they prayed. Twenty-one women, some of whom were pregnant, nine men and fifteen children, mostly under the age of ten and two still infants, were killed in the attack. The state government rejected accusations of complicity and argued that the attack was the product of local conflicts that were 'customary' among the Tzotzil (ibid.: 229). The legal team defending the fifty-seven paramilitaries finally charged with the Acteal massacre gathered 'anthropological evidence' on this point. Aída Hernández (2002) refuted it by observing that although individual women have died as a result of witchcraft accusations as well as domestic violence in highland Tzotzil communities, there are no recorded precedents for mutilation of the bodies of pregnant women, or for mass aggression against an entire group of women and children. She therefore concluded that the Acteal tragedy was a consequence of the new 'rules of engagement' produced by the state's resort to the deniable violence of paramilitarization.

Subsequent journalistic investigations did uncover evidence of state complicity: the guns used were military issue and the *priista* leaders of the paramilitary group responsible had been in communication with both government and army officials (Olney 2004: 2). Yet the official federal government report published at the end of 1998 insisted that the paramilitary groups in Chenalhó were 'security and vigilance committees' that local supporters of the PRI and the Party of the Cardenista Front for National Reconstruction[7] had formed to protect themselves from Zapatista aggression (Moksnes 2012: 229). Since the violence was explained as the result of long-standing local feuds, only men from the municipality were arrested as perpetrators of the killings, although the municipal president and fourteen low-level police and military officials were charged with indirect responsibility for having failed to prevent them from taking place (ibid.). No senior officials were prosecuted. The legal process was, rather typically for Mexico (Gledhill 1999), so plagued by irregularities that twenty-nine men who had been sentenced were released in 2009, and sixteen more were granted new trials and released between 2010 and 2011 (Moksnes 2012: 230). By the time of the sixteenth anniversary of the massacre in 2013, the Supreme Court had ordered the liberation of sixty-nine prisoners, and Las Abejas were denouncing not simply impunity, but the threat that the return of the paramilitaries posed for the survivors (Castellanos 2013b). By January 2014, Acteal had received seventeen families displaced from other parts of the municipality.[8] A Presbyterian pastor reputed to have blessed the arms used in the 1997 massacre accused the remaining two Zapatista militants in the *ejido* in which he lived of poisoning the local well. They narrowly escaped lynching (by being doused with gasoline and burned alive).

The EZLN denounced the new forced displacements in Chenalhó as simply another example of a campaign of aggression and harassment that had forced people to abandon their homes, lands and crops in twenty communities in the five regions in which it had established Good Government Councils (*Juntas de Buen Gobierno*). The Councils are a form of autonomous government above the municipal level that the Zapatistas established from 2004 onwards. Based on the regular rotation of their members, these Zapatista institutions undertake to serve all those who live in the area in a transparent and honest way, whether or not they are Zapatista sympathizers. The Good Government Councils provide health and educational services that are now managed entirely by people from the Zapatista autonomous communities, since ending dependence of the help of professionals from outside is considered an essential part of 'building autonomy'. It is important to bear in mind that the Zapatistas do still enjoy significant financial support from their international network of sympathizers, an advantage that most other indigenous autonomy movements in Mexico do not possess. The work of constructing 'autonomy' at the grass roots has been continued patiently despite the fact that many autonomous communities have continued to face low-level military and paramilitary harassment, enabling the EZLN to break an extended

silence with a demonstration of its ability to prepare a new generation of younger militants by marching them through the streets of
the major cities of Chiapas in December 2012. The marches were
conducted in complete silence in a display of discipline designed to
make Zapatista voices 'speak more loudly'.

Yet although the Zapatista movement continues to display its
mastery of political theatre, its repeated attempts to break out of its
containment in Chiapas to transform wider national political spaces
have not been successful. Although its Sixth Declaration of the Selva
Lacandona and 'Other Campaign' in the 2006 elections that brought
Felipe Calderón to office did slightly increase the number of allies
that the movement had in other regions of the country, it did not
fulfil its aim of creating a strong, pluralistic, anti-capitalist rainbow
coalition of socially diverse forms of dissidence. In rejecting the entire
political class, the EZLN contributed to the electoral victory of the
right, and the defeat of the centre-left candidate, Andrés Manuel López
Obrador, just as it had done in the 1990s in Chiapas (Viqueira 1999).
Nevertheless, the EZLN's scepticism about electoral party politics
could not be said to have been misplaced, especially in Chiapas. The
PRI did eventually lose direct control of the Chiapas governorship in
2000 to a candidate supported by an alliance of eight ideologically
diverse opposition parties, including both the PAN and the PRD, the
evangelical Pablo Salazar Mendiguchía. He was succeeded by Juan
Sabines Guerrero, the candidate of a coalition of the PRD, Labour
Party (PT) and Convergence citizens' movement, although Sabines,
son of a past PRI governor, had been PRI mayor of the state capital,
Tuxtla Gutiérrez, and, like Aguirre in Guerrero, became opposition
candidate only after he was refused the PRI nomination. Sabines had
Salazar jailed on charges of corruption. The present governor, Manuel
Velasco Coello, also son of a former PRI governor, was the candidate
of the Green Party, aligned with the PRI, and is often considered a
clone of Enrique Peña Nieto, spending enormous amounts of money
on publicity with an eye to the 2018 presidential elections. It is difficult to escape the conclusion that although the Chiapas elite may
have 'modernized' in the way that it organizes its electoral machines
(without entirely abandoning the practices of the past), and also in
its visions of the economic future on which its power should be built,
the inner networks of political power at this level remain very much
what they have always been.

There is competition between political rivals, exemplified in the imprisonment of Salazar, and in rivalry between Manuel Velasco and Roberto Albores Gleason, son of Roberto Albores Guillén, who became substitute governor for the PRI after the Acteal killings, and was then expelled from the party for supporting the candidacy of his friend Juan Sabines. But it is *plus ça change plus c'est la même chose* when it comes to fundamental economic class solidarity and the determination of the whole political class to confine and slowly asphyxiate the EZLN, which Velasco Coello now feels secure enough to congratulate publicly for its contributions to the democratic political culture of the state. More important, however, are the underlying conditions that allow that elite to maintain its control over Chiapas and the consequences that flow from that control.

The counter-insurgency strategy employed in Chiapas not only exploited social divisions, but exacerbated them (Gledhill 2002). We have already seen that religious conflicts were important in Chenalhó, and became politicized because they became articulated to external political networks. The paramilitary groups exploited the frustrations provoked by traditional age hierarchies and the unequal distribution of land rights in peasant communities: young landless men were offered the opportunity to enhance their status by carrying heavy weapons and benefiting from the resources these organizations received for building their own patronage networks. Government social programmes were well conceived from the point of view of causing defections from the Zapatista ranks. In 1997, the inhabitants of the village of Hierbabuena, in the Altos region of Chiapas, for example, joined the EZLN to secure land from a rancher in the zone, but abandoned the movement because they felt that they would do better by seeking the support of government programmes, especially the *Oportunidades* conditional cash transfer programme, than continuing along the 'difficult road' of autonomy. Commuting to the highland city of San Cristóbal de las Casas to work several days a week, men acquired the skills to self-construct modern houses, which they built through a programme that covered the entire cost of the materials, co-financed by the federal, state and municipal governments (Otero-Briz 2014). As a result of defections, many EZLN supporters now live in places that are politically divided into Zapatistas, anti-Zapatistas and neutrals. There are some local communities in which Zapatistas and non-Zapatistas have negotiated a peaceful *modus vivendi*. In the municipality of San Andrés Larráinzar, for example, where the EZLN signed the famous 1996 Accords that the government of Ernesto Zedillo then failed to honour, two local authorities, one Zapatista and one PRI, managed to work together well enough to collaborate on some issues of general public interest (Ramírez Sánchez 2012). But there is also conflict, especially where there are disputes over land and other resources over which Zapatistas secured control, as in Chenalhó, although violent agrarian conflicts are not restricted to Zapatista territory.

On 2 May 2014, the Zapatista militant and schoolteacher José Luis López, known as *Galeano*, was killed in the Zapatista stronghold of La Realidad by members of the Independent Central of Farm Workers and Peasants-Historical (CIOAC-H, *Central Independiente de Obreros Agrícolas y Campesinos-Histórica*) (Martín 2014). The CIOAC-H is one of two legacy organizations of a peasant union originally founded at the end of the 1960s by the Mexican Communist Party. It is now aligned with the PRD (which absorbed the communists), another faction having split off and aligned with the PRI. The Good Governance Council declared the assassins members of a 'paramilitary group' organized by 'the three levels of bad government' directed by the president of a non-Zapatista *ejido* and naming a long list of persons involved in a 'band of paramilitaries' called 'los Luises'.[9] In an ironic parallel with the disputes between Zapatistas and non-Zapatistas underlying the conflict in Chenalhó (Moksnes 2012: 217), there was a dispute in this case also over use of a gravel bed, which the Good Governance Council had previously agreed could be shared by the CIOAC members for their participation in the previously mentioned government housing programme. It was now claimed that the 'paramilitaries' were trying to exclude the Zapatistas from using it, having also seized a truck used to transport the gravel that belonged to the Good Government Council and taken it to the CIOAC-controlled *ejido*. The killing of *Galeano* rapidly became an international *cause célèbre*. It was at a ceremony in his memory on 25 May 2014 that the EZLN's *subcomandante* Marcos announced that, as a result of a 'collective decision' of the Clandestine Revolutionary Council of the EZLN, his 'personage' had now outlived its political usefulness and his voice would no longer speak for the organization.[10]

This act confirmed that the military leadership of the EZLN had, as announced the previous year, passed to a Tzeltal indigenous member of the Clandestine Revolutionary Council, *subcomandante* Moisés, who joined the movement in the early 1980s and moved up the ranks. In his valedictory remarks Marcos answered those who argued that the EZLN project had ultimately failed by stressing the way that the movement had changed radical politics. It had replaced 'revolutionary vanguardism' with the principle of 'governing by obeying', the 'taking of power from above' with the 'creating of power from below', 'professional politics' with 'everyday politics', 'leaders' with 'people', 'the marginalization of women' with 'the direct participation of women', and 'scorn for the other' with the 'celebration of difference'. The baton had now been handed from mestizos to a strictly indigenous leadership, although in his own speech *subcomandante* Moisés made it clear that this did not mean that the EZLN's struggle would cease to be an 'anti-capitalist' struggle, a point he emphasized several times.[11]

Both the EZLN and *Las Abejas* insist that the death of *Galeano* is proof that the counter-insurgency war that began in 1994 is still under way, and possibly intensifying (Bellinghausen 2014b). The violence of paramilitary attacks is, they argue, complemented by the co-optative strategy embedded in the new government's *Crusade Against Hunger* programme, loosely modelled on Lula's *Fome Zero* programme in Brazil, and placed in the hands of a new Secretary of Social Development who is a former leader of the PRD, Rosario Robles.[12] The programme was initiated in Las Margaritas, gateway to the original Zapatista heartland of the Selva Lacandona in the Tojolabal region (Bellinghausen 2014a). This perspective is consistent with Armando Bartra's suggestion that the counter-insurgency war in Chiapas is a more sophisticated, neoliberal, version of the attempt to combine development aid with repressive violence pioneered in Guerrero, which prompted Lucio Cabañas to remark that by handing out beans, cows and money, building roads and giving away land, the government 'was going to wear us down' (Bartra 2011: 17).

Embarking on what Bartra calls 'counter-insurgent developmentalism and agrarianism' was made necessary by the *casus belli* used by the EZLN rebels, who declared their uprising on the day that the North American Free Trade Agreement came into force. Both the urban and rural poor had suffered seriously as a consequence of Salinas de Gortari's neoliberal 'shock therapy'. Bartra points out that the government had already known that armed insurgents were building up their influence in the peasant communities of the state in 1993, when it started injecting extra money into programmes targeted on the Selva Lacandona region as a 'preventive' counter-insurgency measure. After the rebellion, the Ministry of Social Development embarked on more ambitious efforts, supported by infusions of World Bank funding, whose purpose was unmasked in a leaked 1996 ministry document that referred explicitly to the use of development funding to reduce support for the EZLN by giving immediate priority to the demands of other organizations and divide members of the armed movement itself (ibid.: 15). Counter-insurgent developmentalism was complemented by counter-insurgent agrarian reform, as the government bought up land to give to peasants (ibid.: 16). Although the government, having theoretically abolished land redistribution, now aspired to deliver land as private property or co-property through state purchase from the original owners and resale to beneficiaries on long-term low-interest credit arrangements, in practice, as we will see shortly, this is not always what happened. There was also plenty of traditional clientelism in the way that these measures were implemented. Yet as Bartra points out, the strategy clearly reflected the influence of post-Vietnam US counter-insurgency doctrines.

Yet as the EZLN steered its demands more along the path of indigenous autonomy, the neoliberal state having shown its military superiority and failed to collapse as a result of wider movements triggered by the Chiapas rebellion, the government was presented with a further problem, demands for self-determination. Mobilization to create forms of regional self-government that would improve the position of indigenous people in fact had a history pre-dating the 1994 rebellion, particularly during the 1980s in the Tojolabal region around Las Margaritas (Burguete Cal y Mayor 2003). The Albores Guillén state government attempted to address the political dimension of the problem of indigenous rights and self-determination with a programme to create new municipalities, backed by the federal government's Coordinator for Dialogue and Reconciliation in Chiapas, Manuel Camacho Solís.

Leyva Solano and Burguete Cal y Mayor (2011) argue that remunicipalization was another facet of the Chiapas counter-insurgency process. Under the Albores plan, new municipalities would weaken the EZLN, not simply by reducing tensions inside the 'conflict zone' where the organization was strongest, but also by turning areas outside the Zapatista 'core' zone into 'buffer zones' in which other social and political actors could be encouraged at the expense of further Zapatista expansion, all within the framework of the combination of carrot and stick embedded in the rest of the counter-insurgency strategy (ibid.: 44). In other regions of the country, 'remunicipalization' had been an indigenous demand, a means of securing greater autonomy for indigenous communities by removing them from the control of local administrative centres dominated by non-indigenous people, but the EZLN strongly opposed the government proposals, precisely because it considered them to have a hidden agenda that had little to do with restoring peace to the region. Seven new municipalities were created in 1999, following a new round of military operations against the rebel-controlled autonomous municipalities. Although the incoming government of Pablo Salazar dropped the original plan to create thirty-three new municipalities after it entered office the following year, the EZLN strategy of creating autonomous regions associated with Good Government Councils was the organization's response to the challenges posed by government actions to reorganize local government, as well as a means to move the politico-military organization of the EZLN into the background to highlight the peaceful and democratic character of the autonomous institutions run by its civilian support bases. Yet as Bartra points out, the ethnographic case studies that Leyva Solano and Burguete Cal y Mayor assemble in their book on the Albores remunicipalization programme demonstrate that:

> In the new municipalities there is much more than just simple counter-insurgency because the government initiatives combine with local interests and demands. The contrary initiatives introduced by the repressive Albores Guillén reactivated previous demands, some of which were quite old, in the new municipalities. They also unleashed regional processes that, while undoubtedly expressing the interests of local caciques or bosses, also created expectations amongst normal citizens interested in improving their well-being through the strengthening of local governments. (Bartra 2011: 20)

Bartra's emphasis on historically rooted local interests and demands is important. Local interests and demands are influenced, at any given moment in time, by the wider networks woven by the EZLN, paramilitary organizations, regional political cliques, and

groups whose influence and economic ascent relied on the support of the federal government, whose interests have not always
corresponded to those of regional elites throughout the modern
history of Chiapas (Ascencio Franco 1998). Local situations are
complex because they involve factional conflicts and realignments
within peasant communities over future generations' access to land,
as well as shifting relationships between peasants, state agencies and
non-indigenous landowners, merchants and political bosses. They
also include the efforts of different sectors of local society to make
Mexico's imperfect democracy work better for them by whatever
means prove viable at the time. This may still include embracing the
politics of clientelism and the buying of votes, practices that once
again became a matter of public scandal, but no further action on
the part of the electoral authorities, during the national contest that
brought the PRI back to power in 2012.

In a study located in the region around the city of Tila in the
northern zone of Chiapas, the region that spawned the *Paz y Justicia*
paramilitary organization, Alejandro Agudo Sanchíz (2008) has shown
how a group of peasants declared themselves Zapatistas after the 1994
rebellion emboldened them to invade land that remained in private
hands despite previous phases of agrarian reform that had greatly
diminished the differences between indigenous peasants and non-
indigenous ranchers as landholders. Their action was opportunistic:
the invaders had no real connection with the EZLN, and had already
begun to coordinate themselves through kinship and neighbourhood
ties (ibid.: 592). Members of the local *ejido* had previously demanded
rights to the same land: they disliked the invaders because these
'Zapatistas' had earlier been clients of a non-indigenous local *cacique*
(ibid.). The *ejidatarios* responded by reassuming a loyalty to the PRI
that they had abandoned for allegiance to the PRD in an earlier
phase of their own struggles over land rights, turning to *Paz y Justicia*,
which controlled the *ejido* council between 1995 and 2001, to drive the
'Zapatista' squatters off the land (ibid.: 595). Yet the 'Zapatistas' now
saw that they had new opportunities to legalize their land invasion
by appealing to the 'agrarian' dimension of the government counter-
insurgency strategy, which sought to damp down insurgency by making
new land grants. They ceased to be Zapatistas and formed an 'apoliti-
cal' civil association (ibid.: 596). Agudo Sanchíz therefore presents us
with an intriguingly paradoxical situation. A group of land invaders

who earlier worked as gunmen for a local boss hated by the *ejidatarios* passed from being Zapatistas to being a group of citizens involved in a peaceful negotiation with the state through institutional channels. The *ejidatarios*, in contrast, abandoned an institutional opposition to the PRI regime through affiliation to an electoral political party in return for support from an illegal paramilitary organization whose violence was, nevertheless, sponsored for a time by legally constituted PRI political authorities (ibid.). In the end, the squatters did achieve their legal land regularization after the government bought the land from its owners and assigned the fifty-five families five hectares each, at a heavily subsidized price, within the framework of a trusteeship. Even more ironically, the families were subsequently granted a new *ejido*, which saved them the money that they would otherwise have had to repay to the trust, and also enabled them to thumb their noses at their old enemies, the existing *ejidatarios*. Although the manner in which they finally acquired title to the land was far from revolutionary, they named their new *ejido* 'Primero de Enero' (First of January), in commemoration of the date of the Zapatista rebellion that had provided the context in which they embarked on their journey to becoming legal landholders (ibid.: 599–600).

This example raises further questions about the place of paramilitarism itself in counter-insurgency. Comparing Mexico and Colombia, Patricia Olney (2004) has argued that the privatization of counter-insurgency operations through paramilitarization reflects a breakdown of elite consensus. She notes that although *Paz y Justicia* received money from the state government, most of the finance for paramilitary groups came from local ranchers and businessmen (ibid.: 3). This is entirely consistent with the involvement of PRI state deputies and municipal presidents, since these figures generally belonged to the same local elite. Olney argues, however, that collaborative relations between local paramilitary leaders and state-level PRI officials and members of the security forces are 'more indicative of internal divisions within the PRI than they are of a national counterinsurgency strategy' (ibid.: 6). Local elites doubted that the federal state was willing or able to defend their economic interests, and tended to offer strong resistance to political democratization (ibid.). Olney also emphasizes that since the local interests that opted for paramilitary violence were, as we have just seen in the case of the Tila region, socially heterogeneous and motivated by localized kinds of conflicts, once paramilitary violence broke out it was difficult for any superior instance of government to exercise control over its development (ibid.: 19).

Under the administration of governor Juan Sabines, critics of the regime began to denounce what they saw as a new counter-insurgency strategy. This seemed to be a continuation by other means of the 'Plan Puebla-Panama' programme with which the Fox administration had proposed to advance the economic modernization of Chiapas and make Mexico's capitalism a sub-imperial node in the articulation of Central America to the United States (Wilson 2013), a programme continued in a low-key way by the current 'Mesoamerica Project', which also includes Colombia. The 'sustainable rural cities' programme promised to reverse what, ten years after the EZLN rebellion, had seemed a deepening rural crisis marked by persistently high poverty indices, fragmentation of landholdings, recession in commercial agriculture and cattle-raising, and growing outmigration (Villafuerte Solís 2005). Population would be regrouped from dispersed rural settlements into rural centres that would sustain a variety of modern manufacturing as well as agro-industrial activities. The concentration of population would also enable the state to deliver high-quality medical and educational services to rural areas more effectively and economically, along with the 'digital connectivity' so essential for twenty-first-century life. For the EZLN and other dissident organizations, this project was designed to break the movement for autonomy and self-determination and subject the rural population to new forms of exploitation and surveillance.

In 2012, I visited the sustainable rural city of Santiago El Pinar, in the Los Altos region. I discovered that the houses neatly arranged along paved streets rising up a hillside were made of flimsy material, not of sufficient size to accommodate a normal rural family, and still lacked electricity and piped water. They were, however, painted blue and made a very pretty photograph from a distance. There were a few people about, since people came to take away items such as stoves that were delivered to the houses in which they did not live in the rural city to the homes in which they continued to live outside it. So it was easy enough to confirm that people were not impressed by the governor's project. Contrary to a press report that I read later, the medical centre was functioning, had a good complement of medical staff and seemed well stocked with medicines. But a cooperative factory that we visited, producing tricycle carts to be used for selling products on city streets, was completely dependent on the state government as the purchaser of its output as well as the supplier of the materials used. A chicken co-op also had no local market, and the costs of selling outside the region clearly made the enterprise non-viable economically without a subsidy from public funds. This project did not seem much like counter-insurgency, nor, for that matter, the kind of neoliberal economics advocated by Milton Friedman and Friedrich Hayek. What it did seem like was the kind of exercise in 'integral rural development' that I had seen driving up the public debt in 'statist' Mexico when I first started doing fieldwork there at the beginning of the 1980s. In this case, international donors had met some of the cost, although the state government's own public debt had risen alarmingly under Sabines, to 40 billion pesos.[13] The political benefit for the governor was the positive publicity from being seen in the cities to be 'doing something' about rural poverty. As we drove out of Santiago El Pinar we saw a billboard in a series with the general slogan of 'Chiapas keeps moving forward' that proclaimed that Chiapas had 'left behind the first place in social backwardness [*rezago social*]'. After Sabines left office, Governor Velasco quietly dropped his flagship programme.

There is one part of the Chiapas economy that shows unquestionable dynamism in various regions: the contraband economy. Conventional images of the 'illegal economy' in Mexico focus on drugs, arms and the trafficking of people. Yet as Rebecca Galemba (2012) has shown, what has kept much of the population of southern Chiapas going is smuggling traditional agricultural commodities, such as corn, sugar and coffee, across the border with Guatemala. She also shows that people involved in this type of smuggling see it as a legitimate form of work, thereby contesting the state's right to define what is legitimate or not (ibid.: 5). The viability of smuggling across unofficial border roads does, however, depend on state agents not interfering in the trade. This is only partly a matter of paying bribes, since Galemba shows that the state apparatus chooses not to inspect certain things and certain routes (ibid.: 7). Local people in this region make a clear distinction between 'licit' and 'illicit' forms of smuggling. Smugglers who become conspicuously affluent in their housing and lifestyles may be suspected of having a foot in the trans-border drugs economy as well. But Galemba emphasizes how people who make a successful business out of smuggling agricultural and everyday consumer products have succeeded in constructing a 'moral economy' that brings together a variety of workers loading cargoes and selling food and drink (ibid.: 9). The local communities put chains across the clandestine border roads to stop passing trucks and collect 'taxes' that are used to fund the provision of basic services such as water and electricity as well as to keep the roads themselves in a good state of repair (ibid.: 5). Asked how they felt about that, people often observed that they were living in an era of free trade imposed by the government through the North American Free Trade Agreement, which ended the guaranteed prices and subsidies that corn farmers used to receive. Since the neoliberal government itself now did little to provide people with business opportunities and livelihoods, smuggling was the way in which ordinary people could claim their 'right to work' in a 'free trade' regime that was anything but free for them, since they now received no government support to compete with subsidized *gringo* farmers, and still faced many bureaucratic regulations that made doing things 'by the book' unprofitable or impossible (ibid.: 9).

At first sight this appears another relatively innocuous example of what Gustavo Lins Ribeiro (2006) calls 'economic globalization from below'. Yet as Galemba points out, it does have its downside. The contraband economy is articulated to the legal economy, as some of the goods end up being traded through legal outlets, but it is becoming impossible to run a retail store that only deals in legally sourced goods, since the competition may sell smuggled goods (Galemba 2012: 10). The boundary between trading in 'licit' and 'illicit' commodities is fragile. Although the overall effects of the illegal economy seem positive in terms of 'development' and rising material living standards, social inequalities in the region are increasing and it has become difficult to enjoy a decent standard of living just by pursuing professional careers such as schoolteaching (ibid.). Although the 'culture of contraband' offers a critique of the state, it is not a challenge to state power (ibid.: 11). On the contrary, leaving aside the way officials benefit from getting bribes and politicians benefit from getting campaign contributions, the tolerated illegal economy solves a lot of the state's problems by giving ordinary people the chance to solve their own problems of economic survival and acquiring basic services, a basic neoliberal goal.

The contraband economy of Chiapas is not restricted to the

southern border area, or to traditional agricultural commodities. The criminal economy is visible too, particularly in the form of really nice houses built in incongruous places, but it is relatively discreet. Levels of overt criminal violence are quite low by the standards of some other parts of Mexico and Brazilian cities, although there are occasional shootouts in the urban periphery of San Cristóbal de Las Casas as well as Tuxtla Gutiérrez. There were also some cases of femicide in poor districts of both cities, which some locals attributed to the fact that 'they' were moving in. In Mexico, as in Brazil, criminals generally have no name, although expressions used can be negative, such as the fairly frequent '*los malos*' (the bad ones) (Sandoval 2012). The relative absence of spectacular violence in Chiapas not associated with paramilitarism and political and agrarian conflict is, however, deceiving.

Chiapas is a region of passage for Central American undocumented migrants heading for the United States and also a node in trafficking networks that meet local and national demands for domestic servants, dancers in bars and sex workers (Casillas 2012). Despite expressions of concern by the state and federal governments, little has been done to end the complicity between migration authorities and criminal gangs, particularly those operating under the franchise of Los Zetas. The kidnapping and extortion of migrants is a form of rent-seeking exploitation of the vulnerable that has filled mass graves elsewhere in the country with those whose relatives could not pay or who refused to work as cartel killers (Cordero Díaz and Figueroa Ibarra 2011). There have even been cases of the enslavement of victims by criminals (L. Sánchez 2013), although the conditions under which Central American migrants have found 'ordinary' employment working in Mexico have also often been akin to slavery.

As Wendy Vogt has shown, migrants in passage are turned into commodities that provide profits and rents to a wide range of actors, including Western Union, which not only makes money from wiring migrants' remittances back home to their families, but also from wiring the money that relatives have to pay to the extortionists and kidnappers (Vogt 2013: 775). Federal police extort money from migrants travelling on buses by threatening to turn them over to immigration officials if they do not pay, despite having no authorization to ask people about their migratory status (Isacson et al. 2014). Mexican municipal police routinely rob migrants. In a newspaper interview in mid-2014, one couple from Honduras argued that it was sometimes better to be assaulted by petty criminals, since the police stripped victims naked in their search for concealed money, and threatened to kill women who complained about abuse, although another interviewee in the same group also recounted how Zetas in Tamaulipas had tied a man to the railway track to be decapitated by a passing train when his relatives in the United States were unable to pay the $3,500 that they demanded as ransom (Gómez and Henríquez 2014). These victims were interviewed in one of the shelters created by Catholic priests to offer migrants moments of safety during their passage, and claimed that even the shelter itself was infiltrated by gangs of extortionists. Vogt shows that the inability of the shelters to afford complete protection is not simply because they can be infiltrated by criminals, but also because some migrants may themselves be tempted to go with the flow of the logic of the commodification of bodies: she gives the example of one man who recruited women from the shelters for strip clubs (Vogt 2013: 776). Although Central Americans do sometimes receive help from sympathetic Mexicans, who may even suffer judicial persecution for their charitable acts (Cordero Díaz and Figueroa Ibarra 2011: 150–1), the nature of their exploitation reinforces stereotypes of gang membership and involvement in prostitution, as well as fear of harm coming to locals from criminal violence and rent-seeking directed at migrants, producing levels of anxiety that have forced some of the shelters to close (Vogt 2013: 776).

Most of the kidnapping of migrants entering by Chiapas has taken place over the border in either Veracruz or Tabasco, although gangs prey upon them in different ways everywhere. One of the most visible sites of victimization remains the freight train called '*La Bestia*' (the Beast), although official promises have been made to restrict migrant use of this means of transport. Migrants may begin their journey in Tapachula, the main city of the Soconusco region of Chiapas, near the Pacific coast and border with Guatemala, or pass via Palenque, in the north-east of Chiapas, to the border town of Tenosique in Tabasco. The two railway routes from the south converge in Coatzalcoalcos, Veracruz, before dividing again into separate routes that pass up the east and west coasts. Assaults on the trains are frequent. Migrants crowded on to the roof of train carriages face extortion and possible murder, especially if they refuse to pay or lack money, but on occasion the train has been stopped and entire groups taken away en masse, with the complicity of the authorities. Even without the attacks of the criminals, the train ride is dangerous, since it is possible to sustain serious injury by falling off. As Vogt points out, calling such tragedies 'accidents' is to abstract from the systemic processes that create 'a global workforce of people whose lives teeter on the edge of disposability in an economic sense but also in an immediate embodied sense' (ibid.: 771–2).

This situation became a public scandal, but Mexican official actions continued to be oriented towards persecution rather than protection. In May 2014, federal police and agents of the National Institute of Migration carried out a violent operation in Tabasco, preceded by an attempt to detain migrants at the railway station in Palenque. They detained over three hundred migrants, along with three Catholic priests from the support network.[14] This is the kind of fruit that 'bilateral security agreements' between the Central American, Mexican and US governments have been producing for some time (Villafuerte Solis 2011), an issue to which I will return in the concluding chapter. The impact of these agreements on the transnational drugs and arms trade has been minimal, while adding another level of victimization to the experience of Central American migrants, an increasing number of whom are unaccompanied minor children (Isacson et al. 2014). The posture of the USA seems especially hypocritical given that the conditions that are driving them northwards are not simply consequences of neoliberal capitalist globalization but also the legacy of US-sponsored counter-insurgency wars (Vogt 2013: 770). One of Vogt's most poignant ethnographic examples is the case of a man who fought on the government side in the Guatemalan military state's genocidal campaigns against indigenous villages, who was now trying to cross into the United States for a third time in order to feed his children, thereby risking twenty years 'in a prison run by the same government that had indirectly supported him 25 years earlier' (ibid.: 770).

Decentring the EZLN

The EZLN was created by urban revolutionaries of the same kind that tried to mobilize the peasants of Guerrero. They moved into a regional space in the Selva Lacandona that had particular social, cultural, political and economic characteristics, as an area of relatively recent peasant colonization (De Vos 2002). The peasant communities of the core zone of the rebellion had previously been influenced by a Catholic diocese committed to Liberation Theology's preferential option for the poor and more culturally sensitive forms of proselytizing among indigenous people, and by activists from leftist political parties and rural union organizers (Leyva Solano and Ascencio Franco 1996; Estrada Saavedra 2013). The failure of these earlier interventions to deliver the results the peasants of the Selva had hoped for, and the deepening crisis provoked by neoliberal transformation, provided the opportunity for the EZLN to build up its influence in this space. Doing so transformed the outlook of the urban revolutionaries involved in the movement. But the EZLN did begin its life as a politico-military organization. As such, it needed to recruit young people as fighters, and (not unlike the paramilitaries) it appealed to young indigenous men who looked forward to benefiting from land redistribution, and to both young men and young women who were frustrated by traditional family and village hierarchies (Estrada Saavedra 2005: 534). Although the EZLN emphasizes the principle of 'bottom-up' control of the organization by its indigenous community support bases, each village had its 'responsible' person who was ultimately answerable to the Clandestine Revolutionary Council of what people called 'the organization' (ibid.: 542). This shadow structure of authority could exercise direction and backstage influence on what local people decided, and people who did not want to go along with what the EZLN proposed at the time of the rebellion faced being expelled from the community and losing their land rights. Marco Estrada Saavedra has argued that once a majority vote in favour of joining the EZLN struggle had been achieved in an assembly, there was an element of fear behind the compliance of those who remained in doubt about the wisdom of that path (ibid.: 538–9).

As a clandestine organization that developed by extending a network that had no visible centre or hierarchy, the EZLN was more resilient against repression than a vertically organized, left-wing political party (Trejo 2012: 102). The EZLN was not, however, able to prevent forced displacement of its supporters by the Mexican army and paramilitary groups, and the movement did not lack a strategic directing hand as it embarked on its different projects to extend its influence beyond Chiapas. Even after the 'organization' announced that it was leaving the building of autonomy to its base communities under the democratic authority of the Good Government Councils, links were still maintained with the EZLN via the 'responsible persons', who exercised considerable influence over grassroots community rep-resentatives. The Good Government Councils helped the Zapatista autonomous communities survive in a hostile environment in which Zapatistas had to share space with enemies and defectors, at times even within the same villages. But the alternative sovereignty that the Zapatistas have established in some regional spaces is not comprehensive, since many non-Zapatistas still prefer to accept the state's sovereignty for many purposes even if they go to the Good Government Council for some services. This, it will be recalled, is the kind of choice that people may also make in contexts where the alternative is the help of criminal organizations, but criminals are not normally in the business of trying to build 'new worlds' in which the state as we know it will be radically transformed by grassroots democratic practice.

There are, however, many parts of Chiapas in which the EZLN has never had a great deal of influence. In others, the influence that it had was indirect. As José Luis Escalona (2010) has shown for the case of two Tojolabal communities that recovered control over their own affairs after agrarian struggles secured the conversion of former *fincas* (landed estates) into *ejidos*,[15] many indigenous people in Chiapas have preferred to confront the social changes produced by the problems of the rural economy, and the challenge of enhancing their citizenship, by continuing to participate in electoral politics and competition for political control of conventional municipalities. Although Chiapas is often thought of as an 'indigenous' state, less than 32 per cent of the total population was indigenous in 2010 according to the National Commission for the Development of Indigenous Peoples (Comisión Nacional para el Desarrollo de los Pueblos Indígenas 2010a). This does not mean that people in Chiapas who think of themselves as mestizos who have little in common socially and culturally with the indigenous people of the Los Altos or Selva Lacandona region cannot perceive that they have shared interests. An example would be people in the municipality of Chicomuselo, on the border with Guatemala, where a gunman on a motorcycle who was never identified by the authorities assassinated the leader of a protest movement against the Canadian Blackfire Mining Corporation's pollution of local water resources. The local priest is a follower of the late Bishop Samuel Ruiz, and has worked hard to sensitize his flock to the problems of poverty, environmental destruction and the decline of the peasant corn economy. Yet the social and ethnic divide remains a profound one.

By the time that the dirty war in Guerrero ended, Mexico was already becoming a largely urbanized society, its rural population reduced to 34 per cent of the total by 1980, and down to 12 per cent thirty years later. With the end of the Cold War, and slow movement towards allowing opposition parties to win electoral contests, many former revolutionaries repented of their past commitment to armed struggle. In the case of both Guerrero and Chiapas, the re-emergence of armed movements might therefore be linked to levels of political closure, electoral fraud and repression on the part of state governments which were no longer typical of the country as a whole.

This is how many analysts explained the different trajectories of Chiapas and Oaxaca in the first half of the 1990s. Coming into office after the fraudulent presidential elections of 1988, Chiapas's new governor, Patrocinio González, reversed the limited openings offered to social movements by his predecessor, drew up new laws to criminalize social protest and unlawfully detained the 'clerical and socialist agitators' at the top of what Guillermo Trejo argues he incorrectly surmised were centralized and vertical organizational networks, thereby driving the decentralized village support networks that provided the popular base of the EZLN along a more radical path (Trejo 2012: 168). In Oaxaca, in contrast, PRI governor Heladio Ramírez played a major role in persuading the federal government headed by Carlos Salinas to embrace ILO convention 162 and pursue a neoliberal multiculturalist strategy. In Oaxaca, the PRI not only abandoned earlier repression to allow the independent Coalition of Workers, Peasants and Students of the Isthmus (COCEI) to take control of the municipal government of Juchitán, but also promoted a change to the state's Constitution that allowed indigenous communities to elect their authorities in assemblies by 'uses and customs' without the participation of political parties or ballots based on individual secret votes. In recognizing the distinctive cultural identities and rights of indigenous Oaxacans, Ramírez deftly played the 'ethnic card' to divert attention, for the moment, from the changes that the Salinas administration made to the national Constitution to end land redistribution and open the way to privatization of the land granted to *ejidos* (ibid.: 166–7).

Yet Oaxaca did not remain tranquil. In 2006, a bitter battle broke out between the PRI state governor, Ulises Ruiz, and a disparate coalition of indigenous and non-indigenous social movements grouped into the Popular Assembly of the Peoples of Oaxaca (APPO) (Norget 2010). The APPO reflected a tendency also found elsewhere in Latin America for socially heterogeneous movements, and in this case predominantly urban groups, to be understood by foreign activists as 'indigenous' despite their plural composition. Another important case is the 'war' against water privatization in Cochabamba, Bolivia (Albro 2005). The notion of indigeneity lends itself well to claims that the movement is practising a more democratic kind of politics, since practices such as making decisions in assemblies on the basis of consensus dovetail nicely with anarchist ideas about how 'prefigurative' politics should be done (Maeckelbergh 2011). This is central to the global appeal of the EZLN to alter-globalization activists. Indigeneity also seems apt for a critique of neoliberal marketization. The Cochabamba protesters argued that Andean people know that 'water is life' and should not be turned into a commodity. In reality, as Norget shows, the groups that came together in the APPO encompassed a broad range of political philosophies. Some of the protesters felt quite comfortable with Stalin as an icon, and grumbled that there wasn't enough class politics or top-down enforcement of discipline in the coalition. Yet it does seem important that 'indigeneity' can be politically resignified by actors who do not see themselves as indigenous in their everyday lives, and by indigenous actors themselves, in a way that goes beyond the issue of special rights for indigenous people. The positive side of this resignification is that it changes the perceived place of indigenous people in the modern world in a symbolically powerful way. It makes them seem relevant to pressing contemporary concerns, such as making democracy more meaningful to everyone and thinking about climate change and economic alternatives, rather than presenting them as historical anachronisms demanding special privileges simply because their ancestors were colonized by Europeans. The downside is that external constructions of movements as 'indigenous' erase the much more complex, and variegated, politics of what indigenous citizens actually do.

With the support of the Fox government, Ruiz won the battle against the APPO by means of outright repression. He was also able to take advantage of the divisions that existed within and between indigenous communities in an ethnically fragmented state whose 570 mostly tiny municipalities comprise almost a quarter of the national total, and of the APPO's failure to articulate its struggle to those of the majority of the indigenous population in the countryside. In this context, it was unsurprising that paramilitary groups enjoyed impunity when they harassed and besieged the Trique community of San Juan Copala, after a group favouring Zapatista-style autonomy became dominant there.

Trejo's thesis about the significance of localized limitations on political opening seems applicable to the state of Michoacán. Indigenous communities there did not embrace armed insurgency despite apparent efforts by guerrilla cells of the EPR to mobilize some of them. The state governorship passed from the PRI to the PRD in 2002 and the PRI had to wait ten years before recapturing it. Yet Michoacán has recently seen both indigenous and non-indigenous citizens participating in a different kind of armed movement, self-defence forces whose existence has been justified by the state's failure to defend its citizens from criminal violence and extortion. Violence developed to a point at which the situation in the state could be defined as a threat to national security, and a new federal intervention justified, under the Peña Nieto government. Michoacán's self-defence forces resemble those of Guerrero, and criminal penetration of local government in Michoacán is at least as significant as in Guerrero. The answers to some of the questions raised by the recent history of Guerrero are, however, perhaps already clearer in the case of Michoacán.

In the next chapter I take issues raised in this chapter further by offering a critical analysis of Felipe Calderón's 'War Against the Drug Cartels' in Michoacán and the Peña Nieto administration's claimed 'pacification' of the state. One issue is the multiplication and ramification of relationships between state agents and criminal organizations, the significance and variety of which are already apparent from the discussion of Guerrero and Chiapas. Another is how criminal enterprises relate to state-sponsored projects of capitalist development, including the way that the 'deniable violence' of criminal paramilitaries contributes to the extension of models of capitalist accumulation that have high social and environmental costs. What we can learn from Michoacán is that Mexico has become a country in which genuinely popular social movements are routinely criminalized and their leaders imprisoned, while persons devoted to illegal activities continue to thrive under the protection of a state that produces rather than alleviates insecurity.

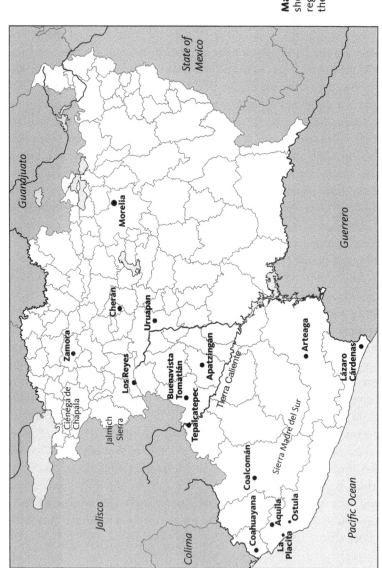

Map 4.1 Michoacán, showing places and regions mentioned in the text

5 | PARAMILITARIES, *AUTODEFENSAS* AND THE PACIFICATION OF MICHOACÁN

I have been doing ethnographic research in Michoacán since the start of the 1980s. Over the years, I have come to know a variety of places and people throughout the state, which in the early years often had to be traversed by bus or car along unpaved roads. My early work focused on the rural economy, peasant and capitalist, agrarian conflicts, and the extensive migration to the United States that enabled both mestizo and indigenous inhabitants of the state to weather successive economic crises and the repeated failure of state-sponsored development projects to deliver what they had promised. Ironically, one of the greatest gifts of the land reform to the *campesinos* of Michoacán was that it facilitated the migration of members of those families that benefited from it (López Castro and Zendejas Romero 1988), although journeying to the North was a long-established local tradition that went back to the period before the great depression of 1929, and had become an obligatory rite of passage into adult status for young men in the places in which I worked by the 1980s.

The Ciénega de Chapala, on the frontier with Jalisco, had been dominated, up to the Cárdenas agrarian reform, by one of the largest landed estates (*haciendas*) in western Mexico. I went to work there because Lázaro Cárdenas and his brothers had been born and raised under the shadow of this vast engine of rural exploitation, which had continued to enjoy the support of Cárdenas's revolutionary predecessors in Mexico City because it was seen as epitomizing the superior rationality of modern agro-industry. This was not an entirely accurate vision. Although the *hacienda* possessed a modern sugar mill and exported wheat and meat outside its region by train, sometimes leaving its workers without corn to make *tortillas* when the external market price was especially high, its economic power also rested on its monopoly of commercially exploitable land and ability to extract what Marx called 'absolute surplus value' from the peasants who worked for it. Whatever the labour laws said, its administrators had virtually untrammelled power to extend the working day, and the *hacienda* obliged its permanent workers to live in shacks that could be demolished by striking the roof supports at the front with the butt of a rifle: entire families could be expelled should any member express dissatisfaction with the regime. This kind of power depended, first, on the fact that the *hacienda* possessed a private army of 'White Guards', called the *Acordada*. The *Acordada* underpinned a regime of coercion that disciplined workers and intimidated sharecroppers who found that they had still ended up in debt with the *hacienda* after securing a bumper harvest. It was also capable of keeping at bay any of the armed bands of revolutionaries and 'bandits' – often difficult to distinguish – that instilled fear and loathing into the peasants who lived outside the defensive perimeter of the large village where the estate's Great House was located. The second basis of *hacienda* power was that it controlled the local judiciary, which declared federal decrees null and void on several occasions during the struggle for land reform.

Lázaro Cárdenas wanted to make the expropriation of this estate the flagship of a radical turn in agrarian reform that would grant land to the previously ineligible permanent workers of the *haciendas*, the *peones acasillados*. His problem was that a majority of the workers of this estate rejected his call to mobilize for the land, and his new agrarian reform movement was forced to rely on more politicized people who had returned from sojourns as migrants in the United States, or become activists in provincial cities where they had made their living as artisans or merchants. The *hacienda* responded with a campaign of terror and assassination, but the situation of agrarian fighters throughout the state had already been compromised by the fact that this was a region in which the *cristero* rebellion of Catholic peasants against the secularizing government of Plutarco Elias Calles had also been strong during the period 1926–29. As a soldier under Calles, and then Michoacán's state governor, Cárdenas had armed the *agraristas* to fight the *cristeros*. He did succeed in pushing through land reform in his native place as president of the republic, in part by offering the owners of the *hacienda* attractive economic terms for abandoning their land and sugar mill altogether, but the violent divisions of the past left a profound legacy of bitterness within the peasant population. This expressed itself in the period after the land reform by violence within the 'emancipated' villages between those who had supported the *agraristas* and those who supported the right-wing *sinarquista* movement (Serrano Alvarez 1997).

This is only one small fragment of a regional history of violent conflicts that were as heterogeneous in their causes as the geographical, climatic, ecological, demographic and economic diversity of a state such as Michoacán would lead us to expect, a diversity reinforced by localized variations in inter-ethnic relations and related disputes over farmland and forest resources. Yet the effects of these local conflicts did tend to coalesce into broader patterns of dissidence that impeded the national state's establishing an undisputed hegemony over this regional space. Lázaro Cárdenas was not only an exceptionally adept statesman, but also pragmatic. In a zone that had been a hot spot of *cristero* armed militancy in the sierras on Michoacán's Pacific coast, for example, he was content to reach personal understandings with local leaders of that movement that allowed them to dominate their subregion's politics into the 1950s, on condition that they abided by the ground rules of the new order established by the consolidated post-revolutionary regime. In the Ciénega de Chapala, his brothers were careful to ensure that the families that had provided the administrators of the old *hacienda* regime were given a place in that new order. Yet because it was a new order created through sustained armed violence, the destruction of the repressive apparatus of the *haciendas* provoked new problems. Everyone who migrated to the United States came back with a gun. Those guns were used to settle old scores between *agraristas* and anti-*agraristas*, and I found this to be a pattern behind killings for decades after the agrarian reform. But the guns were also used in more personal disputes, some of which arose simply from everyday efforts to assert a kind of masculinity that the armed power of the *haciendas* had suppressed but also stimulated through its constant humiliation of those subjected to its violent disciplinary power.

When I began to do fieldwork in the former *hacienda*, I discovered that whenever I asked in which year something happened, the reply would begin with 'it was when X was killed'. My notebooks soon filled up with long lists of family tragedies that occurred during the three decades after Cárdenas left the presidency. In the 1970s, however, homicide rates began to fall substantially. Although people who lived in these *ejido* communities still had plenty to complain about, and there were still some very poor families, the majority had seen substantial improvements in their quality of life by the 1980s. Most of this came from their own efforts as migrants, although the possession of valuable, mostly irrigated, farmland was an asset even if it was rented out to others. The debt crisis and neoliberal restructuring of the 1980s and 1990s were to change things for the worse, but criminal violence took a considerable time to become central to the regional scenario.

The abduction, torture and killing of US Drug Enforcement Administration (DEA) agent Enrique 'Kike' Camarena in 1985 was one visible sign of the increasing importance of the drug cartels in western Mexico. Yet at the time it was read more as another sign of the complicity of Mexican politicians and law enforcement in the 'world of crime' than as something that menaced the security of honest citizens. This was a period in which drug traffickers stuck to their business and only committed violent acts that were related to their business interests. A farmer who refused to allow his land to be used for marijuana cultivation might be killed, but life was fairly tranquil in the zones where drugs were produced, even at the start of the 1990s. I felt quite safe moving around in zones in the *Tierra Caliente* (Hot Country) region of Michoacán that were the major zones of production. Or more precisely, I did not feel that the drug lords and their employees were a threat. It was the agents of public order that scared me.

Even in the Ciénega de Chapala I had experiences such as looking into the barrel of an automatic weapon being aimed directly at my face by a member of the state judicial police who was clearly high on cocaine, obtained, I discovered, as a consequence of having kin in high places in the state judiciary. In later fieldwork in the sugar-producing region around Los Reyes, located on the edge of the Hot Country zone, I encountered judicial police doing the dirty work of some *caciques* who exercised considerable political muscle in the state capital as leading members of the Cattlemen's Association. They were trying to expel a group of peasants from land on which they had built a hamlet that even had its own government school, since their rights to it had been confirmed by a presidential decree. During the 1980s, judicial police did not wear uniforms and were engaged in a variety of forms of theft and extortion. Local judges guaranteed their impunity and received a cut of the proceeds. Justice was a matter of negotiating about money. Money would get the unjustly accused or the guilty released, somebody else unjustly imprisoned, or a favourable decision in a civil case. Particular cases swung one way and another if all parties paid. In agrarian disputes, the decision of the bureaucrat was always a matter of negotiating via money or the traffic of influence. Taking the matter to a higher level became even more expensive, as Monique Nuijten (2003) showed in her analysis of the state apparatus as a 'hope-generating machine'. Peasant farmers who benefited from the agrarian reform had few reasons to love 'the state' as they experienced it through the actions of the local agents who acted in its name. But they were 'between a rock and a hard place'. In the period of the agrarian reform, they needed the state to support their efforts to gain land and support them in their fights with the *cristeros*. After the agrarian reform, their ability to work their land depended on the state offering them cheap credits and subsidized inputs. When that support was not forthcoming, they often had little alternative to handing their land over to a capitalist entrepreneur to cultivate in their place. Which level of government the peasants needed to appeal to for support was a variable, depending on who occupied the governor's chair in Morelia. Yet they often had to hope that the federal government would provide a solution to their problems, since the state government was often controlled by politicians who acted in collusion with commercial agricultural and cattle-raising interests, *caciques* involved in illegal logging, or local bureaucrats who might work for federal agencies but were thoroughly enmeshed in regional clique networks that guaranteed their impunity. This hope was often illusory because the networks in fact extended all the way to Mexico City itself.

Extortion of one kind or another should therefore be seen as a regular, everyday, feature of the way that the power that different levels of government bestowed on its authorized agents was exercised, whether we are talking about the bribes habitually paid to facilitate routine bureaucratic transactions, or the much larger sums that could be extracted via judicial impropriety, plundering state-owned enterprises, or the frauds committed by bureaucrats on the publicly funded system of insurance against crop failure, which required the collaboration of peasant farmers. Government functionaries, leaders of PRI trade unions and a host of other elements in the corporate apparatus of the state also accumulated wealth off the backs of street traders and anyone else who was engaged in an economic activity that could be 'regulated' by extra-official means. The practices of extortion, and indeed much of the rest of what criminal organizations now do, were already firmly established in the era in which Michoacán was supposedly 'governable'. Many of them were, in fact, embedded within 'government' itself.

Given this situation, which was scarcely peculiar to Michoacán, it becomes difficult to talk as if 'the rule of law' ever existed in the conventional sense. Where the law was actually invoked and used to produce a particular outcome, such as a decision about property rights, or responsibility for a homicide, it was quite possible that it would be administered in a way that produced demonstrable injustice. The hated judicial police presented serious threats to the security of ordinary people. Their capacity to instil fear that would discourage individuals from offending the interests that they served was certainly reinforced by the daily sight of peasants being driven off to jail slumped in the back of a pickup with obvious signs of physical abuse. Everyone knew of specific cases that confirmed the habitual use of torture on witnesses as well as on accused persons in police 'investigations'. Yet it was difficult to make oneself safe simply by avoiding any kind of action that would involve the police, because they also robbed and extorted money from people who had no problem with the law or interest in causing political trouble. Many people concluded that the only way that it was possible to deal with the *judiciales* was to ambush and kill them on the road before they arrived.

It is important to remember that much of what has happened recently in Michoacán is rooted in this longer-term historical experience. This does not mean it simply represents an intensification of past patterns. On the contrary, in the rest of this chapter I will place more emphasis on what is new. But a historical perspective is also essential for deciding whether the problems faced by the citizens who live in a state such as Michoacán result from their having been abandoned by 'the state', or from the nature of the presence that 'the state' has had in their lives over an extended period. Following Daniel Goldstein's perspective on the role of the state's 'phantom presence' in the production of insecurity in Bolivia (Goldstein 2012), I argue in this chapter that the nature of the state's presence has been and remains crucial in the case of Michoacán. I turn first to how that idea illuminates the growth of drug trafficking in this part of Mexico.

The state and the development of the drugs trade

It will be clear from what I have already said that the hegemony of the national state and PRI apparatus over Michoacán was always patchy. The limits to hegemony were configured by a history of political dissidence that pitted Catholics against the secular state, and conflicts relating to the ways in which agrarian reform excluded many, and often did not work well even for those who received land. When the state did take a more active role in the rural economy, from the late 1960s onwards, the new opportunities for graft provided by renewed support for the *ejido* system and state-sponsored agro-industrial projects strengthened subregional systems of boss rule. These were tied together at regional level through the negotiation of power within a state government that generally supported the reproduction of impunity. The other important quality of state economic intervention was that it promoted the technical modernization, industrialization and internationalization of the rural economy. Even peasants became users of pesticides and herbicides produced by transnational companies, and certain kinds of capitalist agriculture, such as growing tomatoes, expanded by renting high-quality irrigated land in the *ejidos*. Migration to the United States continued to increase, since it offered better returns for the landless children of *ejidatarios* than working in local agriculture. This pattern of development is important for understanding the development of the drugs trade in Michoacán from the 1980s onwards, especially after state support for the rural economy was withdrawn again after neoliberal policies were introduced to deal with the deepening crisis that began in 1982.

As Salvador Maldonado (2013) shows, there are three zones of Michoacán that are particularly important for understanding the development of the drug economy. Each needs to be defined in terms of its sociocultural and political as well as its ecological characteristics. One is the mountainous sierra occupied by non-indigenous people called *rancheros* (literally ranchers, although the category includes people who farm as well as people who raise cattle, activities usually combined in this zone). The agrarian class structure of the *ranchero* population is based on private property relations. The sierras had a landlord class, obliging some inhabitants to pay rents, traditionally as a share of the crop or of calves bred. As demographic densities increased in the nineteenth century, families began to migrate to other areas in search of new pasturelands that would be free of the burden of rent (Cochet 1991).

Rancher migrations transformed the second important zone of drug trafficking, the Pacific coast, because the infiltration of ranchers into the territories occupied by Náhuatl-speaking indigenous peoples turned into a conquest that gave mestizos political domination over the region. The indigenous communities are today located in the municipality of Aquila, one of the largest and poorest not only in Michoacán but also in the country as a whole. The rancher invasions extinguished two of the colonial indigenous communities that had managed to survive into the twentieth century,[1] Aquila and Maquilí, and transformed another two, Coire and Pómaro, into invaded territories in which relations between indigenous and mestizo inhabitants were tense (Gledhill 2004). The remaining Nahua community on the coast, Ostula, did succeed in keeping the mestizos at bay. A small group of families encouraged by a political boss in the county seat of Aquila invaded Ostula's territory in 1928, but were contained in an enclave on its borders and never allowed to participate in the institutions of self-government or the religious life of the indigenous community. The mestizo invasions did, however, create a problem for Ostula that proved long standing, the creation of a new mestizo settlement on the coast called La Placita, located on the border of Ostula's territory. La Placita was granted an *ejido* during the presidency of Lázaro Cárdenas.

Despite the class-stratified nature of their social organization, Michoacán's *rancheros* projected a cultural image of rugged independence of masters, including the state, and strong devotion to family and Catholicism, underpinned by a patriarchal masculinity that glorified the skilled horseman who always carried his gun and would not hesitate to defend his honour. A teacher who began his career in a primary school in a *rancho* at the end of the 1960s once told me how nervous it had made him when the boys sat down at their desks and laid their pistols down on them. *Ejidatarios* were despised as people without honour because they had received their land as a 'gift' from the government (Barragan 1990). In Los Reyes, the juxtaposition of *ejidos* on the irrigated plain and *ranchero* communities in the surrounding hills tended to produce a mutual construction of stereotypes, in which the people of the valley floors would argue that the people of the *ranchos* were 'uncivilized' and violent. In practice many families in this region occupied both worlds because they had access to different kinds of property, but the stereotypes emerged frequently for rhetorical effect in political contexts, such as heated debates over the leadership of the cane growers' union. When someone adopted a *ranchero* subject-position, the emphasis would be the corruption of the state and all who had worked with it in the *ejido* or sugar mill during the period in which the mills had been state owned. On the other side, there was often an explicit insinuation that *rancheros* lived from the profits of cultivating marijuana.

As Maldonado points out, the less accessible sierras of the Sierra Madre del Sur, stretching from Jalisco down to the border with Guerrero, had a long history of cultivating marijuana and opium poppies, just like the equivalent zone in Guerrero. He describes some points along this chain of mountains as 'small golden triangles' because the state's security apparatuses 'simply have no presence there' (Maldonado Aranda 2013: 49). When the state did attempt to provide services to these communities, particularly schools, airstrips were built to allow teachers to fly in alongside other personnel and supplies. Traffickers could also use these landing strips to export drugs. For the most part, however, even the people who lived in the small towns of this zone 'had contact with the State only through caciques, the army, or on sporadic visits from some government agency' (ibid.). Since these populations tended to experience the state only at its corrupt and violent worst, the presence of the *narcos* was generally welcome, since, in contrast to the old-style *caciques*, they did not make themselves rich at the expense of the locals, but gave something back to the communities that harboured them, enabling them to share in some of the benefits of technological modernity, such as satellite television. Maldonado concludes that in this type of community 'internal codes weave a web of silence and solidarity that envelops everyone who grows or distributes narcotics, so when the drug trade becomes integrated into regional economies and cultures, people adopt it as part of a lifestyle, in fact, a road to social ascendance' (ibid.: 50).

It was, however, state investment in infrastructure modernization which stimulated the growth of drug production in the coastal region. In the 1980s, a new coastal highway was built to link the deep-water port of Lázaro Cárdenas, in the extreme south of Michoacán on the border with Guerrero, with Zihuataneco, 92 kilometres further south, and the port of Manzanillo in Colima, 338 kilometres to the north. Marijuana could now be moved easily by road, sea and air, but more importantly, cocaine base could be delivered by sea from Colombia to processing labs located on the coast.[2] The cocaine business was restricted to the mestizo communities. People from the indigenous communities did try to participate in what became a 'boom' of marijuana cultivation, but most soon became dispirited, since indigenous people were generally not well enough armed to avoid being robbed of their money while they were returning home after delivering the product to buyers on the coast. There were, however, exceptions. The large village of San Pedro Naranjestil, located towards the south of the indigenous territory of Pómaro in the direction of Lázaro Cárdenas, is divided between indigenous and mestizo families that tend to keep apart. But in the indigenous *ranchos* higher up in the sierra, young indigenous men had fully adopted the *ranchero* model of masculinity, packing pistols in their belts and carrying AK-47s over their shoulders. The parish priest, a deeply committed follower of Liberation Theology who had abandoned a promising scientific career to minister to the poor, told me how he had tried to persuade the young men not to bring their weapons into the church. They finally agreed, although the reason they carried them all the time was fear of attack by other groups or the military. The priest said he had looked into their eyes as they talked and was disturbed that he saw nothing in them with which he knew how to communicate. This interview, conducted in 2002, gave me a preliminary insight into the way things were going as levels of violence associated with drug trafficking increased and the nature of the violence began to change.

The third zone of southern Michoacán to become a major centre of drug production was the Tierra Caliente region centred on the city of Apatzingán, although during the 1970s the drug trade had also been extended into the *ranchero* communities of the Jalmich highlands, on the border with Jalisco to the north-west, and into the temperate zone around Uruapan to the north of Apatzingán, whose avocado orchards provided an effective way of laundering drug money (ibid.: 52–3). Unattractive to Spaniards because of its hot climate, and considered a place where only imported black slaves and their descendants could work, the Tierra Caliente remained marginal to the rest of Michoacán until 1947, when the state in the form of the Tepalcatepec River Basin Development Commission led by ex-president Cárdenas embarked on a massive new development initiative (Barkin and King 1970). An extensive peasant colonization programme was undertaken through the creation of new *ejidos* which offered generous allocations of land to those willing to put up with what were initially very challenging conditions on a social frontier with an enervating climate. In the early days the risks were considerable: some of the pioneer settlers whom I met over the years told me that they had slept in their fields with a gun beside them at harvest time. Yet life did improve after major investments were made in roads and irrigation works, hydroelectric and mining projects. The mining was related to a later phase of Cárdenas's grand vision for the socio-economic and political transformation of the entire Balsas river basin, the construction of the country's second-largest steel works in Lázaro Cárdenas city, inaugurated as a state-owned company in 1969 and privatized in 1991 (Aparicio 1995; Williams 2001).

Peasants from other regions of Michoacán came to see the *ejidatarios* of the Apatzingán region as 'the spoiled children of Lázaro Cárdenas' (Stanford 2000: 80). But the agricultural development model adopted in the region made its farmers dependent not only on state support but also on the particular export commodity chains to which the state directed their production, and on the US companies that controlled access to US markets (ibid.: 81). The economic history of the region was punctuated by a boom-and-bust cycle that started with cotton and ended with cantaloupe melons. Although, as Lois Stanford (ibid.) documented, the *ejidatarios* tried to improve the terms of their incorporation into markets dominated by a monopsonistic alliance between the state and transnational agribusiness, or to bypass controls entirely, the neoliberal shift to free market policies did not work out well for them. Crisis and structural adjustment led to reduced state spending on infrastructure, and elimination of subsidies and government guaranteed farm prices, but not to reduced corruption and collusion between government bureaucrats, private property owners and the leaderships of associations of *ejidatarios* (Maldonado Aranda 2013: 10). International prices also fell, and the transnational companies cancelled the agreements with producers that had enabled them to sustain an export economy based on chemical fertilizers, herbicides and pesticides that had taken a heavy local environmental toll (ibid.: 11).

As Maldonado points out, drug production and trafficking were already well established in this region before the crisis of the statized economy. The traffickers took advantage of the same infrastructure and commercial networks that were created for the legal agro-export economy (ibid.: 6). As these legitimate activities became less profitable or even viable, some of the *caciques* that had previously fed on the corruption of state institutions, along with other members of local elites, themselves turned to trafficking (ibid.: 10). Neoliberal measures to promote administrative decentralization strengthened the nexus between local politicians and traffickers, with the support of a state government that argued that the police, also part of this nexus, should take the principal role in maintaining public security, rather than the military (ibid.: 12). Yet although the drugs economy helped some existing elites to rescue themselves from economic disaster, blurring the traditional lines of distinction between traffickers, *caciques*, landowners and businessmen, the lines did not dissolve completely.

As Victoria Malkin shows for another town in the Tierra Cali-ente,[3] the old landed families of the area were sometimes able to adapt to changing times by developing new businesses, but found their power as *caciques* and their wealth increasingly challenged by more successful international migrants, prosperous *rancheros* from outside the town, and some *ejidatarios* who had done especially well during the agro-export boom years (Malkin 2001: 108). Although marijuana grown in the surrounding sierras had been the principal product trafficked in the 1970s, by the 1990s local traffickers were also dealing not only in cocaine but methamphetamines as well. As Malkin points out, methamphetamines require access to chemical ingredients and technical knowledge, but they do not require control over land, making this branch of the industry more open to new entrants than marijuana or opium poppies (ibid.: 110). The principal base of the traffickers was a neighbouring town that locals classified as a '*rancho*' in the denigrating sense that I mentioned in the case of Los Reyes (ibid.: 112–13). Yet their 'new money' not only had a substantial impact on the economy of the more 'civilized' urban settlement, but also presented a significant challenge to the political patronage networks of 'old money'. Malkin argues that the success of this challenge depended not simply on their spending money in ways that local people would approve, by building swimming pools open to the public, or by donating money for the renovation of churches, but on their ability to enact a cultural transformation (ibid.: 115). This transformation was simultaneously linked to disillusion with past models of progress and moral personhood associated with the old orders of the big landowners and the *ejido*, and to positive affinities with the neoliberal order of things, including entrepreneurialism, and a valuation of individual consumption, leisure and 'fun' (ibid.: 116). In a context in which the masculinity of young landless men was challenged by their inability to play the 'breadwinner' role, attracting women was a motive for participating in trafficking that worked very well, since women *were* attracted, and would stress the virtues of their husbands or boyfriends as 'providers' to silence moral challenges (ibid.: 117).

Participation in trafficking was not necessarily a route to riches and social success. Throughout Michoacán in the 1990s, drug lords recruited young international migrants to act as 'mules', in an environment which had been made much more difficult by new US immigration controls (Maldonado Aranda 2013: 11).[4] Many of them ended up in a US jail (Malkin 2001: 114). Yet the visible success of the traffickers, and their willingness to 'help out' families in need by giving them marijuana seeds to sow or offering other kinds of participation in the traffic, did convince many that 'honest work' of the kind that traditional international labour migration had offered was no longer an effective way of securing the basics, such as having enough money to get married and build a house, let alone of 'progressing' to a better future (ibid.: 122).

Violence was the downside of the expansion of the drugs economy. Yet in the 1990s, the violence that *narcos* might bring to a community was not seen as different in kind to the kinds of fights over land, political power and women that had existed in these communities in the past (ibid.: 119). In a town in the Tierra Caliente it was difficult to make a moral case against drug trafficking (as distinct from addiction), since corruption and illegality had been so integral to the order presided over by a state that had now abandoned people. Furthermore, even in its relative 'absence', the state continued to be a problem. The main kind of violence that local people worried about in the 1990s when they thought about drug trafficking was the violence committed by the state judicial police and the military in the name of eradicating the drug trade. As Maldonado notes, the Salinas de Gortari administration used drugs and arms searches as a pretext for military operations that resulted in widespread abuse of the human rights of supporters of the candidate that he defeated by fraud in the 1988 elections, Cuauhtémoc Cárdenas (Maldonado Aranda 2013: 18). Michoacán became the principal bastion of the *neo-cardenista* movement that gave birth to the PRD, which meant that anti-drug operations remained intimately entangled with efforts to keep candidates out of elected office or even to remove them after they had been elected. I learned personally of killings carried out in tiny *ranchos* simply to send a message to everyone else about the dangers of supporting the opposition. Threat was omnipresent even in places that had PRD mayors, often stigmatized by their opponents as people who had been put into office by 'the *ranchos*', i.e. traffickers, or by indigenous communities that had 'lost their respect for institutions' by having the temerity to protest about their lack of public services or the illegal logging of their communal forests. PRI propaganda in Los Reyes made it abundantly clear that the choice was between voting for 'peace' or voting for 'war' and desolation.

From cartel wars and wars against cartels to mafias

By the late 1990s, Michoacán had its own cartel, run by the Valencia brothers, members of a rural merchant family that epitomized 'traditional' *ranchero* values. They had previous experience of marijuana and poppy cultivation but had developed a transnational entrepreneurial vision as migrants to the United States (ibid.: 20). Making contacts in Colombia, they secured control of the cocaine route along the Pacific coast and also formed an alliance with the Amezcua brothers in Colima to develop the production and sale of methamphetamines (ibid.). Their Milenio cartel apparently enjoyed the protection of the PRI state governor and invested its profits in avocado orchards in Uruapan and in Periban, near Los Reyes (ibid.: 20–1). In 2001 the governorship of Michoacán finally passed to the PRD, represented by Lázaro Cárdenas Batel, grandson of President Cárdenas. By this time the Milenio cartel had allied with the Sinaloa cartel through the intermediation of 'Nacho' Coronel, a trusted right hand of Sinaloa's boss, 'El Chapo' Guzmán. Guzmán had originally worked for traffickers based in Guadalajara, Jalisco, and had been imprisoned in 1993 for drug trafficking and alleged participation in the murder of Cardinal Juan Posadas Ocampo in the city's airport, after being detained in Guatemala. But he had already taken over the leadership of the Sinaloa cartel from his prison cell before his escape from jail in January 2001 (Hernández 2012). The success of the Valencias only underscored the attractions of Michoacán for the bigger cartels, since the state was not only strategic from the point of view of shipping drugs to the United States, but also close to the vast domestic markets of Guadalajara and Mexico City, ever more important as national consumption of cocaine and crystal meth increased.

The Valencias aided the Sinaloa cartel militarily in its battle with the Gulf cartel for control of Tamaulipas, and the latter responded by moving into Michoacán (Maldonado Aranda 2013: 23). The instrument of the Gulf cartel's intervention was the Zetas, founded by former Mexican military Special Forces officers (Grayson et al. 2012). The Valencias turned to former Guatemalan Special Forces soldiers, *kaibiles*, to train their own gunmen, and the entire conflict took on an increasingly paramilitary character (Maldonado Aranda 2013: 24). By the time I began fieldwork in the Nahua community of Ostula on the Michoacán coast at the end of 2001, the Zetas had begun killing mayors aligned with the Valencias in towns in the Tierra Caliente, including the town in which Victoria Malkin worked.

In 2002, nine men were assassinated in a ranch used as a cocaine laboratory located on the main road to the Aquila county seat. Ing. Mames Eusebio Velázquez Mora, Aquila's municipal president from 1996 to 1998, had sold the ranch to a purchaser from Sinaloa. Its new occupants forced a neighbouring adult education centre to close down. Velázquez Mora, who stood as candidate for the Party of the Cardenista Front for National Reconstruction, although he remained close to the PRI, brought about significant changes in the place of the indigenous communities in the politics of Aquila. He secured huge increases in the budget of his impoverished municipality by obtaining more funding from the Ministry of Social Development, following the politically convenient appearance of an armed group supposedly affiliated with the EPR, although indigenous people who rejected their invitation to 'join the struggle' suspected that they might be cartel gunmen. Velázquez Mora's administration invested in public works in Ostula's central village and other indigenous communities, sponsored indigenous cultural events and the marketing of artisan products, and paved the way for indigenous candidates to win mayoral elections in the future. His successor, who stood as candidate of the PRI, was a schoolteacher from Ostula.

Yet although people in Ostula spoke well of 'Ing. Mames', they displayed anxiety about discussing him. A mestizo friend, who subsequently became mayor of the neighbouring mestizo municipality of Coahuayana for the PRD, also told me that 'researching Mames' would be a very bad idea. When I did interview him in 2002, in relaxed mood after an evening at the cockfight, he proved extremely friendly and showed me videos of the indigenous forum that he had organized. A few weeks later, Velázquez Mora, along with the former Aquila police chief who was driving him, died in a hail of bullets in Guadalajara near the upscale Plaza del Sol shopping centre: their car had been bought in Los Cabos, Sinaloa, and contained a large quantity of US dollars and a basket of imported wines.

From 2002 to 2004, the municipal president of Aquila, also from Ostula, although he lived on a single-family ranch located on the coast, was Martín Santos Luna, of the PRD. Santos Luna played an active role in the wider indigenous politics of the state, sometimes signing up his community to radical declarations of which most of its members remained unaware. 'Disappeared' in the wave of violence that engulfed Ostula from 2010 onwards, he was one of the Ostula leaders to whom *subcomandante* Marcos paid homage in his valedictory speech in La Realidad in 2014. He was succeeded in 2005 by Mario Alvárez López, a member of the PRI who in 2012 became regional coordinator of the Ministry of Rural Development for the municipalities of Aquila, Coahuayana and Chinicuila, under the PRI state government headed by Fausto Vallejo. This change reflected the return of mestizos to control over the municipality.

The municipal president from 2008 to 2011 was José Cortés Ramos, once again of the PRI. Cortés Ramos was one of the municipal presidents arrested when Felipe Calderón launched the mega-operation known as the 'Michoacanazo' in his native state in May 2009, during the governorship of Leonel Godoy of the PRD. Since this operation, involving both the military and the federal police, took place on the eve of elections, many concluded that the real motives of Calderón's intervention were political, although two mayors from his own party were arrested as well as mayors of the PRD and, principally, the PRI. Released after a month in jail, Cortés Ramos was interviewed by a researcher for a *Washington Post* news story (Booth 2010). An indignant Cortés explained that he had been accused of receiving money from 'organized crime groups' to fund his election campaign in return for giving them protection. Arguing that the local police did not 'even have the guns they need', Cortés insisted that it would have been impossible for him to protect anybody. This proposition only makes sense if we understand that rival groups were engaged in violent competition for control of a municipality that had decades of involvement in drug trafficking but by that time, according to US security specialist George Grayson (2010), boasted one of the largest crystal meth labs in the country. Cortés himself hinted at the underlying conflict when he went on to say that he didn't think the federal government's operations against organized crime were a bad thing, but added that 'we don't see any results because the number of violent shoot-outs and killings isn't going down. Just the opposite' (Booth 2010).

The 'Michoacanazo' was one of the most criticized incidents in the entire 'war against drugs' that Calderón launched against the cartels, with US encouragement, after assuming office in 2006. In addition to the arrests of eleven mayors, federal security forces detained twenty-five others, including a judge, various policemen and a former director of public security and other functionaries of the state government. One argument in defence of launching the operation without informing the state government was that the governor's own half-brother, Julio César Godoy Toscano, elected a PRD congressman for the Lázaro Cárdenas district, was accused of having a close relationship with Servando Gómez Martínez, aka 'La Tuta', a native of the *ranchero* municipality of Arteaga to the north-east of the port city. La Tuta, so called because he was originally a primary school teacher, was one of the founders of the La Familia Michoacana cartel. This split off from the still-united Gulf cartel and Zetas in the same year in which Calderón became president (Grayson 2010). It was the influence that the Familia Michoacana established over local government which provided the justification for the Michoacanazo. Yet although one former mayor had to endure nineteen months in prison, the Federal Attorney's Office failed to produce evidence that would sustain a prosecution against any of the accused. The operation did, however, have an additional downside. The aggressive and arbitrary behaviour of the large federal invading force increased the alienation of large sectors of the local population from the government. Calderón's militarized 'war on the cartels' cost, at a conservative estimate, nearly 60,000 lives, many of them lost as 'collateral damage'.[5] The strategy was based on efforts to 'decapitate' the cartels by targeting their principal leaders and trying to persuade captured lieutenants to act as protected witnesses. This increased distrust within the criminal organizations and created struggles over succession to leadership that exacerbated tendencies towards fission within the larger organizations and continual shifting of alliances between different groups that was already under way when Calderón launched his grand national offensive.

Journalist Anabel Hernández (2012) has argued that the 'war

against drugs' in Mexico was a fraud from the very beginning of the PAN's entry into national government, marked as it was by 'El Chapo' Guzmán's extraordinary escape from jail early in the Fox administration. Although the use of the military and federal police in operations such as the Michoacanazo was justified by the assumption that state and local police were already corrupted by the *narco*, Hernández seeks to demonstrate that a corruption of public power that offered systematic protection to criminals, and especially to the Sinaloa cartel, reached right to the top of the federal security apparatus itself. Even if we discount Hernández's very detailed case against Calderón's Secretary of Public Security, Genaro García Luna, it became impossible to deny that some elements of the federal police were compromised in the light of a series of dramatic incidents that occurred in the last year of PAN government, including a firefight between two different federal police squads in the domestic terminal of Mexico City's airport (Castillo García 2012). There are scant historical grounds for believing that the military are beyond infiltration either, although they are probably more likely to obey orders that come from the heart of government, or, more precisely, the clique that currently controls the commanding heights of federal power, which may have its own relations with organized crime.

The growing fragmentation of the cartels also reflected the ramification of chains of complicity between state agents, politicians and criminals. As state agents and politicians began to profit more directly from criminal activities, what had always been a corrupt system of power transformed into an increasingly 'delinquent' one, protecting and nurturing the growth and diversification of the illegal economy. As a result, the passing years have produced a parallel process of fragmentation in the 'shadow' state and in the cartels themselves. This is driven, on the one hand, by the impunity offered by the protection of politicians and elements of the official security forces, and on the other hand by the struggles to control *plazas*, the territories in which particular groups control the production, transport or sale of drugs. Different groups of criminals enjoyed the protection of different political patrons and elements of the public security system located at the municipal, state and federal levels of government. Shifting alliances and divisions between criminal groups and their protection networks created a complex dynamic that varies between regions and changes over time.

In accordance with this dynamic, in 2010 the Zetas became completely independent of the Gulf cartel, embarking on a war for control of Michoacán's *plazas* with the local group whose gunmen they had originally trained, the Familia Michoacana. La Familia found itself obliged to rebuild bridges with the Sinaloa cartel to ward off the Zetas' assault. In Mexico's twenty-first-century drug wars violence has become communicative: decapitated and dismembered corpses are used, along with banners placed on bridges, to send messages to the enemy and to the population in general. Yet violence was not the only means by which the Familia Michoacana constructed its power within local society. One of its founders, Nazario Moreno González (nicknamed 'the Craziest One' and 'the Rosary'), was not simply adept at acting as a patron to cash-strapped farmers and local schools and churches, but created his own religious cult, based on an eclectic mix of heterodox Christianity and US self-help philosophy. Members of the organization were expected to obey a 'code of conduct' that gave La Familia a mafia-like quality. In December 2010, the Calderón administration announced that Moreno had been killed in a federal police operation while carrying out one of his philanthropic missions in a village outside Apatzingán, the municipality of his birth. Devotees who revered him as a saint never believed this to be true, since no body had been recovered. It became evident that large numbers of people had known that it was not true after he was finally killed in 2014 in another federal operation by the Peña Nieto administration in Tumbiscatío, a sparsely populated municipality located in the sierras between Apatzingán, Coalcomán, Aguililla and Arteaga (Mosso 2014). This episode tarnished the image of Calderón's 'war' against the cartels even further.

After Moreno González moved backstage, three of La Familia's founders, Enrique Plancarte Solís, his uncle Dionisio Loya Plancarte and Servando Gómez Martínez, 'La Tuta', announced the formation of a new organization, the Knights Templar (*Los Caballeros Templarios*). This reproduced the code-bound ethos of its precursor and added new rituals to emphasize its character as a 'fellowship' of crime. José de Jesús Méndez Vargas ('El Chango', the Monkey) took over the leadership of the original Familia Michoacana, but as more of its original battalions chose to follow the new organization (hardly surprising if they knew that Moreno was still alive), the Knights Templar succeeded in driving the rump of the original Familia Michoacana out of the state. Yet despite its displacement from its home turf, La Familia survived, becoming a significant player in drug trafficking, kidnapping and extortion rackets in the neighbouring State of Mexico. By 2013, the Templarios' principal enemy was Jalisco state's 'New Generation' cartel. New Generation is led by members of one of the splinters that formed from the break-up of the Milenio cartel that followed the capture of its principal leader in 2009, and the death of Nacho Coronel, which disrupted its ties to Sinaloa. As the name implies, some are still members of the Valencia family.[6] The Knights Templar accused New Generation of arming some of the local self-defence forces that emerged in the Tierra Caliente with the express purpose of eradicating their own organization.

In their extensive public propaganda (through *narco*-banners, the media and YouTube) both La Familia and Los Templarios denied being criminal organizations. They presented themselves as 'social organizations' that were simply seeking to defend the people of Michoacán from abusive federal police forces (although they insisted that they 'respected' the military and the federal government), and from other bands that they stigmatized as not only 'criminal' but also 'terrorist'. The Jalisco New Generation cartel adopted a similar rhetorical posture towards its enemies, asserting that it had no quarrel with the government and was simply determined to 'cleanse' Jalisco of Zetas and Michoacán of Templarios. Its aim is clearly to control the Guadalajara *plaza* and become the hegemonic force in the world of crime throughout western Mexico. Cleansing is, of course, also the term used earlier by the Colombian paramilitary *autodefensas* (Taussig 2005).

Although patronage relations and cults may produce some positive local support for criminal organizations, it was probably the human rights violations perpetrated during federal operations in Michoacán under the Calderón government which encouraged a larger number of alienated citizens to accept the Knights Templar as the lesser of two evils, despite the fact that their talk of defending the people of Michoacán was inconsistent with the increasing importance of extortion in the organization's business model. Operating through a cellular structure dispersed through rural communities, the Templarios not only established their control over a good deal of municipal government but also provided services in the administration of justice and resolution of individual personal problems, including conflicts with other members of the community and powerful outsiders. The strategy was bold and brazenly hypocritical: the organization demanded payments from the local managers of major transnational companies such as Pepsico, attacked their installations when payment was denied, but justified such actions by accusing the companies of covert collaboration with the federal police, all the while assuring the public that they had no intention of damaging legitimate businesses that dedicated themselves to their proper task of bringing jobs to the people. The Templarios ran drug rehabilitation centres and recruited the reformed addicts as gunmen. Their claims that their code forbade them to allow drugs to be sold to children and mandated respect for women were equally hypocritical. Yet by combining material support for politicians' electoral campaigns with threats to the electorate, and sporadic acts of political violence against individual candidates, first the Familia Michoacana and then, even more comprehensively, the Knights Templar acquired the power not only to determine who won local elections, but even which candidates would be allowed to contest them. The level of control over local life achieved by this criminal organization, in which La Tuta played a central role from the beginning in the area of political networking, therefore undermined the limited democratic gains that had been achieved since the hegemony of the original PRI apparatus had entered its phase of decadence. Whatever they said publicly, politicians of all parties in Michoacán were obliged to maintain cordial relations with members of a criminal network that had become part of normal social life in many towns and villages throughout Michoacán.

The pragmatic choice was to go with the flow, and as people did so, the Templarios grew ever stronger and their ambitions, and greed, ever greater. Signs of local resistance had, however, emerged by 2012, and it is important, in a state dominated by mestizos, that they emerged initially from some of Michoacán's indigenous communities. During the previous year, members of the Purhépecha community of Cherán, in the central highlands of Michoacán, had rejected their elected local authorities for complicity with criminals, and formed an armed self-defence force to challenge what people now regularly called 'the Michoacán mafia',[7] which had taken control of illegal logging of Cherán's forests and was also practising *cobro de piso*, the extortion of protection money from local businesses (Turati and Castellanos 2012).

As I emphasized in Chapter 2, generalized extortion and the reproduction of a 'subculture of violence' are only two of the downsides of rule by mafias that are apparent from the comparative literature. In terms of the weaving of backstage relationships between criminal organizations and 'legitimate' social and political actors, there is, as we will see in more detail later, strong evidence of links between mining and energy interests and the paramilitary violence perpetrated by cartel gunmen in rural contexts in Mexico and Guatemala. Such violence has the advantage of easy 'deniability' by both the companies and government, since it can be attributed to competition over *plazas* or 'settling of accounts' between drug traffickers. This is one of the key issues to emerge from a deeper exploration of the 'resistance' that has developed to the rule of the Michoacán mafia, and the ambiguous role of all three levels of government in relation to that resistance.

Indigenous and mestizo self-defence forces

Although the PRI administration of Ernesto Zedillo failed to honour the agreements made with the EZLN in 1996, a new federal indigenous law was finally approved by the Mexican congress in 2001. But all references to indigenous 'territories' and rights to political association above the level of municipalities were removed by amendments made by the Senate to the original draft bill proposed by the multiparty Commission of Concord and Pacification (COCOPA). In states such as Michoacán, where indigenous people are estimated to make up slightly less than 5 per cent of the total population by the CDI (Comisión Nacional para el Desarrollo de los Pueblos Indígenas 2010b), even indigenous organizations that made more radical autonomy demands found themselves obliged to negotiate with state governments more preoccupied with other constituencies in an effort to secure state legislation more favourable to their cause than the federal law.

The largest part of the indigenous population of Michoacán is concentrated in the central highlands, and belongs to the Purhépecha ethnic group, although the state has smaller populations of other ethnicities, including the Nahuas of the coastal region. The connection with the Cárdenas family is a special factor in Michoacán's politics, and after the electoral fraud of 1988, a significant part of the Purhépecha indigenous leadership abandoned the PRI to join the PRD (Pérez Ramírez 2009). The capture of the governorship for the PRD by

Lázaro Cárdenas Batel gave Purhépecha leaders even more incentive to negotiate with the state government, but their expectations were quickly dashed. Despite having been trained as an anthropologist and having expressed his support for indigenous rights, as a senator Cárdenas Batel had voted for the emasculating amendments to the COCOPA law. Although he subsequently apologized for this 'error', as governor he rejected proposals by the radical Purhépecha Nation organization to create regional autonomies via remunicipalization and creation of levels of indigenous self-government above municipal level (Gledhill 2004). Another contradiction in the political situation under the governorships of Cárdenas Batel and his successor Leonel Godoy was the fact that the principal Purhépecha leaders, many intellectuals quite socially distanced from the 'bases' in whose name they spoke, had strong motives to support the continuing participation of their communities in party-based electoral politics. Their party was in power regionally. It not only had power to implement social programmes, but also powers of patronage of interest to individuals (Jasso Martínez 2010). Nevertheless, the Cherán autonomists who took up machetes and hunting rifles, organized patrols, and mounted guard around fires at night to defy the Templarios, did also break with the political status quo by advocating the elimination of electoral political parties from communal political life, and fought successfully for the election of constitutionally recognized municipal authorities by 'uses and customs'.

Cherán is a community long noted for its internal disputes as well as for conflicts with neighbours over resources. The autonomists blamed infighting between PRI and PRD factions for creating the situation that allowed organized crime to impose its grip on a divided community. In opting for armed self-defence, they followed a path already taken by the Nahuas of Ostula, with which Cherán had been building alliances since the time of my first fieldwork on the coast. Both communities agreed that no ballot boxes would be installed in their communities for the elections of November 2011 and that no proselytization for political parties would be allowed (Martínez Elorriaga 2011). In seeking constitutional recognition of Cherán's right to elect municipal authorities by 'uses and customs', however, Cherán's autonomists pursued a more state-oriented path of insurgency than Ostula, where a group of more militant leaders had decided to throw in their lot with the EZLN in 2006, receiving a personal visit from *subcomandante* Marcos, who, as we saw earlier, did not forget the sacrifices his allies were to make. The election of Cherán's authorities by 'uses and customs' was eventually declared constitutional by the highest electoral judicial tribunal and state congress after a remarkable legal campaign by Cherán's lawyers (Aragón Andrade 2013). In February 2012, the Michoacán Electoral Institute delivered papers ratifying the election of the twelve members of a new communal council, the *K'eris*. Despite these advances, the Cherán self-defence forces did not succeed in eliminating violent confrontations with neighbouring communities. Harassment of *comuneros* by paramilitary forces continued, obliging the new authorities to continue to demand action on the part of federal security forces. Cherán's 'autonomy' therefore remained dependent on the state in several respects. Cherán is, however, a municipality in the centre of the state that has good communications by paved highways with other centres of population and an urbanized centre with 10,000 residents. Living in a poorer and more geographically isolated community of villages, hamlets and dispersed *ranchos*, people in Ostula were far more vulnerable to repression and the 'deniable' violence of paramilitary gunmen.

At first sight what happened in Ostula appeared simply another episode in an agrarian conflict between the indigenous community and its mestizo neighbours that was already long standing when I did my original fieldwork on the coast early in the new millennium. Although the government re-recognized Ostula's *de jure* rights to communal lands – over which it had never lost control *de facto* – in the 1960s, defects in the technical administration of the procedure, along with fundamental conceptual differences between indigenous conceptions of territoriality and the modernist bureaucratic principles of land reform, made continuing boundary disputes inevitable. On 29 June 2009, a large number of men and women from Ostula invaded an area of more than seven hundred hectares of land close to the coast that was known as La Canahuancera. They were supported by people from the neighbouring indigenous communities of Coire and Pómaro, and, most important of all, by Ostula's communal police force, which was the first of the modern self-defence forces to be established in Michoacán, although the people of Ostula prefer to avoid calling it an *autodefensa* to underscore the fact that it represents a long-standing indigenous institution. Ostula replicated the communal police model of the CRAC in Guerrero, a region with which the Michoacán Nahuas have historical ties of trade and pilgrimage.

Ostula insisted that mestizos from La Placita had usurped La Canahuancera for more than forty years. One mestizo who claimed to own part of that land was none other than Mario Alvárez López, former PRI mayor of Aquila. The need for armed protection reflected the violence that the conflict was now provoking. A year earlier, the teacher acting as president of Ostula's Commission for the Defence of Communal Property (CDBC), Diego Ramírez Domínguez, had been kidnapped and murdered, while leading an attempt to resolve the boundary problem by peaceful legal means in the Unitary Agrarian Tribunal in Colima. Frustration with lack of progress through legal channels, and revulsion over this murder, strengthened the hand of those who advocated taking direct action over La Canahuancera. On their first attempt, the Ostulans were forced to retire after men armed with automatic weapons fired upon a group that included women and children. After the second, successful, invasion, the Ostula communal police captured some of these aggressors, who were subjected to 'moral condemnation' by an indigenous tribunal. Nevertheless, despite their long-standing commitment to maintaining their autonomy, the Ostulans continued to respect the state's official justice system in matters involving persons from outside the indigenous community, and subsequently handed the prisoners over to the public attorney.

The invasion of the disputed land was planned in advance through lengthy discussions in the communal assembly. La Canahuancera was given a new Nahua name, Xayakalan, and forty families were sent to establish a new settlement there. The assembly determined that each of the twenty-one administrative divisions of the indigenous community that were recognized by the municipal government, the *encargaturas del orden*, should take responsibility for the construction of palm and adobe houses for the settler families. Taken by surprise by the Ostulan action, the PRD state government promised to broker a definitive solution to the agrarian problem. The landowners from La Placita would receive indemnification in return for renouncing their rights. The new settlement of Xayakalan would be officially recognized as the twenty-second *encargatura del orden* of Ostula. The state government would also secure official recognition of Ostula's communal police as a 'rural defence force' from the Ministry of Defence (Sedena). Leonel Godoy's administration failed to deliver on any of these promises.[8] The fact that the communal police were denied legal recognition proved disastrous. Early in 2010, Marines disarmed the force, setting in train a series of killings by figures that the Ostulans called 'assassins [*sicarios*] and paramilitaries' that robbed the community of its principal leaders and activists. As the death toll mounted, the Inter-American Court of Human Rights instructed the Calderón government to take preventative measures to protect Ostula. None was taken. By the end of 2011, twenty-eight people had been killed and eight more 'disappeared'.

Two of these killings demonstrated that links with external organizations of national significance were no protection against the kind of impunity that reigned on the Michoacán coast. Pedro Leyva Dominguez, killed in October 2011, had gained support for the defenders of Xayakalan from the national Movement for Peace with Justice and Dignity (MJPD). Founded by the poet Javier Sicilia, whose own son had been a victim of *narco*-violence, the MJPD strongly questioned the effectiveness and human cost of Calderón's public security policies. This phase of the violence was linked to attempts to resuscitate negotiations over the judicial status of Xayakalan through the Programme of Attention to Rural Social Conflicts of the Agrarian Reform Ministry. Two months after Pedro Leyva was killed, the head of the unofficial *encargatura* of Xayakalan, Trinidad de la Cruz Crisóforo (Don Trino), was kidnapped by a group of heavily armed hooded men when he tried to return to the community accompanied by MJPD activists. Don Trino had taken refuge in Colima for fifteen days after being publicly beaten and threatened with death inside Ostula by a group of gunmen. He returned to participate in discussions about the posture that the community should adopt in its negotiations with the ministry. All the middle-class activists were eventually released without serious physical harm, but some of them had to endure listening to the screams of seventy-three-year-old Don Trino as the paramilitaries tortured him to death.

When the original threats had been made against Don Trino, Ostulans had denounced known individuals to the local authorities, sometimes by name and surname, sometimes by their nicknames. No action was taken. After his death, there were a few more patrols by Marines in the Xayakalan area, but their main purpose seemed to be keeping those trying to defend the settlement disarmed. The 'paramilitaries' attacking Ostula's leaders continued to move about freely within the coastal communities. It was not only local authorities which were complicit in this impunity: the escort of federal police that was supposed to protect Don Trino and the MJPD activists accompanied them only to the entrance to Xayakalan and then suddenly disappeared, without explanation. After the elimination of Don Trino, murders continued, bringing the number killed to thirty-two, some leaders who did not share his political perspective. In January 2012, gunmen once again denounced by name by members of the indigenous community killed Crisóforo Sánchez Reyes, in charge of La Ticla's irrigation system. In May the body of Teódolo Santos Girón appeared at the entrance to the La Ticla cemetery. Another schoolteacher, fifty-two-year-old Teódolo belonged to the PRD and was regional organizer of the presidential campaign of Andrés Manuel López Obrador and his Movement for National Regeneration, despite the fact that the other leaders of the Xayakalan invasion supported the rejection of electoral party politics. He remained popular because he was sympathetic towards the Zapatistas, combining his militancy in the PRD with service as Ostula's delegate to the pro-EZLN National Indigenous Congress.

The immediate perpetrators of the violence are easy to identify. Federico González Medina, 'El Lico', controlled drug trafficking in La Placita. He had been popular in his own community for the 'help' that he offered to its residents, although in his final criminal incarnation as Knights Templar regional boss for the Aquila–Coahuayana region he had been ordered to extort protection money from everyone. La Canahuancera had served as a collection point for marijuana brought down from the sierras for shipment out of the region by sea. Yet much more was at stake in the conflict than what would only have been a minor inconvenience from the point of view of a criminal mafia for which marijuana was now of secondary importance, and even drug trafficking itself only one of a series of extremely lucrative operations.

The indigenous communities in general, and Ostula in particular, as the most militant of them, had become an impediment to various twenty-first-century projects for making the coastal region contribute more to processes of capitalist accumulation. The area possesses beautiful beaches and the mountains remain suitable for ecotourism despite the ravages of illegal logging. Ostula's *comuneros* had rejected attempts by the state government to persuade them to turn their beaches over to tourist developers in return for compensation in the form of cattle or other rural development resources. An ambitious state tourism development plan involved the construction of a new

Pacific highway that would cut directly through the communal territory of Ostula. This offered another motive for mestizos to retain control of La Canahuancera. More importantly, however, the zone still had significant untapped mineral resources, which the Italian-Argentinian company Ternium, operator of the Las Encinas iron ore mine in Aquila, sought to develop, along with a new local port for bulk shipment of ore. The indigenous community of Aquila had agreed that mining should be carried out within the land assigned to it in the year 2000.[9] But the company did not honour its commitments on royalty payments, and the political factions aligned with the PRI and PRD in Aquila battled with each other about whether the money should go only to recognized members of the indigenous community or be distributed in a way that would benefit the whole population of Aquila. At the end of 2011, members of the Aquila indigenous community began a campaign to persuade Ternium to negotiate by blockading the mine, which provoked violent interventions by federal police in 2012. Ternium had secured government concessions to mine in areas that lay inside other indigenous territories, but the legally constituted assembly of the Ostula agrarian community had always rejected proposals for mining in its territory which did not give the indigenous community complete powers of co-management.

Mining in Michoacán is not, however, always carried out legally. Minerals were exported illegally to China. Chinese partners of the Michoacán mafia supplied the precursor chemicals used in the manufacture of methamphetamines in return, through the international port of Lázaro Cárdenas. Chinese buyers were also interested in acquiring the precious types of wood that could still be extracted from Ostula's communal forests. This trade was also illegal since the trees were protected species. In 2014, the president of the Communal Property Commission of Aquila's indigenous community, Octavio Villanueva Magaña, accused 'El Lico' González of collaborating in illegal mining operations with a group of 'corrupted' members of the indigenous community and the delegate of the agrarian reform ministry responsible for the region; the scale of illegal mining was demonstrated by the seizure of more than 100,000 tons of illegal iron from two ships in the port of Manzanillo, following similar operations in Lázaro Cárdenas (Dávila 2014: 11). That there was an intense internal struggle for control of Aquila taking place is indicated by the fact that one of the *comuneros* accused of participation in these activities, Fidel Villanueva, had actually been elected president of the Indigenous Community in October 2012, only to be removed a few months later accused of misappropriation of funds and links with the *narco* (Flores et al. 2014). By 2013, however, the main problem facing the Aquila *comuneros* was simply that once Ternium did start paying the royalties, and publicized the amount of money involved in the press, 'El Lico' made them targets of extortion, demanding a monthly payment (Dávila 2014).

In June 2013, a self-defence force emerged in Aquila, led by people who had supported the ousting of Fidel Villanueva. Their opponents accused them of pursuing purely personal ambitions related to the control of the mining royalties (Martínez and Ocampo 2013), but the *autodefensa* succeeded, for the moment, in expelling the Templarios. Although its leader, Agustín Villanueva Ramírez, invited the mayor of Aquila, Juan Hernández, to support the movement, he chose to flee the community. In August 2013, state police supported by the Marines and an army Special Operations Unit invaded Aquila, put down resistance from the *autodefensa* and detained forty-five of its members, including Agustín Villanueva (Dávila 2014: 12). According to Octavio Villanueva, there was cooperation between the state police, Aquila's mayor and the Templarios of La Placita in the course of this operation (ibid.). At the time of these events, Octavio Villanueva, who is not related to Agustín Villanueva and had had his own differences with him during the disputes over the distribution of royalties, had rejected the contention of the acting state governor, Jesús Reyna, that the group behind the *autodefensa* was motivated by a desire to take back control of the mining royalties, insisting that Agustín Villanueva and his followers simply wanted to stop the extortion (Martínez Elorriaga 2013b). Reyna himself was arrested as a Templario collaborator in 2014 after the release of a video that showed him participating in a meeting with La Tuta. Octavio Villanueva insisted that the original Aquila *autodefensa* was different in nature from other self-defence forces that emerged in the Tierra Caliente of Michoacán during 2013: its objective was simply to create a local communal police force similar to that which had been established in Ostula, replacing a municipal police force controlled by the Templarios (Dávila 2014: 13). He also listed a series of *comuneros* who had been killed by the Knights Templar after the Aquila *autodefensa* was dismantled.

It is clear that the local politics of 'self-defence' in Aquila were enmeshed in factional disputes which the management of the Ternium mine had some interest in fostering, in order to reduce the size of the royalties that the company would have to pay out, and to remove impediments to the extension of its operations into new areas. Yet these events also revealed an extensive chain of complicities between PRI politicians and the Knights Templar cartel. Government intervention served in the short term only to give the Templarios a little more breathing space. A new *autodefensa* emerged in Aquila in January 2014, announcing that it had been formed by people who had not supported the original movement on the mistaken assumption that the Templarios would 'have compassion' on those who did not rebel.[10] They now realized that the only time during which they had enjoyed freedom from 'extortions, rapes, killings and kidnappings' was the period between 24 July and 13 August 2013 when the communal guard had taken control.[11] After the first *autodefensa* was dismantled, the Templars had returned, eager to make up for the money that they had lost by extending and increasing their extortion. The new *autodefensas* invited other towns and villages in Aquila to join them.

By this stage, however, the Templarios were under strong attack from *autodefensas* elsewhere in the state, and January 2014 also brought a major new federal intervention. This was directed by a new Commission for the Security and Integral Development of the State of Michoacán (*Comisión para la Seguridad y el Desarrollo Integral del Estado de Michoacán*), headed by presidential appointee Alfredo Castillo Cervantes, who had been Attorney General of the State of Mexico when Enrique Peña Nieto was its governor. These developments also changed the situation in Ostula, as we will see in the next section, but first it is necessary to look in more detail at what the internal situation in Ostula had actually become in the years since the 2009 invasion of La Canahuancera. It was not only Aquila whose internal divisions reflected the deep penetration of the social life of rural communities by criminal networks.

Ostula was no stranger to factional conflicts, but the defence of territorial boundaries had tended to bring contending groups together in the past. Important divisions had, however, emerged over the La Canahuancera situation. According to his own testimony, Don Trino, principal promoter of the invasion, mobilized a group of *comuneros* to pressure the communal assembly not to wait until the problem was solved by legal means. Another group, headed by a former president of the Common Property Commission, continued to advocate a judicial solution even after the Agrarian Procurator's office found in favour of La Placita. Don Trino's supporters accused this group of being fifth columnists, leaking information to 'the enemy'. But drug trafficking itself was a potent dissolver of community bonds. As methamphetamine trafficking became increasingly important, some young indigenous people began consuming these drugs, and their parents began worrying about the behavioural changes that they produced. Some of the Ostula schoolteachers were recruited by 'El Lico' González to become drug distributors. At least four of them were killed between 2009 and 2012, two belonging to families in the group advocating a legal solution to the dispute with La Placita.

The relationship between members of the community and organized crime was complicated by violent struggles to control the local *plaza*, which prior to the achievement of complete hegemony by the Knights Templar were struggles between the Zetas and La Familia Michoacana. La Familia took advantage of the interest of some young people in the idea of armed self-defence. Presenting themselves as 'Zapatista sympathizers', traffickers offered young indigenous men an escape from the everyday humiliation that they had previously suffered at the hands of mestizos, whose ability to dominate had been based on possession of automatic weapons. Small groups of young people involved in the defence of Xayakalan were led in the night along mountain trails that took them to hidden training grounds in the mountains. At the same time, gunmen identified by *comuneros* as 'Zetas' appeared in the house of one of the Ostula teachers who was a member of the PRI. According to their host, they were 'municipal security guards' sent to protect the communal centre, over which his house presented a commanding view. Some other young Ostulans joined that side. As a result of the violence generated, some young people 'disappeared' without their deaths becoming a matter of public record, and others fled for their lives. As we have seen, in 2011 armed killers working for the drug lord in La Placita walked about freely even in Xayakalan, menacing the leaders of the autonomy movement, whose members began to suspect everyone of being an informer or traitor. Emerging social and religious differences were also damaging solidarity in Ostula. Some of the settlers in Xayakalan had been disliked by other *comuneros* because they were Evangelicals or Jehovah's Witnesses. One of the younger leaders had served a prison term. In this sense, Xayakalan served as means of hiving off undesirable individuals and dissident minorities from the heart of a community whose Catholic identity had always been central not only to its autonomous religious life but also to its management of secular affairs (Gledhill 2004). The use of Catholic ritual as social glue was also undermined by insecurity: it became necessary to abandon rituals that bound dispersed settlements into a coherent 'community' defined by its occupation of a territorial space through processions carrying images of the Virgin and saints between different areas.

Although the teacher who brought the *sicarios* to his house was forced to leave and live in Aquila, *narco*-violence left a strong legacy of division. When some of the young men who had gone into exile in fear of their lives as 'El Lico' consolidated his grip returned to the community and revived the communal police force in February 2014, the Ostula assembly allowed it to become known publicly that some members of the community had 'joined the mafia' (Cano 2014c).[12] The young returned exile appointed to lead Ostula's refounded communal police force, Semeí Verdía, promised that these people were 'under observation', and added, ominously, that when there were no 'invitees' (i.e. press) present, it would be decided what to do with them. He quickly added, however, that 'the law will enact justice, not us'.

As mentioned in the previous chapter, the leadership of the CRAC in Guerrero distinguished their organizations from the more recently formed UPOEG *autodefensa*s in precisely these terms. Indigenous communal police forces are long-established institutions. Serving in the communal police in Ostula at the time when I first studied its communal organization was a form of service that most adults would perform at one or more points in their lives, and without pay. Leaderships and members are subject to election by community assemblies. Such organizations may work in terms of specifically indigenous concepts of security and the administration of justice, which take violence as an inevitable aspect of social life, and use a mixture of punishment and negotiation of settlements calculated to prevent conflict escalating (Speed and Collier 2000). Ostula's traditional dispute settlement processes always followed that logic. But it is also necessary to remember that the first Ostula self-defence force handed over the gunmen it detained to the appropriate government authorities. Semeí Verdía's remarks were clearly intended to reassure everyone listening that they were not creating a vigilante organization, that the rights of people accused of collaborating with the Templarios would be respected, and that everyone would receive due process. What due process can mean in a place like Michoacán, where the official judiciary are part of an apparatus of power heavily influenced by propertied, political and criminal interests, remains open to further discussion. Yet it seems important to recognize that the leader of Ostula's self-defence force was making a strong statement of commitment to the *principle* of the rule of law.

Semeí Verdía made his statement in the context of a reaffirmation of the principle of indigenous autonomy. The same public commitment to the rule of law is also characteristic of Ostula's allies, the Cherán autonomists, who have repeatedly criticized the state government for failing to ensure that it exists. During my fieldwork in 2012, the Fausto Vallejo administration accused Cherán of an attack on another community that caused deaths on both sides. The inhabitants of El Cerecito were accused of complicity with the criminals organizing illegal logging by the Cherán autonomous council, but the Cherán version was that there had been no confrontation and that twenty unarmed workers on a Temporary Work project funded by the Ministry of the Environment and Natural Resources had been ambushed by gunmen (Muñoz Ramírez 2012). The council held the state Public Attorney's Office responsible for any consequences that might follow from the diffusion of the incorrect account of the incident. The Miguel Agustin Pro Human Rights Centre concluded that this was yet another proof that the state authorities were failing to provide rural communities with the security that they deserved and that the Calderón government's approach to dealing with organized crime was misguided. The irony of the situation in which Michoacán was living in mid-2014, after the Peña Nieto administration's new intervention, was that it was far from clear whether the rule of law was being strengthened by the government's strategy for dealing with what, in the course of the previous year, had become a proliferating number of self-defence forces.

In April that year, the federal commissioner announced a programme for legalizing *autodefensas*, now occupying twenty-five of Michoacán's municipalities, as a uniformed and trained Rural Defence Force (the Fuerza Rural), provided that they agreed to the registration of their weapons by 10 May. This was ironic given that the proposal to make Ostula's communal police an officially recognized Rural Defence

Force during Leonel Godoy's governorship was rejected by federal authorities. The immediate reaction of the Marines to the reformation of Ostula's force in February 2014 had also been to attempt to disarm it, although Semeí Verdía successfully negotiated his way out of that situation (Cano 2014c). Nevertheless, official concern about Ostula's continuing commitment to armed autonomy may have increased after the community's lawyer not only affirmed Ostula's determination to continue to occupy Xayakalan, despite previous judicial decisions in favour of the non-indigenous landholders, but also explained that he had discovered that a dozen mining concessions had been granted in Ostula's territory without the community's authorization (Castellanos 2014).

Michoacán's other *autodefensas* were different in nature to the organizations developed in Ostula and Cherán, and different too from the original *autodefensa* of Aquila, since this did not show any ambition to expand its activities beyond its locality during its short life. By March 2013 there was significant *autodefensa* activity in Buenavista Tomatlán and Tepalcatepec in the Tierra Caliente. By May, when the Peña Nieto government sent the army into Michoacán, new groups had emerged in Coalcomán, Periban and Los Reyes. I have no doubt that many who participated were simply ordinary citizens tired of extortion. Nevertheless, the leaders who played a key role in subsequent developments tended to have a similar kind of social profile, and some had somewhat dubious pasts. The *autodefensa* of La Ruana, 20 kilometres from Tepalcatepec and part of the Buena Vista Tomatlán municipality, was led by the lemon-grower Hipólito Mora. The *autodefensa* of Parácuaro, to the north of Apatzingán, was commanded by 'Comandante Cinco', Alberto Gutiérrez, a native of Tepalcatepec, who administrated lemon orchards. Tepalcatepec was the epicentre of *autodefensa* mobilization. One of its *autodefensa* leaders was medical doctor José Manuel Mireles, a former migrant to the USA from a family that owned mango orchards. Another was Estanislao Beltrán, a cattleman nicknamed 'Papá Pitufo' (because his long beard made him resemble a Smurf).

Hipólito Mora was supposed to have agreed the date of 24 February 2014 for declaration of hostilities against the Templarios with another cattleman from Tepalcatepec, Juan José Farías, El Abuelo ('the Grandfather'). The Tepalcatepec cattlemen supposedly decided to throw off the Templar yoke because the criminal organization was attempting to impose its own candidate as president of the Cattlemen's Association, with a view to tightening its extortion further. There is, however, another version in circulation as a result of declarations made in the United States by the former mayor of Tepalcatepec, Guillermo Valencia Reyes, who fled the country after claiming to have been threatened by 'El Abuelo' and pressured to resign by Commissioner Castillo (Martínez Elorriaga 2014a). Valencia claimed that Farías, who has strong family connections with the military, and whose brother was detained in Calderón's 'Michoacanazo' while serving as municipal president, received a delivery of arms from the army and had prior connections with Castillo (Cano 2014b). On this reading, the Peña Nieto administration would have had a direct hand in orchestrating the appearance of the non-indigenous *autodefensas*. Yet 'El Abuelo', who became a member of the legalized Fuerza Rural established by Castillo, had not simply been accused of links with the Milenio cartel by Valencia Reyes and others: in 2009 he was actually arrested on drug-trafficking charges that kept him in jail until 2012 (Muedano 2014).

Beginning their activities in an apparent spirit of harmony and collaboration, the original group of *autodefensa* leaders in the Tierra Caliente formed a General Council of *Autodefensas y Comunitarios* to coordinate their activities, initially under the leadership of Mireles. Despite the operation against the Aquila *autodefensa* in August 2013, those of the Tierra Caliente continued to advance, announcing their intention to drive out the Templarios, recover properties that the criminals had appropriated, and end the reign of extortion. Two people died when the *autodefensas* of Buenavista and Tepalcatepec joined forces in November to take over the town hall of Tancítaro, a centre of avocado production, disarming the municipal police. The state government assured the public that no further advances would be permitted, and the Templarios did fight back, destroying avocado packing plants and causing some displacement of population (Martínez Elorriaga 2013a). But by the end of January 2014, the important Tierra Caliente *ejidos* of Nueva Italia and Antúnez had fallen, along with parts of Coahuayana. The federal security forces had initially impeded the entry into Apatzingán of the combined *autodefensas* of Tepalcatepec, Buenavista, Coalcomán, Aguililla and Chinicuila in October 2013. But in February 2014, a force led by Estanislao Beltrán and Comandante Cinco was finally permitted to 'take' the Templarios' principal base in the Tierra Caliente, accompanied by state and federal police. Fifty people were arrested on the day of the occupation, and although it became clear that the Knights Templar did have the support of part of the population, Apatzingán's PRI mayor, Uriel Chávez, was arrested for participation in that criminal organization two months later (Becerra Acosta 2014).

On 13 February 2014, the Ostula communal police force, supported by the self-defence forces of Aquila, Coalcomán and Chinicuila, occupied La Placita. Locals told the journalists who accompanied them that 'El Lico' and the rest of his Knights Templar band had abandoned the community several weeks before the *autodefensas* arrived.[13] This action reflected the way that the wider balance of forces had been transformed after months of advance by the *autodefensas* that were receiving financial support from commercial farmers and cattlemen, an advance assisted by federal security forces. Actions taken directly by the federal state seemed to confirm its determination to 'cleanse' Michoacán of the Knights Templar. The death of Nazario Moreno on 9 March 2014 followed the capture of his brother and a half-brother who was cousin of Templario leader Enrique 'Kike' Plancarte (Méndez 2014). Marines killed Plancarte himself in a rented house in Querétaro at the end of the same month (Aranda et al. 2014). Although La Tuta remained at large, and was rumoured to be constructing new alliances, the number of local operators of the Templarios also killed and captured suggested that a serious effort was being made to dismantle this cartel, an impression reinforced by the arrest of Jesús Reyna.

At first sight, the federal government appeared to have carried out a relatively successful operation to dismantle the Knights Templar cartel by making use of the local knowledge of the criminal network that the mestizo *autodefensas* of the Tierra Caliente possessed, and the support that they enjoyed among a population tired of extortion, even if that support was not total. The state followed this up by obliging the *autodefensas* to register their arms and enrol in an officially recognized, uniformed, rural police force, thus avoiding the Colombian-style paramilitarization that many critics of a permissive attitude towards the *autodefensas* feared. Yet on closer inspection, all was not quite as it seemed.

Not seeing, like a state

Questions continued to be asked about the federal operation, including whether it was really any different from Calderón's 'Michoacanazo'. Commissioner Castillo seemed to be selective about which local politicians were brought to account, releasing videos and photos of meetings with La Tuta at what seemed politically convenient moments, no doubt making those who suspected that there might also be such circumstantial evidence against them on file somewhat nervous. Some of those accused claimed that the meetings were involuntary, a reflection of the cartel's power to menace individuals and their families. Fausto Vallejo, the PRI state governor, had already taken one leave of absence on health grounds, leaving the subsequently arrested Jesús Reyna in charge. Vallejo finally used his health as a pretext for resignation in June, after his son had been accused, with probable justification on the basis of other evidence, of being an active participant in the 'Michoacán mafia', following the release of a photograph of him socializing with La Tuta on the Internet (Martínez Elorriaga 2014b; Olmos 2014).

It is hardly surprising that a commissioner appointed by a PRI federal administration would act in a way designed to limit the damage to his own party in a state in which it faced serious competition from both the PRD and the PAN. But the commissioner's position was constitutionally anomalous. Michoacán's political class began to refer to him as the 'Viceroy', since it had been obvious that Fausto Vallejo possessed little control over events before Castillo, Peña Nieto's personal protégé, finally told him to step aside. PRI members of the state congress meekly accepted the appointment of a substitute governor who was not a member of any political party, the respected former rector of the University of San Nicolás de Hidalgo in Morelia, Salvador Jara, who thanked both Enrique Peña Nieto and 'his friend' Alfredo Castillo Cervantes for the trust that they had placed in him (Martínez Elorriaga 2014c).

Selene Vázquez Alatorre, a former PRD state congresswoman who declared herself an independent, was less complimentary about the work of 'the Viceroy'. Arguing that the conversion of the *autodefensas* of the Tierra Caliente into officially sanctioned 'rural guards' had simply served to generate more violence, she said that the commissioner had

> ... created a strategy in which there has been an abuse of the pursuit of justice and security. To such a degree that at the beginning Michoacanos used to fear the Templarios and now they are afraid of these people, the rural guards and the authorities, because there

have begun to be illegal detentions, searches, seizing of people and kidnappings. People don't know if they are police or thieves. (Martínez and Martínez Elorriaga 2014)

The situation that the congresswoman was complaining about was the result of a deftly orchestrated series of manoeuvres on the part of the commissioner to take advantage of emerging conflicts among the principal leaders of the *autodefensas* to oblige them to accept the Fuerza Rural system. Key moments in this process were the arrest on murder charges in March 2014 of Hipólito Mora, founder of the La Ruana *autodefensa*, and an increasing distance between José Manuel Mireles, who supported Mora, and both his former friend Estanislao Beltrán and Commissioner Castillo, following Mireles's hospitalization after a helicopter crash in January 2014.

Mora and his followers had become embroiled in a dispute with the Buenavista Tomatlán *autodefensa* and its leader, Luis Manuel Torres, known as 'El Americano', since he was born in the United States, although his parents came from La Ruana. Mora accused Torres and his group of being former Templarios. Driving upmarket trucks marked with the insignia H-3 and carrying heavy weapons, El Americano's group had acted as shock troops in the advance of the *autodefensas* to take control of Los Reyes and other towns. 'El Americano', for his part, had accused Mora of being responsible for the killing of Rafael Sánchez Moreno and José Luis Torres, who certainly were 'reformed' Templarios, but had become members of a rival self-defence unit. Mireles, who had himself once been accused of sowing marijuana, arrested and tortured, defended 'El Americano' as well as Mora, but argued that Mora's arrest was a government betrayal. On 9 May, towards the end of the process of arms registration, Mireles was removed from his position as spokesperson for the *autodefensas*, and replaced by Estanislao Beltrán, in a meeting in the headquarters of the 43rd Military District in Apatzingán presided over by Castillo. A week later Hipólito Mora was released from jail, 'for lack of evidence', something that certainly invited comparison with Calderón's Michoacanazo.

Mireles continued to insist that the destruction of the Templarios was far from over, but he too was soon embroiled in controversy for alleged responsibility for an order that cost the deaths of five unarmed people at a checkpoint on the coast. Semeí Verdía, now in effective command of all the coastal *autodefensas*, defended Mireles (Cano 2014d), who claimed that the doctor sent by the Public Attorney to the crime scene had tricked him into appearing in a photograph in which he was holding up the head of one of the victims.[14] Yet with Estanislao Beltrán and Comandante Cinco now firmly in the commissioner's corner and publicly criticizing their former friend and ally, Mireles was being marginalized, although he continued to enjoy respect from those who saw him as the only remaining leader willing to question official claims that the battle against organized crime was virtually won. Hipólito Mora and 'El Americano' were obliged to appear in a photograph in which the commissioner joined their hands together in a gesture of reconciliation, for subsequent diffusion via his Twitter account.[15] By combining threats of prosecution and incentives to collaborate in the form of state legitimation, Castillo dragooned the leaders of the Tierra Caliente *autodefensas* into accepting incorporation into the Fuerza Rural, and he was soon to show what would happen to those who continued to resist this federal government dispensation.

At the end of June 2014, José Manuel Mireles and more than seventy others accused of illegally bearing arms were arrested in the community of La Mira, close to Lázaro Cárdenas (Cano 2014a). Mireles was in La Mira by invitation to set up a citizen council that would control a new local self-defence force. Seized while eating chicken in a restaurant in a massive operation by police, soldiers and Marines, Mireles was hooded, bundled into a helicopter, and shipped off to a distant federal prison in Hermosillo, Sonora, although the judge responsible for his case was based in Uruapan (Morales and Oterol 2014). Arms and drugs were allegedly found in the doctor's vehicle, but his lawyer insisted that they had been planted, that those who planted them had also stolen money left inside the truck, and that Mireles had been mistreated after arrest, to the point of initially being denied medication for his diabetes. Commissioner Castillo made it clear that his crime was that of 'defying the state' by not honouring his part in the agreement that the *autodefensas* would lay down their arms (Martínez 2014b). Formally charged with illegal possession of both arms and drugs, and humiliated by the shaving of his head and removal of his moustache, Mireles declared himself a 'political prisoner'. Highway blockades set up by the *autodefensas* of Aquila, Chinicuila and Coahuayana were followed by protests in other parts of the country. But the federal authorities made it clear that they were not for turning in the matter of a still widely respected 'loose cannon'.

Yet as we have already seen in the case of 'El Abuelo', Alfredo Castillo and the federal state were strangely selective in what they chose to 'see' when it came to 'rigorously applying the law' to leaders of *autodefensas*. As owners of lemon and avocado orchards and cattlemen, some of those leaders were taking control of rural properties and animals that had belonged to Templarios or Templario allies who fled in the face of their advance. In many cases this may have been a matter of recovering property that the Templarios had acquired from its original owners by violence or the threat of violence, but since these were local organizations operating in a local social context, it is difficult to distinguish between property that was being recovered for its rightful owners from criminals and property being appropriated in a settling of old scores or simply in an arbitrary way. The relatives of one of the men that Hipólito Mora was accused of killing claimed that Mora had seized properties of people who refused to support the movement and had taken control of other properties whose owners lived in other municipalities or in the United States.[16] Another complaint that began to emerge about the conduct of the *autodefensas* was that young men were being intimidated into joining 'the struggle' in very much the same way as the Knights Templar had coerced people into joining them. There were also complaints that some *autodefensas* seemed to want to engage in the same kind of extortion as the criminals. Although in some cases this may have been a demand for a 'contribution' towards the costs of maintaining patrols and other expenses not being met by wealthier patrons from their own pockets, in other cases the situation took a more sinister turn.

In the case of Aquila, Octavio Villanueva Magaña claimed that he was threatened with death if he did not pay the reconstituted *autodefensa* the same monthly 'protection payment' as was previously extorted by the Templarios from the indigenous community, and that the new *autodefensas* were using their AK-47s to menace residents (Dávila 2014: 12). Sympathizers of the original *autodefensa* had turned to a long-established agrarian social movement, the Coordinadora Nacional Plan de Ayala (CNPA), for support. In January 2014 the CNPA opened up a line of negotiation with Alfredo Castillo, who at that time tried to convince Aquila to align itself with José Manuel

Mireles and Hipólito Mora, at this juncture still enjoying official favour. Aquila's negotiators explained that they simply wanted to re-establish a local community guard, not an expansionary self-defence force, and that the best approach would be to create a local citizens' council that could elect trusted people to serve in it (ibid.: 13). Castillo promised to assist with the release of the detainees but what he actually did was send a team of lawyers to visit the prisoners in the two jails in which they were imprisoned to try to persuade them to drop their relationships with the CNPA and its lawyers (ibid.).

On the basis of this evidence, it would appear that the 'Viceroy' of Michoacán had little enthusiasm for community-based security forces that would be appointed in a democratic way by members of the communities that they served. His preference is for groups that are controlled by more affluent rural property owners. The government instituted 'confidence tests' on police, and both state and municipal police were dismissed on the grounds that the tests provided evidence that criminal groups had suborned them. It was not clear, however, what, if any, controls were being applied to the elements enlisted as members of the Fuerza Rural, which included the H-3 group, already accused of being a new mafia in formation by a variety of independent voices. One of these voices was the priest Gregorio López of Apatzingán, widely respected for his public denunciations of the Templarios' hold over the municipality and the role of Mayor Uriel Chávez. Recently returned from a visit to Europe after receiving death threats from the Templarios, 'Padre Goyo', as he is known locally, was a strong supporter of the *autodefensa* movement, a man who has said that Christ himself was a revolutionary and the first *autodefensa*. His assessment of the work of Commissioner Castillo is worth quoting:

Alfredo Castillo is committing the sin of naivety. He is naive be-cause he has allowed the command to be bought by some leaders who sweeten the pill well. He thinks you can keep the dogs on the leash with sausages. They served Castillo *atole* [a sweet corn drink] with the finger. It's going wrong. He's admitting all the rats to the rural police, all the Templarios. That police is only just beginning and it's already very corrupted ... Those pseudo-leaders like Papá Pitufo, Los Viagra, El Cinco, and others, have pardoned mayors for millions of pesos; they pardon some magnate, some Templario, for 500 or 600 thousand pesos, they've delivered them properties for millions of pesos. It's a vile filth what they're producing and the government is part [of it]. I don't know if they're receiving a cut. Money corrupts. (Martínez 2014a)

Little seems to stand in the way of the new Fuerza Rural reproducing the abusive exercise of local power that has long been typical of states such as Michoacán. The National Human Rights Commission is not an adequate instrument for regulating everyday police conduct. It is, ultimately, a question of deepening the rule of law. The way in which Michoacán was 'pacified' did not seem to do that. None of this sounds promising from the perspective of an indigenous community such as Ostula, which has been fighting to defend its territory against powerful outside economic interests which appear to have been able to call on cartel gunmen, under conditions of impunity to which all three levels of government have contributed.

In Michoacán, the state, including the federal state security apparatus, has long only been 'seeing' what it is convenient to see. One of Commissioner Castillo's apparent successes was the seizure of illegally mined iron ore in the ports of Lázaro Cárdenas and Manzanillo, along with the closure of some illegal mines in Arteaga (García Davish and Miranda 2014). Rumour has it that illegal mining soon started up again, but the obvious question to ask about the pre-intervention situation is how this vast quantity of ore, which can be transported only in large trucks, managed to make its way to the port from the mining sites over a very extended period along a federal highway guarded by federal security forces. The state, including the Marines, also failed to 'see' armed paramilitaries wandering around threatening people in the full light of day. There was no effective official response even when the gunmen were denounced by name. The person who controlled them, 'El Lico' González, was able to escape with his men without hindrance from government security forces either. Yet those forces were ready enough to take weapons off indigenous self-defence groups. What the state does make a considerable effort to 'see', and neutralize, are those who threaten to subvert politically connected economic interests.

It appears that Commissioner Castillo was determined not to 'see' that his new rural defence force was riddled with persons who have criminal antecedents, or at any rate determined not to pay any serious attention to the claims of any of the journalists and public figures who asserted that this was the case. Michoacán was not taken over by a mafia overnight, so this omission is hardly novel in itself. When they began to fall out with each other, the *autodefensa* leaders from the Tierra Caliente engaged in mutual accusations of 'links' with organized crime. It was, in practice, difficult for anyone living in Michoacán over the past twenty or thirty years (including visiting anthropologists) never to have any social contact with people involved in drug trafficking and money laundering activities. It was also extremely imprudent to get on the wrong side of these people. This is not the same kind of sin as collaborating in systematic extortion, as Apatzingán mayor Uriel Chávez was accused of having done. Yet if Calderón's 'Michoacanazo' did nothing else, it did signal that Chávez's kind of sin was not exclusive to members of the PRI, but a more deeply rooted cancer in the state's political life.

It is not clear that Peña Nieto's intervention in Michoacán has done more than produce changes in the personnel running the state's criminal networks. It is also not clear that a simulated 'pacification' that leaves underlying problems untouched because it is the actors rather than the script that are changed can prevent a resurgence of resistance. It is, however, clear that political damage limitation would be imperative for a national PRI regime that is seeking to reconsolidate its control over the country and push forward major economic 'reforms' that are welcome to foreign investors but likely to be less popular with Mexicans. What this 'pacification' may have done is buy off the resistance of more economically privileged actors who were smarting under the criminal yoke, by giving them new rent-seeking as well as commercial opportunities. This could only be more bad news for the socially disadvantaged sectors of Michoacán's population, especially if promised new public investments in the 'development' of the state are not oriented towards improving the economic circumstances of those segments of the population, and new poverty reduction measures turn out to be no more than 'smoke and mirrors'.

6 | ACHIEVING HUMAN SECURITY: THE CONTRA-DICTIONS OF REPRESSIVE INTERVENTION

This study has examined the contradictions of public security policy in two countries, focusing on processes that are similar in the sense that they are couched in the language of 'wars' and 'pacification', but different in the sense that the Brazilian study is focused on metropolitan cities and the Mexican study on areas that are rural, although they also contain medium-sized cities. Brazil's limited land reform, the limited success in changing that scenario of Latin America's largest social movement, the Landless Workers' Movement (MST), and the continuing importance of agro-exports produced by highly capitalized large farms in that country's economy, have long made life on the urban periphery the fate of the majority of the country's poor. It seems fairly clear that elite thinking in Mexico over the past quarter-century has also been based on the assumption of continuing expulsion of rural populations towards the cities. In the past, Mexican elites also saw international labour migration as a useful safety valve, and in a state such as Michoacán, work in the United States is still an important contributor to the reproduction of rural life. Nevertheless, it may be less significant for the next generation. Economic conditions facing migrants in the United States have deteriorated, and a continuing process of border securitization that increases the costs and risks of an undocumented migrant way of life in the North has been complemented by an unprecedented persecution of migrants inside the United States that has earned Barack Obama the soubriquet 'the deporter'.[1] Rural places and populations will continue to exist in both Brazil and Mexico, because they are assets for domestic as well as international tourism. Tourism entails conservation and even rehabilitation of built environments as 'heritage' and of natural environments as something to be non-destructively consumed. Yet conservation is not the destiny that capitalist elites seem to have in view for the whole of the countryside in an era in which extractive industries will be competing for space and water with plantation-style agribusiness as well as tourism in many regions.

Rural and urban dystopias

We have seen that wherever they live, poorer Brazilians and Mexicans, like poorer citizens throughout Latin America, may be victims of a variety of forms of violence and rent-seeking behaviour. In the case of Mexico, 'spectacular' criminal violence has come to be virtually synonymous with the country in recent years, despite the fact that it is concentrated in particular regions. Yet even in regions such as Michoacán, severed heads, bodies hanging from bridges, or mutilated corpses left in public view with *narco*-messages placed on their chests or carved in flesh do not tell the whole story of the suffering to which the population is subjected. Although people have few options but to live with the situation, everyday life has become blighted by petty, and sometimes not so petty, acts of extortion, and a pervasive sense of threat that may turn into a life-changing catastrophe for some unlucky individuals. Those with economic assets, however modest, may be the most vulnerable, but this kind of insecurity has now been generalized in the zones where criminal gangs are able to operate in a relatively unrestrained way. Furthermore, as we have seen, whether it is a criminal gang or an *autodefensa*, coercive methods of recruitment often leave people with flight as the only alternative to acquiescence. At least part of the exodus of citizens from Central America and internal displacement within Mexico results from this kind of everyday violence. In the case of Brazil's *favelas*, attention also tends to focus on the most visible forms of violence resulting from armed confrontations between police and traffickers. Yet the claims of traffickers that they 'respect' community members do not always stand up to close scrutiny, while the dominion of militias is equally preoccupying.

Whether it is Brazil or Mexico, armed guardians of order authorized by the state may prove as much part of the problem of achieving personal security as a solution to that problem, and in multiple ways. Some of these ways are related to the privatization of security services, whether we are talking about the way state agents can be captured by a variety of private interests, about the way the private security that better-off citizens and companies can afford to hire can escape state regulation and violate the rights of the less fortunate, or about the formation of mafias like the Brazilian militias or what some of Michoacán's former *autodefensas* may be becoming with the tacit consent of government. Yet if the nature of the state is part of the problem of lack of human security, it is only part of a bigger problem. That problem can be defined in terms of the centrality of 'accumulation by dispossession' in contemporary capitalism. This logic transcends the rural–urban distinction. There is, of course, a difference between the results of the capitalist drive to valorize space. The 'gentrification' of *favelas* leaves something behind that may seem an improvement from the point of view of the urban landscape, whereas open-pit mining that decapitates mountains leaves nothing behind, and may very well contaminate the surrounding environment as well if governments eager for foreign investment at any cost do not enforce clean-up agreements. Yet both these processes displace people, will probably rob them of their modest capital, and in the absence of vigorous development in other areas of the economy may also swell the ranks of the population that is surplus to the current requirements of the capitalist labour market.

The urban situation is especially preoccupying. Mexico's rural peasant economies have been unravelling for decades as young people have preferred migration to cities or across international borders to the hardships of a traditional rural production regime plagued by falling maize prices and environmental deterioration (Fitting 2006). Although poorer migrants from the indigenous south of the country often filled low-wage rural jobs abandoned by natives of other regions who chose international migration, they too began to look for better opportunities. Were it not for the growth of the narcotics economy, rural outmigration would clearly have been even greater than it is, and where that kind of illegal economy has flourished, it has undermined any security advantages rural areas might once have possessed relative to the urban periphery. Dystopian future scenarios should include a further round of reduced employment opportunities produced by advances in robotics and intelligent machines, and major problems of shortage of water, likely to be exacerbated in the Mexican case by the open-door policy that the Peña Nieto administration has adopted towards allowing US companies to develop the extraction of shale oil and gas through fracking technologies. Although it may be possible to argue, as former Peruvian president Alan García argued, that current technologies permit extractive industries to operate in a safe way and limit their environmental impact, even technological optimists should concede that recent Latin American experience demonstrates that the political conditions under which they will actually do that are difficult to achieve, especially when transnational companies are involved (Bebbington 2009: 13). García's views also stand squarely at that intersection of nineteenth-century liberalism and neoliberalism which insists that land and resources should be fully privatized and placed in the hands of entrepreneurs equipped to make them 'productive', as distinct from 'backward' mestizo peasant farmers and indigenous people (ibid.: 12).

What, as I stressed in the opening chapter, does not represent a simple return to the nineteenth century is the contemporary role of financialization, as illustrated, for example, by the transformation of hedge funds from institutions designed to reduce risk into contributors to market instability (Maurer 2002). As Laura Carlsen points out, citing the *Wall Street Journal*, Mexico's oil privatization may not be as important to the Mexican government and the oil companies for the flow of oil it may generate as for the flow of capital it will generate: US oil companies face a gap between spending and revenue that they need to plug by selling shares, taking on debt, and liquidating less remunerative assets (Carlsen 2014). Resource extraction is as much about speculation as it is about providing raw materials and energy essential to the reproduction of the industrial economy. In this sense it can be equivalent to a nineteenth-century 'bubble'. As Anna Tsing (2000) pointed out, using Canadian mining as an example, getting financial investors on board is a kind of conjuring trick. All kinds of actors, including small investors, foreign governments and perhaps some local people at the site of extraction, become enthralled by promises of untold riches, but even if the 'amazing investment opportunity' is not simply a scam, the project has to materialize in a regional landscape inhabited by real people, and it is they who have to pick up the pieces (ibid.: 141). As I emphasized in the opening chapter, financialization has deeper consequences than just the creation of 'bubbles': it produces inequalities and insecurities that affect the process of meeting 'basic needs'. The lack of a sense of social responsibility associated with the alchemy of making money out of turning all manner of things into objects of financial speculation also seems, as Jean and John Comaroff (2000) suggested, to impact on the way that sectors of society that cannot take their seat in the global casino respond to its ethos. Extorting money from a poor person by threatening to harm their children may be one such response. It is often difficult to find much moral distinction between 'illegal' forms of dispossession and rent-seeking and what is made legal by the privilege given to private enterprise as the means of securing the public good. It is not for nothing that many Mexicans are apprehensive about the powers that the Peña Nieto government has assumed to expropriate[2] land in favour of foreign companies through the secondary legislation that has followed its constitutional revision of the terms of the state monopolies in the energy industry.

Securitization has become a means of holding this kind of world together and diminishing the challenges that its injustices create. It is not simply about repression, since securitization involves the production of stories about risks, and the necessary means of reducing them, that will resonate with at least part of the population. It may also involve, as we saw in the case of the Brazilian UPP programme, some promises that have proved difficult to deliver, such as major investments in social development and a police force that respects the poor. In the case of the 'pacification' of Michoacán, securitization involved a good deal of cultivation of 'appearances' that seem to have little to do with reality, another kind of conjuring trick that seeks to restore a less conflictive kind of coexistence between the capitalist and criminal economy without worrying too much about the everyday security of the population at large. Yet securitization seems to point the way to another dystopian situation in which inequality is armoured, yet again, by coercion, much of it administered not by the state, but by private entities.

Transnational perspectives

Private security companies have not only become ubiquitous in domestic contexts but also in the international interventions by the United States and its allies. One company that became particularly controversial because of its role in New Orleans after the Hurricane Katrina disaster, as well as for its shooting of civilians in Iraq, is Blackwater Security Consulting. Founded by former Navy SEAL Erik Prince, Blackwater rebranded itself in 2009, was then sold to a private equity company that changed its name again, and finally merged with its competitor Triple Canopy, becoming part of Constellis Holdings (Scahill 2008; McCabe 2014). In his subsequent role as head of his own private equity company, Prince built an oil refinery in southern Sudan and then decided to go back into the private security business by advising Chinese firms on how to avoid the risks of investing in extractive projects in Africa (Wright 2014). The private security industry is therefore not a simple extension of North Atlantic geopolitical power. But the lucrative contracts that governments award to such enterprises, including companies that run prisons and migrant detention centres, have been a major factor in the industry's growth. It is considerably easier for governments to continue to award these contracts despite public questioning of the way private corporations conduct their business and accusations of gross human rights violations by their employees, when the persons whose rights are being violated have been converted into 'threats' by the process of securitization.

As a Washington Office on Latin America (WOLA) report emphasizes, US concern with security on Mexico's porous southern border with Guatemala has been progressively escalating (Isacson et al. 2014). In terms of the costs of the electronic surveillance equipment being delivered, 'creating a twenty-first-century border' in the south as well as the north of Mexico became the most important facet of the police and military assistance provided to Mexico under the Mérida Initiative programme, with the enthusiastic backing of the Peña Nieto government. In 2014, an upsurge in the number of 'other than Mexican' migrants being detained in the United States began to be seen as a crisis because of the number of children crossing the border. More than 52,000 unaccompanied minors were apprehended in the United States between 1 October 2013 and 15 June 2014 (Muñoz Ríos 2014). Homeland Security announced that the number of unaccompanied children arriving in south Texas from Guatemala, El Salvador and Honduras had overwhelmed the capacity of the Border Patrol and child welfare services, creating a situation that Obama declared a 'humanitarian crisis' on 2 June (Isacson et al. 2014). Most of these children were making no effort to evade detention. Under US law, Central American children, unlike Mexican children, cannot be summarily deported. They have to be handed over to officials of the Department of Health and Human Services within seventy-two hours of detention, and be given a hearing in a US immigration court to be considered for asylum or some other kind of permission to stay. By mid-July, the courts had accumulated a backlog of 40,000 cases that could take up to 578 days to process.[3] Although some Central Americans, including children, also seek asylum in Mexico, generally after having been victims of violence in their own countries, the approval rate is very low, and conditions in Mexican detention centres are so squalid and dangerous that many drop their petitions and attempt to make it to the United States, without receiving the international protection to which they are theoretically entitled (ibid.). The response of both Obama and the Mexican government to this 'humanitarian crisis' was to issue public warnings to children in Central America planning to try their luck that they would be deported. Obama made an emergency request to Congress for powers to secure the 'fast track' deportation of children from Central America entering the country illegally, thereby overturning the special protection that had been given to them in 2008 under the administration of George W. Bush (Lewis 2014).

One of the pretexts offered by the Department of Homeland Security for strengthening Mexico's southern border is the 'risk' that terrorists from outside Latin America will use it to infiltrate their way into the United States. In 2012 Homeland Security staffed an office in the Chiapas border city of Tapachula 'to build capacity in the identification of aliens from countries of national security concern who are released from the Tapachula detention facility', yet that office has yet to identify a single migrant from the dozens from the Middle East, Africa and Asia released every year who had links with transnational terrorist networks (Isacson et al. 2014). The border continues to be crossed freely in both directions by members of violent drug cartels, including the Zetas. I have already discussed its significance in terms of human trafficking and the creation of a population in transit subject to rent-seeking, violence and abuse by a wide variety of actors, including Mexican migration officials and police as well as criminals. It is clear from the stories that unaccompanied minors tell that many are fleeing not simply from poverty and lack of jobs but from gang violence and extortion, situations that would entitle them to international protection and asylum in the United States. In a United Nations High Commission for Refugees survey 'violence in society' was cited as a reason for leaving by 66 per cent of the children interviewed from El Salvador and 44 per cent of the Hondurans, although the Guatemalan children that the UNHCR team interviewed cited deprivation more frequently than violence in society and abuse in the home (ibid.). The most important reason for all in this survey was 'family and opportunity', and it is clear that the accelerating exodus was related to a perception that the

United States did open its doors to children in pain. Obama, unable to enact immigration reform because of Republican opposition, felt obliged to make it clear that it does not. The society over which he presides is divided. Sympathetic border residents horrified by the stories that both adults and children tell them continue to offer charitable support, while armed self-defence militias are once again calling for volunteers to 'finish the work that the Border Patrol isn't doing' (Gomora 2014; Dart 2014).

The fact that the 2014 'humanitarian crisis' posed by Central American migration through Mexico revolved around unaccompanied children gave it a special moral resonance in the global North. Yet it is important not to allow this particular kind of sensibility to cloud the larger issue. Many of these children had adult relatives in the United States who endured the hardships of getting there in earlier years. Not all of them were unaccompanied. Some were taken by mothers who decided that the risks were outweighed by the opportunities that their children would have that they would not have at home, although the decision might have been precipitated by threats made by extortionists to the mother herself (Dart 2014). Some parents may fulfil Obama's hope that the costs (and extra debts), plus the suffering, incurred in reaching Mexico's northern border only to find a closing door will change perspectives. Yet Central American migrants are persistent despite, and perhaps even because of, the psychological and monetary costs of their passage. It is important to contest the argument that those who seek opportunities in life that are not available at home even to young people with education are morally underserving, and that only those who face a direct threat to life should be allowed to cross the 'biopolitical divide' between North and South. As we saw in Chapter 4, the situation of adult migrants is also a multidimensional humanitarian catastrophe. In terms of human security, the situation in Central America is dire on all fronts, but these problems are interrelated because of the development model that is being imposed on the whole Mesoamerican region.

My own research strongly supports the WOLA report's observation that residents of Chiapas see the joint interest of the United States government and Mexican authorities in enhancing regional 'security' as related to large-scale plantation, mining and energy projects, projects about which nobody is consulted and little information is made available in the public domain. The report's authors observe that:

Especially in Chiapas, residents also had misgivings about the increased presence of federal security agents in the state. Many have experienced violent repression against their organizing and advocacy in the recent past. We repeatedly heard a view that new security forces were being stationed in the state for reasons other than to seize drugs and weapons or to detain migrants. Human rights defenders and community groups speculated that the positioning of security forces may owe more to preparations to respond to potential social conflicts as development projects are put into place, mines are opened, and highways are built or expanded through communities. (Isacson et al. 2014)

Both the transnational crime and migration issues have produced new promises of intergovernmental collaboration. Yet the framework for that collaboration is 'Project Mesoamerica', created specifically to continue the kind of development model that sees plantations and assembly manufacturing that feed off abundant supplies of cheap displaced peasant labour, accompanied by neo-extractivist projects, as the way forward.

One of the partner states that is a major source of migrants moving northwards, Guatemala, was led at the time of my research by Otto Pérez Molina, a former soldier and Director of Military Intelligence. Pérez might be congratulated for accepting the failure of the 'war against drugs' and advocating decriminalization as the only realistic solution. But he has also presided over a militarization of security in the north of Huehuetenango province that has focused on suppression of pacific local opposition to the imposition of the same kind of development projects that concern people in Chiapas (Rasch 2012). In the 'Ixil Triangle' of northern Quiché, scene of some of the worst violence of the 1980s, hydroelectric and extractive projects with participation of capital from a variety of countries are at the heart of a complex series of conflicts involving 'old actors' such as large landowners, continuing legacies of the civil war such as evangelical groups linked to the military, and 'new actors' in the form of criminal organizations (Corvo 2014).

Honduras, whose modern history was shaped by the power of the US United Fruit Company (now Chiquita) to extinguish any move towards democracy prior to the 1970s (Moberg 2003), suffered another coup in 2009. The ousted president, Manuel Zelaya, who was elected as candidate of the Liberal Party, one of Honduras's two established oligarchic parties, made an unexpected move to align his country with Hugo Chávez's Bolivarian Alliance. Zelaya's return from exile was clearly conditional on his accepting the rules of the game that have guided the Central American country with the highest homicide rate and level of income inequality in the region following its return to 'democracy'. His wife, Xiomara Castro, stood as a third-party candidate in the 2013 presidential elections, but was declared in second place behind conservative Juan Orlando Hernández, candidate of the ruling National Party, who was credited with 36.8 per cent of the vote. Four activists of Castro's new Libre party were murdered, and there were widespread accusations of intimidation, fraud and vote buying (Welsbrot 2013). President Hernández has blamed his country's *coyotes* (people smugglers) for the upsurge in emigration of young people, linking the *coyotes* directly to the *narco*. He ascribed Honduras's increased significance in the transnational movement of drugs to the United States to a migration of Colombian and Mexican traffickers produced by those countries' campaigns against the cartels. Although he also promised a clean-up of corrupted public institutions, his main proposal for combating the criminal violence that he asserted was a cause of reduced economic opportunities as well as a direct driver of migration was 'to place a soldier on every street corner in Honduras' (Michel 2014a).

El Salvador has a similar history of gang violence, accompanied by continuing political violence, to the other two main sources of Central American migration since a UN-brokered peace agreement brought a formal end to the twelve-year civil war between its US-backed and military-led regime and left-wing guerrillas of the Farabundo Martí National Liberation Front (FMLN) in 1992 (Moodie 2011).[4] It has also participated in the development of low-wage export manufacturing typical of the region. Yet El Salvador is an exception to broader patterns in the region because it declared a moratorium on new mining operations in 2008, on the grounds of their low social utility and threat to the country's contaminated water resources. This policy is likely to be continued following the narrow 2014 electoral victory of Salvador Sánchez, a former leader of the FMLN, which frustrated the ambitions of the right-wing ARENA party to return to power. Sánchez also rejected his ARENA opponent's calls for the military to take over internal security. El Salvador's reward for putting people and the environment before extractive industry profits was, however, a massive $301 million lawsuit from the Pacific Rim mining company against the government's refusal to grant it a gold mining permit, being heard at the World Bank's International Centre for the Settlement of Investment Disputes (Provost 2014). The Canadian-Australian company Oceanagold acquired Pacific Rim in 2013, despite the fact that the company was virtually bankrupt, in evident expectation of a successful outcome, since international tribunals have regularly found in favour of the investors in disputes with states that attempt to implement environmental safeguards or close down operations that have violated them, awarding compensation for lost profits. The role of international arbitration bodies presents an increasing threat to national state sovereignty and democracy that US-sponsored international trade agreements are designed to reinforce.[5] Based on a jurisprudence completely grounded in Western economic liberalism (Wolf 2004), they represent a form of 'soft power' that may prove more effective in bringing states that try to contest the terms of capitalist globalization to heel than the more violent interventions that the United States has continued to sponsor outside Latin America.

El Salvador, with a population of just over six million, is the smallest, although also the most densely populated, country in Central America. Even the largest Central American country, Guatemala, only has a population of slightly over fifteen million. Costa Rica, which abolished its army in 1948, although it created a new internal security force in 1996, is scarcely more populous than the Mexican state of Michoacán. Panama, a staunch ally of the USA since the administration of George Bush Senior ordered the military invasion that overthrew Manuel Noriega in 1989, is even smaller. Nicaragua might appear to be another exception to the rule in the region, given its affiliation to the Bolivarian alliance, and income inequality has fallen since the return to government of the Sandinistas under Daniel Ortega in 2006. Yet as Dennis Rodgers has shown, Managua's urban infrastructure now replicates the repressive class segregation of other neoliberal cities in Latin America, a reflection of the way in which the Sandinista leadership merged with the old oligarchy (Rodgers 2012). The prospects of a major paradigm shift in the economic model dominating the Project Mesoamerica countries are not, therefore, very strong. The weight of Mexico and Colombia in the partnership is as preponderant in economic as in demographic terms, and behind them stands the United States. Although Colombia's president, Juan Manuel Santos, secured re-election in 2014 despite strong attacks from the elite faction led by former president Álvaro Uribe on his determination to continue peace negotiations with the guerrillas of the FARC (Revolutionary Armed Forces of Colombia) and initiate talks with those of the ELN (National Liberation Army), Santos's commitment to Colombia's established economic development model is unquestionable. Colombia's approach to internal security is also taken as paradigmatic in Mexico, so current thinking remains somewhat entrenched on the role of repressive force in managing the social consequences of domestic inequalities, addressing the problems of crime and violence, and securing the conditions necessary to perpetuate the model of economic development that dominates the region. The main debate is simply over how much of the task of policing should be placed directly in the hands of the military. The question of how much further privatized provision of citizen and corporate security should be allowed to develop is scarcely debated at all.

There are, nevertheless, a wide variety of social movements, moral voices associated with churches, and electoral political alternatives that are actively questioning various aspects of the status quo. Although truly democratic politics still faces serious impediments in many countries, and it would be quite wrong to discount the electoral support that defenders of the current order of things do actually enjoy – *mano dura* public security policies certainly do not lack electoral appeal, for example – issues such as the treatment of migrants from other countries, whether controls on mining projects should be strengthened or moratoriums on extraction declared, and the extent to which public security should be subject to local democratic control, do fall into the domain of the politically contestable. So do basic issues such as the public versus private provision of public services, the proportion of state budgets that should be spent on healthcare and education, the extent to which the tax system is progressive, and the responsibilities of government in regulating the economy. A good deal of the contemporary Latin American politics of protest is about attempts to assert some kind of local sovereignty, particularly evident in indigenous autonomy demands, but equally characteristic of non-indigenous movements to conserve local environments and ways of life against transnational capitalist mega-projects, or opposition to media monopolies. As I have argued in this section, a major issue today is preserving the degree of national sovereignty that is needed to implement democratic decisions about the future path of the economy and the kind of society in which citizens wish to live. This means not signing international agreements that give such sovereignty away. For Mexico and its immediate neighbours less disadvantageous forms of international partnerships are more likely to be achieved by pursuing closer integration with South rather than North America.[6]

I have stressed throughout this book that the United States bears a heavy historical responsibility for the growth of organized crime and violence in this region as well as for the continuing deficiencies of its democratic institutions. The current approach of the United States government to providing security assistance, and the role of US-based corporations and an international judicial apparatus in regulating commercial relations that favours US interests, is exacerbating the human security problems of the region's population and further undermining local sovereignty. The growth of Chinese demand for Latin American minerals changed the traditional economic scenario significantly, especially for South America but also to some extent for Mexico. It did not, however, change the fundamental acquiescence of Mexico and its Project Mesoamerica partners in a US-sponsored model of economic development that seems incapable of creating the kinds of conditions that have enabled China's own rise in the world economy (Gallagher and Porzecanski 2010). In this respect, Brazil's path of economic development under PT governments differed substantially from Mexico's in terms of the control that the state has exercised over the terms on which foreign companies operate in the country, as well as emphasis on genuine poverty reduction, formal job creation, and promoting social mobility through improvements in real wages.

Security that creates insecurity

I have argued that the use of armed force in 'pacification' operations justified by the need to eliminate criminal violence in Brazil and Mexico has had negative consequences for the human security of the targeted populations, produced perverse consequences, and been shaped by various kinds of hidden agendas. Unintended consequences of great magnitude have also tended to follow from international military interventions designed to provoke 'regime change'.

It might be argued that incapacitating Iraq as a regional power was an unvoiced objective of some of the strategic thinkers behind the US invasion, and that the country's break-up would be the best way of achieving that goal. Yet it is difficult to see any great advantage to the USA or its Israeli allies in the direction in which things were heading by mid-2014. Iran might be inconvenienced by the Iraqi Shiites losing control of much of Iraq's resources, especially by the loss of control over oil to what could become a separate Kurdish state. Yet it is difficult to see how the USA could feel happy about the development of ISIS, the Islamic State of Iraq and Syria, in a position to control the supply of water to the southern part of Iraq through their occupation of the upper reaches of the Tigris and Euphrates rivers. One might argue that US policy was constrained from the beginning by its inability to recognize Saudi Arabian Wahhabism as the principal financial and ideological motive force behind the expansion of violent expressions of political Islam. Timothy Mitchell (2011) has argued that this paradoxical historical relationship between US imperial power and fundamentalist Islam makes sense in terms of an overriding US interest in stopping the consolidation of socialist states in the Arab world. Yet it would seem a leap too far to see the creation of a Shia-dominated sectarian successor state to the secular Baathist regime as something that the USA engineered to ensure the break-up of Iraq, in full consciousness of the probability that this would reproduce the al-Qaeda problem in a potentially still more serious form. The same could be said about the mess that intervention has made of Libya. Both interventions have produced a profusion of new armed actors. Arming actors that Western governments have no hope of controlling in the long term is to stock up problems for the future, as Western support for Osama Bin Laden's mujahedin against the Russians in Afghanistan and the arming of rebels in Syria have demonstrated.

The 'war against drugs' in Latin America abounds with similar contradictions because operations against criminals become entangled in political and geopolitical projects to an extent that can even result in different agencies of the United States government or national governments working at cross-purposes. Admittedly, the contradictions are infectious, since drug trafficking is a very effective way of financing what might once have been more noble insurrectionary causes, as illustrated by the Colombian FARC. Yet the contradictions are intensified, as I stressed in Chapter 3, by the way in which insecurity is co-produced by violent state responses to violent criminal actors and the responses that this generates among the people who are affected by the process.

There would, of course, be less armed violence in the world if there were fewer arms and they were more difficult to obtain. In the case of Brazil, homicide rates fell over several years after 2003, when the Lula government introduced a disarmament statute that imposed tougher restrictions on gun possession and offered an amnesty if guns were handed in for destruction (Cavalcanti 2013; Waiselfisz 2014). Yet a referendum on radical gun control mandated by the new law was voted down in 2005, despite the fact that surveys showed it had strong support among those most affected by violence, residents of low-income neighbourhoods, people from the poorer and especially violent states of north-east Brazil, and women (Cavalcanti 2013: 12). Brazilian pro-gun lobbyists were energetically supported by the US National Rifle Association, which found an impressive number of Brazilians susceptible to its message of the right to individual defence of one's family and home. Roxana Cavalcanti argues that this was a neoliberal message of the private right to security, put across by a spirited media campaign that determined the balance in a form of democratic decision-making that is itself individualized and favours well-organized pressure groups, the referendum (ibid.: 13). The pro-gun lobby naturally included the domestic arms industry, but the fact that the 'no' campaign had a transnational dimension is clearly significant as well. So is the fact that much of the negative campaigning was directed to convincing middle-class people living in less secure condominium buildings or family homes that they could not rely on the police to protect their families.

As we have seen, there are domestic issues to consider in the case of the acquisition of advanced weaponry by criminal groups, including their supply by corrupt members of the security forces. Policing the borders of a country of continental scale is also a genuine challenge for Brazil. Yet in the case of both Brazil and Mexico, the transnational role of the United States is important, not simply as an arms manufacturer and trader, but also as a country whose permissive approach to the sale of weapons reflects a 'gun culture' that is vigorously defended in terms of libertarian values that seem unshakeable despite regular classroom massacres and racist murders by white homeowners committed in the name of self-defence. Nevertheless, wherever the guns come from, and however strongly ideologies of personal security are travelling to

Latin America, we have also seen that there are problems associated with state authorization of the right of off-duty police to bear weapons, state legalization of certain kinds of armed actors as complementary forces in public security, and the use of arms in the private security sector. In the case of Mexico, where the state theoretically exercises stronger control over the right of citizens to bear arms than Brazil, the fact that this control is exercised selectively is another problem: some kinds of people have more rights to self-defence than others.

The argument that police should be armed at all times does make some sense in the Brazilian context, since they may encounter armed criminals who will kill them while off duty. If they use the gun while off duty to murder their unfaithful wives or husbands, or a completely innocent member of the public, there is a strong probability that they will be brought to account. Yet if they use the gun while working for a private security company we get into a much greyer area. There clearly is scope for more effective regulation, and this was the official logic behind the Michoacán commissioner Alfredo Castillo's demand that members of *autodefensas* submit their weapons for test firings when they registered them, so that they could be brought to account should they subsequently use the weapon to commit a crime (a technique applied in the case of the Blackwater agents accused of murdering civilians in Baghdad). Confidence in such a system does, however, depend on the existence of a police force and judiciary that can be trusted to act correctly. Such confidence is very limited in Mexico, particularly where killings are thought to be politically motivated, such as in the case of the human rights lawyer Digna Ochoa in 2001, in which an initial assumption of homicide was changed to a verdict of suicide that was implausible on both motivational and forensic grounds. It seems clear that these problems can be resolved only by profound reforms of the police and justice system.

At this juncture, however, we need to revisit the question of 'the rule of law'. Procedural reforms are certainly important. Mexico's scheduled change from presumption of guilt to presumption of innocence in criminal cases from 2016 onwards should have some impact on the class- and ethnically biased nature of Mexican justice, but there also need to be major changes in police investigative work in addition to other reforms in a judicial process that does not involve trial by jury. Despite the presumption of innocence, the quality of justice in the United States remains influenced by differences of race and income inequality, which affect the quality of defence that is available to different kinds of people. In the case of Brazil, a number of proposals for constitutional amendments relating to police reform are currently on offer to the congress, of which the most extensive and most radical is PEC-51, proposed by Senator Lindbergh Farias of the Rio de Janeiro PT and drafted with the assistance of Luiz Eduardo Soares. As Soares explained in an interview, PEC-51 not only proposes the demilitarization of the police and an end to the current, highly dysfunctional, separation between the investigative civil police and enforcement-preventative military police, but a single career structure that would abolish the present gulf between those who enter as officers and soldiers in the military police, and delegates and non-delegates in the civil police (Tavares 2014).[7] The object of demilitarization is not simply to end the rigid, centralized and vertical structure of the corporations, but also to end the disproportionate use of force and restrict use of armed violence to what Soares considers the 1 per cent of police work that involves exchanging fire with armed criminals. Community policing techniques should be used to deal with everything else. Soares also stresses, however, that police reform alone is not enough. To end the idea that policing is a kind of warfare, society also needs to stop criminalizing the poor and adopting mass incarceration as a solution. Extrajudicial executions and torture added to the violent nature of stop-and-search generate a deep hatred of the police on the part of young men which perpetuates violence (Rovai 2013).

Soares is in favour of the decriminalization of drugs (as is ex-president Fernando Henrique Cardoso), but he is also in favour of an end to the selective application of the law that gives more fortunate citizens impunity. It is clear that this is an ambitious political agenda, but what the UPP experience has now shown is that it is important for Brazil to start advancing along the road of structural reform of the police and ending selective application of the law, abandoning the politics of securitization. The 2014 World Cup was not disrupted by mass protests, since the police firmly dispersed the small groups that tried to form, using pepper spray and baton charges against peaceful and orderly groups as well as those that did seem to have more violent intent. My monitoring of Rio de Janeiro's newspapers showed that the gun battles between police and traffickers continued in the *favelas* on a daily basis, producing casualties on both sides, but in a way that was predictably invisible to the tourists whose security had been one of the justifications for the renewal of this pointless war.

Beyond procedural reform we have the question of the substantive content of the law. This is the most difficult area of all. Presumption of equality before the law does not necessarily produce something that is accepted as just by all citizens when those citizens are not in fact equal in some of the crucial areas identified by the human security paradigm. An obligation to accept undignified work or loss of the right to shelter can be legal, for example. We have also seen that there is a major problem in the way international legal tribunals can override sovereign democratic decisions and protect the 'rights' of transnational corporations and financial speculators, to a point that does significant harm to the rights of people in foreign countries not to suffer environmental and health problems. Nor is this simply a problem of tribunals that are technically international. In the case of Argentina and the hedge fund 'hold-outs', a New York court had enough power over international financial markets to threaten a sovereign nation with economic meltdown that would do untold social damage. I am not making an argument for the tsunami-like nature of globalization here, but it is clear that individual states will not find it easy to change these aspects of the current global order acting alone. It will require strong coalitions, ideally not simply of Latin American states. A step in this direction has now been taken by the creation of an alternative multilateral investment bank for infrastructure development by the BRICS countries (Brazil, Russia, India, China and South Africa). Making these coalitions work is one of the grand challenges presented by a more multi-centric world. Yet it is a challenge that must be met if the potential of the human security paradigm to address the range of global issues proposed by Fukuda-Parr (2003) is to be realized.

There are also, as we have seen, people whose rights are easily discounted by tribunals, especially when they have become objects of a securitization process. The Central American migration crisis scandal did not prompt the Mexican government to review its own asylum provisions, nor to take any effective measures to combat the abuse of this vulnerable population by its own public officials, despite repeated promises and some practically meaningless legislation on the part of the state government of Chiapas. Promising to stop migrants using *La Bestia* is hardly a solution to any of those problems. In both Brazil and Mexico, the securitization of social problems is made possible by feelings of insecurity that have permeated society and are important factors in the political choices that better-off citizens make even when those citizens are not actually objectively those who are most at risk. Fears cannot be totally discounted. Better-off Brazilians and Mexicans are sometimes victims of armed assault or kidnap. When rent-seeking criminals prey on vulnerable migrants, this is a real problem for the generally less affluent local people who live near migrant shelters, for example. Yet the only real solution to that problem is to go for the criminals, not add to the victimization of the migrants.

In principle, all citizens should benefit from a reduction of corruption and abuse of power by public officials. Unfortunately, this is not necessarily the case, since this is another aspect of the class-selective application of the law. Furthermore, both criminals and co-opted guardians of public order can perform useful services for powerful people, as I have shown in a variety of contexts in the course of this book. In both Brazil and Mexico, corrupt practices of various kinds are widespread in business and politics, and politicians at the highest levels have taken payoffs directly from organized crime. I have shown how the rhetoric of securitization can be used to advance capitalist projects by legitimizing interventions that crush resistance. Yet it can also be deployed in ways that deflect attention from wrongdoing at the highest level by making crime seem external to the world of elites and focusing on its immediate perpetrators rather than intellectual authors. Asking military security forces to get their hands dirty in defence of elite interests also demands efforts to protect their reputations and impunity. Charges were brought against soldiers in the case of the extrajudicial execution of members of a criminal group in Tlatlaya in the State of Mexico in June 2014. Yet Tlatlaya is the tip of an iceberg that is largely kept hidden because of the elimination of witnesses or use of torture to secure the silence of survivors (Camacho Servín 2014). The case of Iguala provides a clear illustration of how containment and damage limitation become the order of the day for the federal government and higher-level elites once the links between local political figures and organized crime are unambiguously exposed. In Brazil, right-wing politicians and media moguls have encouraged the public to focus on corruption associated with the state oil company Petrobras. Yet we may learn more about shadow networks of power in Brazil by considering other cases. Politicians and businessmen associated with the numbers game boss (*bicheiro*) Carlinhos Cachoeira have been able to sleep easy simply because too many colleagues from too many parties were entangled in these networks to make the prosecution of anyone politically viable (Decat and Matais 2012). Ironically some of the politicians involved in this scandal are enthusiastic exponents of *mano dura* public security policies who assert that the poor are lazy scroungers who do not deserve government assistance.

Nevertheless, although the kinds of social changes that have taken place in recent years in Brazil have promoted more individualism, they also seem to have promoted an increasing antagonism towards corruption and impunity that cost the PT some of its support in the 2014 elections. Mexican social and political conditions may make reforms more difficult to achieve, particularly if the government in power continues to persecute figures such as Dr Mireles who dare to ask too many questions about the real state of the country. Yet the fact that outright repression has continued to be necessary in Mexico does indicate that civil society remains active. Furthermore, the reputation of the Peña Nieto administration has suffered not only from growing scepticism about its achievements in the field of public security and crime reduction, but also from revelations about the stake of companies directly associated with the president in government-awarded mega-projects. Such revelations hardly come as a shock since Peña Nieto is associated with the Atlacomulco Group, a powerful element of the PRI shadow state that has always had this kind of quality. One of the group's founding figures, the late Carlos Hank González, along with his sons Carlos and Jorge, was accused of having strong links with organized crime, although no charges have ever stuck to the Hanks (Gledhill 1999).

Given that transforming elite behaviour remains a challenge, this leaves us with the question of what measures might be taken at other levels of society to reduce crime and violence within the framework of actually existing power relations. Educational programmes and community actions designed to turn young people away from crime of the kind that are on offer in Bahia's *Pacto Pela Vida* programme are potentially productive, especially if they incorporate efforts to wean adults as well as adolescents away from violent forms of behaviour. This is not just a matter of reducing homicides but of reducing domestic and sexual violence, and road rage, so it is also a matter of working on socially acceptable expressions of masculinity, an issue which is, as we have seen, integral to the problem of criminal and police violence as well. Yet these kinds of interventions clearly work more effectively in a context in which other aspects of human security are also being attended to, including conditions of work, decent housing, and leisure and sporting facilities, since social humiliation and excessive inequality are what make criminal life and violent forms of behaviour attractive despite their risks. I have argued that it is impossible to end crime by slaughtering or incarcerating criminals who will instantly be replaced by others, and especially undesirable to adopt this approach when it will provoke more fragmentation of criminal groups and even more violence. It may be true that local street gangs have become quite dangerous in Mexican cities such as Ciudad Juárez in recent years, and it is probably no accident that this has happened in the wake of a campaign of repressive policing in the urban periphery. In the case of Central America, Oliver Jütersonke, Robert Muggah and Dennis Rodgers (2009) have argued that repressive public security policies have tended to 'radicalize' youth gangs, leading them to engage in more organized, and violent, forms of criminality. In the case of Juárez, it seems that the smaller fry may even have become inconvenient for large-scale organized crime itself, but both Brazilian and Mexican experience support the view that it is vital not to have a public security policy that drives even more young people into the arms of criminal organizations. This is why community policing and avoiding mass incarceration of disadvantaged youth are so important.

The best way to attack large-scale organized crime is to 'follow the money' and not just the illegal products. This is more important than ever when trafficking has diversified beyond drugs, and extortion is providing an important proportion of the income of criminal organizations. The practical problem is where following the money will take one, and whether any actually existing police force in Latin America will be allowed to go as far as it takes, even when it has officers who are willing and able to go down this road. Following the money will likely lead one into the upper levels of politics, the public security services and the international banking system, especially the banking system of the United States (Gledhill 1999; Garzón 2008; Vulliamy 2010). Just as some banks proved 'too big to fail' whatever damage their greed and irresponsibility inflicted on North Atlantic societies and the rest of the world, it seems that some political-criminal networks are 'too big to fall', whether they are national or, as is now more likely, transnational. This underscores the importance, emphasized throughout this book, of reconstructing a public domain ravaged by neoliberal prescriptions, rebalancing the relationship between the public and private, and tackling the structural causes of inequality. Securitization, in all its variants, tends to work in the opposite direction, producing more insecurity for the relatively poor and 'inconvenient' populations that have the most urgent need for the promises of the human security paradigm to be fulfilled. If the money currently being spent on ineffective repressive security and fortifying borders, not to mention the considerable amount of criminal capital still being laundered through the international banking system, were to be spent on strengthening genuinely 'pro-poor' development, it would be far easier to reverse the utter devaluation of human life characteristic of much of the contemporary violence of Latin America.

NOTES

1 Securitization, the state and capitalism

1 Real wages as money wages adjusted for prices are not completely reliable indicators of how much better off in material terms people might be becoming, since that also depends on the changing relative costs of essential items of consumption such as food and housing in relation to other items used to construct indices of price inflation. The proportion of the income of the poorest households that has to be spent on rents and food can change over time, and international comparisons are complicated by differences in what is included in official statistics. But in the Brazilian case, the improvements in living standards are real.

2 For a broader analysis of the profitability of civil conflict and its relationships to the development of illegal economies, see Nordstrom (2007).

3 Biopolitics refers to the part of Michel Foucault's theory of 'modern government' that stresses the significance of state interventions that are concerned with the 'vitality' of the whole population, through public health interventions, for example. As Diane Nelson points out in comparing the Guatemalan military regime's malaria eradication campaigns with its counter-insurgency war, 'protection' of the population, capitalist interests and 'national security' can become entangled in complex ways. Most Guatemalan peasants were willing to collaborate with the state to improve their health, but the effective implementation of medication programmes meant allowing that state

to obtain an intimate knowledge of the population at the household level, which could subsequently be used against them in counter-insurgency warfare, while the campaign against malaria also made capitalist expansion into tropical lowland environments more viable and reduced the problem of 'the lazy natives' being too sick to work productively (Nelson 2005: 233).

4 China has the world's second-highest prison population, but its incarceration rate is substantially lower than that of Mexico, Brazil and, indeed, England and Wales, where 148 people are in jail per 100,000 population.

5 Where journalistic work has explicit bylines, the reference is listed in the bibliography. Contributions attributed to unnamed editorial staff or editorials are referenced in endnotes.

2 Violence, urban development

1 There were only five cases of *latrocínio* in Salvador in 2012 according to Public Security Secretariat statistics. This number increased to twenty-seven in 2013. See www.ssp.ba.gov.br/wp-content/estatistica/2013/CAPITAL/03_CAPITAL_2013.pdf, accessed 28 April 2014. In Rio de Janeiro, *latrocínio* increased from 118 cases to 140 between 2011 and 2012 (Damasceno et al. 2013).

2 'Bahia campeão nacional em homicídios', *Correio da Bahia*, 12 November 2014.

3 High-profile episodes in Bahia during 2012 that received extensive

publicity were the serial rape of two young women by the members of the musical group New Hit inside the band's bus, and a sexual assault perpetrated on a prosecuting attorney while she and a judge whom she had accompanied for a drink in a bar in an upscale neighbourhood were held for twelve hours by a gang of teenage kidnappers.

4 This was how a crime that might otherwise have gone unreported came to the attention of the police. 'Três colegas torturam adolescente de 14 anos após traição amorosa, diz PC', g1.globo.com/bahia/noticia/2012/11/tres-colegas-torturam-adolescente-de-14-anos-apos-traicao-amorosa-diz-pc.html, accessed 1 December 2012.

5 Despite the Bahian origin of the name, irregular settlements in Salvador were traditionally called 'invasions' or, as is also the case in São Paulo, 'periphery'. The term periphery is, however, misleading in Salvador since lack of affordable housing for the growing number of rural–urban migrants in the second half of the twentieth century meant that 'invasions' occurred wherever there was unoccupied space, which means that there are few middle-class residents who do not have poor people as relatively close neighbours (Gordilho Souza 2000). The term 'favela' (along with 'favelados' for residents of favelas) has been used more in recent years in Bahia as communities struggling for 'the right to the city' have come to see themselves as part of a national movement.

6 'Juíza concede liberdade provisória a patrichinhas', Correio da Bahia, 13 April 2013.

7 The word patricinha, abbreviated to 'Pats' in some of these reports, is a slang term for a consumption- and fashion-crazy young woman spoiled by her parents.

8 Ironically, the government of São Paulo aided the expansion of the PCC network by dispersing prisoners to jails in other states.

9 Neither rapists nor homosexuals are invited to become 'brothers' in the PCC (Biondi 2010).

10 Cabral and Garotinho, originally a protégé of Brizola, are bitter political enemies. Garotinho used his contacts in the military police to make life difficult for Cabral by supporting a strike by firemen (who belong to the same corporation). His hand was subsequently to be seen in the strike by military police in Bahia that caused problems for the PT government there in February 2012, discussed in the next chapter.

11 'O fim do governo de Sérgio Cabral e o suposto sucesso da segurança pública', Jornal do Brasil, www.jb.com.br/rio/noticias/2014/04/06/o-fim-do-governo-de-sergio-cabral-e-o-suposto-sucesso-da-seguranca-publica/, accessed 7 April 2014.

12 Interview with Júlia Dias Carneiro, 23 December 2011, www.bbc.co.uk/portuguese/noticias/2011/12/111222_rio_mexico_narcotrafico_jc.shtml, accessed 20 March 2012.

13 'Polícia identifica suspeitos de matar líder comunitário da Rocinha', g1.globo.com/rio-de-janeiro/noticia/2012/03/policia-identifica-suspeitos-de-matar-lider-comunitario-da-rocinha.html, accessed 30 March 2012.

14 'Policiais e traficantes entram em confronto na Rocinha', Jornal A Tarde, 7 April 2012.

15 'Em depoimento de 8 horas, PMs negam agressão sexual na Rocinha', g1.globo.com/rio-de-janeiro/noticia/2012/04/em-depoimento-de-8-horas-pms-negam-agressao-sexual-na-rocinha.html, accessed 21 April 2012.

16 'Após semana de violência, Rocinha ganha reforço de 130 PMs em estágio', g1.globo.com/rio-de-janeiro/noticia/2012/03/apos-semana-de-violencia-rocinha-ganha-reforco-de-

130-pms-em-estagio.html, accessed 24 April 2012.

17 'Patrimônio de PM suspeito de chefiar esquema de propina é de R$ 4 milhões', g1.globo.com/rio-de-janeiro/noticia/2014/09/patrimonio-de-pm-suspeito-de-chefiar-esquema-de-propina-e-de-r-4-milhoes.html, accessed 25 September 2014.

18 'Caso Amarildo: major, tenente, sargento e dez soldados se entregam após prisão decretada', *O Globo*, 5 October 2013. More officers were accused of participating in the cover-up of the crime later in the month.

19 'Com o "selo" da Copa', *Meia Hora*, 27 May 2014.

20 'Niterói terá mais uma Companhia Destacada', *Meia Hora*, 23 April 2014.

21 The brutality of this eviction, which also violated statutory legal procedures, provoked the NGO *Justiça Global* to make a formal complaint to the office of the UN Special Rapporteur for the Right to Adequate Housing. See 'Justiça Global denuncia à ONU despejo de moradores da Favela da Telerj', agencia brasil.ebc.com.br/direitos-humanos/noticia/2014-04/justica-global-denuncia-onu-ilegalidades-no-despejo-das-familias-da, accessed 22 April 2014.

22 Having a gun to hand at all times may have tragic personal consequences, such as murdering an unfaithful wife or girlfriend, or amorous rival, in a fit of jealous rage, or killing some member of the public who shows 'disrespect' to the officer in an off-duty encounter, as exemplified by the case of a student shot by a policeman, analysed by Daniel Linger (Linger 1992: ch. 10).

3 Pacifying the urban periphery

1 Originally elected for the PDT (Democratic Labour Party), Carneiro switched to the PMDB for his re-election campaign, receiving the support of the principal opponents of the PT state government, Geddel Vieira Lima of the PMDB, and his own eventual successor, ACM Neto of the Democrats. Mounting decay of the urban infrastructure and repeated rejection of his administration's accounts by state auditors brought Carneiro's administration to a level of unpopularity that led the PMDB to ditch him, and he completed his term as a member of the right-wing Progressive Party (PP).

2 Most of the land on which Bairro da Paz's residents have built their homes is public property, since the city government acquired it from its original private owners after the invasion became a consolidated occupation in settlement of unpaid tax liabilities. The regularization programme concedes a 'special concession of use for residential purposes', subject to a number of restrictions that include limits on the size of the area that can be occupied by a single beneficiary family and restrictions on commercial, as distinct from residential, use – a problem for communities in which small family businesses as well as production cooperatives make a significant contribution to the residents' livelihoods. For the history of land regularization in Salvador, see Gordilho Souza (2007).

3 Act of an Extraordinary General Assembly of the Residents of Bairro da Paz, 25 May 2013; Meeting of the FPEBP, 28 May 2013. For more information on the history and vicissitudes of the FPEBP, see Gledhill and Hita (2014).

4 Off-duty officers identified by armed thieves robbing bus passengers may well be killed even if they do not 'react' to the assault, for example, a problem that was a great cause of anxiety for officers interviewed in my project.

5 Bairro da Paz does have a *Balcão de Justiça e Cidadania*, which offers free legal advice and conflict mediation to

citizens on low incomes. Although the limitations of this state programme for 'democratizing access to justice' are evident enough in light of the willingness of some residents to turn for support to the traffickers, some of the interviewees did mention this institution as a positive aspect of public provision. The neighbourhood also has a CRAS unit (Centro de Referência de Assistência Social), which administers government programmes of social assistance to poor and vulnerable families.

6 Candomblé is a religion with African roots practised throughout Brazil but especially important in Bahia, where it now enjoys considerable government recognition as cultural heritage.

7 The circuits that connect zones of production, trans-shipment, processing, distribution and consumers in the Brazilian drugs trade involve a multitude of actors, many of whom disguise their involvement behind other activities. Although there are no equivalents of the Mexican cartels, there are transnational family-based criminal organizations that control the production and shipment of drugs across the borders from Paraguay and Bolivia and generally own farms on both sides of the borders. Those frontiers are of a length that makes their effective policing extremely difficult.

8 'Protesto contra morte de criança bloqueia avenida Paralela', *Jornal A Tarde*, 30 January 2014.

9 This information is published on the Facebook pages of Bairro da Paz Eu Sou, a community journalism project, www.facebook.com/Bdapazeusou/posts/264638467033992, accessed 31 January 2014.

10 'O desabafo!', 4 February 2014, online at www.facebook.com/BairrodaPazNews, accessed 5 February 2014. For obvious reasons this public post remained anonymous, although since I received the text privately, I can vouch

for the fact that the author is no friend of the traffickers.

11 One of the interviewees argued that all officers should start as soldiers, so that they could acquire a real understanding of police work in practice.

12 In Japan, central police stations are complemented by small stations (*Kōban*) located within the local neighbourhoods that they serve, establishing everyday face-to-face relationships of trust between officers and residents.

13 In one case, a Candomblé priestess who was the mother-in-law of a victim, and had herself suffered violence at the hands of her own husband, nevertheless encouraged her son to beat his wife, who excited his ire by refusing to turn a blind eye to his multiple infidelities. The wife's problem, beyond her refusal to be 'docile', was that her husband and his mother came from the founding family of the community into which she had married, hoping to escape the drudgery of her life as a domestic servant who had come to the capital from an interior city (Hautzinger 2007: ch. 1).

14 *Cachaça* is the Brazilian name for alcoholic liquor distilled from sugar-cane juice.

15 The case offers a tragic demonstration of the need to avoid simplistic assumptions about 'female nature' in police work. This young woman had joined the police to fulfil lifestyle ambitions that focused on owning a powerful motorbike. An accident with the bike left her in permanent pain, dependent on medication that absorbed all of her salary (SanMartin 2012).

16 'Não há negociação salarial dessa forma, diz governador sobre greve de PMs', *Correio da Bahia*, 17 April 2014.

17 'Governo diz que nova proposta dos PMs está acima do orçamento: "Um retrocesso"', *Correio da Bahia*, 17 April 2014.

18 'MPF afirma que Marco Prisco fez uso da violência para liderar greves', *Correio da Bahia*, 19 April 2014.

4 State transformations

1 Although land was in practice bought and sold within the *ejidos*, and could also be acquired by outsiders, the lack of juridical security in these informal land market transactions did lower its value relative to land fully in the private domain, and prevented its use as collateral for a bank loan.

2 'The world's most powerful people', www.forbes.com/powerful-people/list/, accessed 10 June 2014.

3 The draft report and an open letter from three of its authors to the Fox administration are available at www2.gwu.edu/~nsarchiv/NSAEBB/NSAEBB180/index.htm, accessed 10 February 2012.

4 The text of their communiqué is available at www2.gwu.edu/~nsarchiv/NSAEBB/NSAEBB209/Reaccion_al_Informe_del_Fiscal.pdf, accessed 14 December 2012.

5 In May 2014, the National Human Rights Commission (CNDH) announced that it had records of 24,800 cases of disappearance since 2005. In 612 of these the CNDH had direct evidence that state agents were responsible. 'Editorial/Desaparecidos: actuar ya', *La Jornada*, 21 May 2014.

6 'Desplazados, tragedia silenciosa en México', *El Economista*, 7 January 2012.

7 This party, successor of the old Socialist Workers' Party (PST), had previously been in opposition to the PRI, but formed an alliance with the PRI municipal authorities after 1996, after losing adherents to the Zapatistas (Moksnes 2012: 58).

8 'Conozca los testimonios de los desplazados', *El Universal*, 3 January 2014.

9 'Junta de Buen Gobierno hacia La Esperanza', *La Jornada*, 6 May 2014.

10 'Anuncia "Marcos" la desaparición de su "personaje" en el EZLN', *La Jornada*, 25 May 2014.

11 'Palabras de la Comandancia General del EZLN, en voz del subcomandante insurgente Moisés, en el homenaje al compañero Galeano', *La Jornada*, 25 May 2014.

12 Robles caused considerable scandal in her new job by suggesting that the benefits offered by the *Oportunidades* programme should not be given to indigenous women with more than three children, since they were procreating simply to get the money (Rojas and Camacho 2014).

13 'Sabines deja en Chiapas deuda superior a la de Moreira', www.animalpolitico.com/2012/10/sabines-deja-en-chiapas-deuda-superior-a-la-de-moreira/#axzz2kYKvD2QQ, accessed 12 October 2012.

14 'ONG condena la agresión contra migrantes en Tabasco', *La Jornada*, 6 May 2014.

15 One of these, noted for the subsequent religious and political intolerance of the group that became dominant in the community, completed the takeover of the last vestiges of the former *finca* only after the Zapatista rebellion broke out.

5 Paramilitaries, *autodefensas*

1 A *criollo* (white) elite based in the city of Coalcomán had already begun the process of destroying the indigenous communities by revaluing their communal forests for tax purposes in terms of their notional value to capitalist logging companies, creating unpayable debts. But manipulating the liberal laws that laid the basis for privatizing communal land and dispossessing its former owners were not sufficient to end the

resistance of the indigenous community in Coalcomán itself, which finally had to be finished off by a massacre of its remaining defenders (Sánchez Díaz 1979).

2 The development of Michoacán's Pacific coast as a zone for production and shipment of drugs to the United States was related to US-sponsored operations against the drugs industries of Colombia, Bolivia and Peru, as well as to US operations against routes that transported drugs from Colombia to the United States via Mexico's eastern coast (Maldonado Aranda 2013: 11).

3 Although she uses a pseudonym in the paper cited here, the same town will figure later in this chapter in another context with its real name.

4 Thanks to the sagacity of some of those who organized the networks that took migrants into the United States, a new generation of migrants did succeed in legalizing their presence in the USA by a fraudulent manipulation of provisions in the 1986 Simpson-Rodino Act designed to maintain the supply of migrant workers to US agriculture. This did, however, involve taking on considerable debt, and the younger siblings of the migrants who benefited from this loophole did not enjoy an equivalent opportunity.

5 A figure of 57,449 deaths is widely accepted as a minimum by the Mexican press. There are problems with the way that the Mexican government distinguishes homicides relating to the actions of the cartels and the security forces from other kinds of homicides, and many independent organizations place the death toll considerably higher than this figure (Molloy 2013).

6 Another splinter, which called itself 'The Resistance', broke ties with the Sinaloa cartel and briefly aligned with the Zetas, although both later competed with the New Generation cartel independently.

7 After more than a century of extensive migration to the United States, people in Michoacán were very familiar with the world of 'organized crime' in the North. In my early fieldwork in the 1980s, I met people who had got involved in that world during extended stays in major cities such as Chicago during the 1970s or even earlier.

8 Because the state government failed to grant official recognition to Xayakalan as an administrative unit, its residents could not be assisted from public funds when a hurricane destroyed their houses and crops in June 2011. They did, however, receive aid from their allies the Cherán autonomists.

9 Although the original indigenous community of Aquila ceased to exist both juridically and de facto at the beginning of the twentieth century, a petition by a group of residents was successful in securing its reconstitution in 1981 under the post-revolutionary agrarian reform laws. The discovery of important iron ore deposits in the 1970s provided a stimulus to the movement to reconstitute the indigenous community in what had become a bastion of mestizo power.

10 Their statement was published in English translation on the website of El Enemigo Común on 19 January 2014 ('First statement from the Self-Defense Group of Aquila, Michoacán', elenemigocomun.net/2014/01/self-defense-aquila-michoacan/, accessed 5 May 2014).

11 The new group renewed the attack on Fidel Villanueva and others associated with the Templarios, and also condemned the municipal president, Juan Hernández, adding that he had not actually won election, despite the support of the Templarios, who had been obliged to burn ballot boxes and finally threaten to kill the rival candidate if he dared to take office.

12 Reference was also made in this meeting to the 'bigger cacique' of the

region, Mario Alvárez López, who, as I mentioned earlier, was now occupying a senior regional administrative position in the PRI state government headed by Fausto Vallejo and had a personal claim to land in Xayakalan.

13 'Autodefensas toman La Placita ante una amenaza de desalojo', *La Jornada*, 14 February 2014.

14 'El MP me pidió bajar un cadáver y sostenerle la cabeza para una foto: Mireles', *La Jornada*, 13 May 2014.

15 'Hipólito Mora y "El Americano" liman asperezas', *Milenio*, 21 May 2014.

16 'Tras la captura de Hipólito, relatos de despojo y amagos', *El Universal*, 17 March 2014.

6 Achieving human security

1 Revisiting communities in Michoacán with long migrant traditions in 2012, I met a number of people who had been deported and many more who had lost their jobs because their employers had shut down through fear of police raids and fines. The impact was visible in villages in the form of half-finished houses that their owners now despaired of completing.

2 PRI and PAN legislators decided to change the sensitive word 'expropriation' to 'temporary occupation'. What 'temporary occupation' could possibly mean in practice remains to be seen.

3 The children are initially housed in government-contracted shelters, but they will be released into the custody of a relative resident in the United States, another sponsor or foster family, while they await their court hearing (Isacson et al. 2014).

4 It is worth emphasizing that the historical origins of Central America's transnational gangs, the *maras*, were not in the region itself, but among the population living as refugees in Los Angeles during the period in which Central America was a 'frontline against communist subversion' (Jütersonke et al. 2009).

5 The North American Free Trade Agreement, for example, made Mexico more vulnerable to this type of action. A city government in the state of San Luis Potosí refused to allow the US company Metalcad to operate a hazardous waste dump on environmental grounds. The corporation took the Mexican government to the ICSID for violation of NAFTA rules and obtained $15.6 million in compensation plus an order that the decision not to allow the dump to operate be rescinded (Vincent 2014).

6 Because of the significance of Mexican migration to the United States, and Mexico's current level of dependence on the US market, such a reorientation would certainly be painful in the short term, but perhaps less so in the medium term if South America continues to reorient itself to other global centres.

7 As we saw in Chapter 4, a single career structure would be a very welcome reform for some serving police.

BIBLIOGRAPHY

Acharya, A. (2001) 'Human security: east versus west', *International Journal*, 56(3).

Adesoji, A. (2010) 'The Boko Haram uprising and Islamic revivalism in Nigeria', *Africa Spectrum*, 45(2).

Agamben, G. (1998) *Homo Sacer: Sovereignty and Bare Life*, Stanford, CA: Stanford University Press.

Agudo Sanchíz, A. A. (2008) 'Land recuperation and conflict on the margins of state formation in northern Chiapas', *Identities*, 15(5).

Ahmed, M. (2012) 'Tráfico fixa cartazes no Jacarezinho proibindo venda de crack na favela', *G1 Rio*, g1.globo. com/rio-de-janeiro/noticia/2012/06/trafico-fixa-cartazes-no-jacarezinho-proibindo-venda-de-crack-na-favela. html, accessed 20 June 2012.

Alban, R. (2013) 'Nordeste de Amaralina: dois baleados em operação da PM', *Correio da Bahia*, 18 February 2013.

Albro, R. (2005) 'The water is ours, Carajo!: deep citizenship in Bolivia's water war,' in J. Nash (ed.), *Social Movements: An Anthropological Reader*, Oxford: Blackwell.

Alejandro, J. (2012) 'EPR y ERPI se fortalecen con lanzacohetes: Marina', *El Universal*, 27 November.

Alencastro, C. and S. Ramalho (2013) 'Caso Amarildo: Cabral afirma ser prematuro acusar PMs', *O Globo*, 2 August.

Alves, M. H. M. and P. Evanson (2011) *Living in the Crossfire: Favela Residents, Drug Dealers, and Police Violence in Rio de Janeiro*, Philadelphia, PA: Temple University Press.

Aparicio, J. M. (1995) 'Integración y transformación de las formas del poder local en Lázaro Cárdenas, Michoacán', *Política y cultura*, 5.

Aragón Andrade, O. (2013) 'El derecho en insurrección: el uso contrahegemónico del derecho en el movimiento purépecha de Cherán', *Revista de Estudos e Pesquisas sobre as Américas*, 7(2).

Aranda, J., G. Castillo and M. Chávez (2014) 'Kike Plancarte fue abatido en Querétaro por la Armada, afirman fuentes federales', *La Jornada*, 1 April.

Arantes, P. E. (2012) 'Uma digressão sobre o tempo morto da onda punitiva contemporânea', in V. M. Batista (ed.), *Loïc Wacquant e a questão penal no capitalismo neoliberal*, Rio de Janeiro: Editora Revan.

Arias, E. D. (2006a) *Drugs and Democracy in Rio de Janeiro: Trafficking, Social Networks, and Public Security*, Chapel Hill: University of North Carolina Press.

— (2006b) 'The dynamics of criminal governance: networks and social order in Rio de Janeiro', *Journal of Latin American Studies*, 38(2).

Arias, E. D. and D. M. Goldstein (2010) 'Violent pluralism: understanding the new democracies of Latin America', in E. D. Arias and D. M. Goldstein (eds), *Violent Democracies in Latin America*, Durham, NC, and London: Duke University Press.

Ascencio Franco, G. (1998) 'Clase política y criminalización en Chiapas', *Ciudades*, 40.

Barbassa, J. (2012) 'Brazil drug dealers ban crack: slum dealers say drug "destabilizes" communities', *Huffington Post*, www.huffingtonpost. com/2012/08/22/brazil-drug-dealers-ban-crack_n_1822870.html, accessed 22 August 2012.

Barcellos, C. and A. Zaluar (2014) 'Homicides and territorial struggles in Rio de Janeiro favelas', *Revista de Saúde Pública*, 48(1).

Barkin, D. and T. King (1970) *Regional Economic Development: The River Basin Approach in Mexico*, Cambridge: Cambridge University Press.

Barón, F. (2011) 'Detenido Nem, el narcotraficante más codiciado de Río de Janeiro', *El País*, 10 November.

Barragan, E. (1990) *Más allá de los caminos: los rancheros del Potrero de Herrera*, Zamora: El Colegio de Michoacán.

Bartra, A. (1996) *Guerrero bronco: campesinos, ciudadanos y guerrilleros en la Costa Grande*, Mexico City: Ediciones Era.

— (2011) 'Foreword', in X. Leyva Solano and A. Burguete Cal y Mayor (eds), *Remunicipalization in Chiapas: Politics and the Political in Times of Counter-Insurgency*, Mexico City: CIESAS and IWGIA.

BBC (2014) 'World prison populations', news.bbc.co.uk/1/shared/spl/hi/uk/06/prisons/html/nn2page1.stm, accessed 3 July 2014.

Bebbington, A. (2009) 'The new extraction: rewriting the political ecology of the Andes', *NACLA Report on the Americas*, 42(5).

Bebbington, A. and D. Humphreys Bebbington (2011) 'An Andean avatar: post-neoliberal and neoliberal strategies for securing the unobtainable', *New Political Economy*, 16(1).

Becerra Acosta, J. P. (2014) 'Cae por "narconexos" alcalde de Apatzingán', *Milenio*, 16 April.

Bellinghausen, H. (2014a) 'La actual etapa contrainsurgente inicia en Las Margaritas con la Cruzada Contra el Hambre', *La Jornada*, 24 May.

— (2014b) 'Sigue vigente en Chiapas la guerra sucia diseñada desde 1994', *La Jornada*, 24 May.

Biondi, K. (2010) *Junto e misturado: uma etnografia do PCC*, São Paulo: Editora Terceiro Nome.

Boltvinik, J. (2014) 'Elementos para la crítica de la economía política de la pobreza', *Desacatos*, 23.

Booth, W. (2010) 'Mexico hobbled in drug war by arrests that lead nowhere', *Washington Post*, 26 April.

Borger, J. (2014) 'Protesters rage at Bosnia's politicians', *Guardian*, 13 February.

Borges, T. (2012) 'Líder do tráfico no Boqueirão é preso', *Correio da Bahia*, 27 November.

Bottari, E. and S. Ramalho (2013) 'Soldado que deteve Amarildo já tinha sido alvo de denúncia', *O Globo*, 17 August.

Bourdieu, P. (1989) 'Social space and symbolic power', *Sociological Theory*, 7(1).

Briceño-León, R. and V. Zubillaga (2002) 'Violence and globalization in Latin America', *Current Sociology*, 50(1).

Brito, G. and H. Cirino (2012) 'Delegado suspeita que PMs executaram 30 durante greve', *Jornal A Tarde*, 15 February.

Burawoy, M. (1998) 'The Extended Case Method', *Sociological Theory*, 16(1).

Burguete Cal y Mayor, A. (2003) 'The de facto autonomous process', in J. Rus, R. A. Hernández Castillo and S. L. Mattiace (eds), *Mayan Lives, Mayan Utopias: The Indigenous Peoples of Chiapas and the Zapatista Rebellion*, Lanham, MD: Rowman & Littlefield.

Buzan, B. and L. Hansen (2009) *The Evolution of International Security Studies*, Cambridge: Cambridge University Press.

Caldeira, T. P. R. (2002) 'The paradox of police violence in democratic Brazil', *Ethnography*, 3(3).

Caldeira, T. P. R. and J. Holston (2004) 'State and urban space in Brazil: from modernist planning to democratic intervention,' in A. Ong and S. J. Collier (eds), *Global Assemblages: Technology, Politics and Ethics as an Anthropological Problem*, Malden, MA: Blackwell.

Camacho de Schmidt, A. and A. Schmidt (2007) 'Introduction. Translating fear: a Mexican narrative of militancy, horror and redemption', in *Alberto Ulloa Bornemann, Surviving Mexico's Dirty War: A Political Prisoner's Memoir*, Philadelphia, PA: Temple University Press.

Camacho Servín, F. (2014) 'En Tlatlaya al menos 15 personas fueron ejecutadas, conclusión central de la CNDH', *La Jornada*, 25 October.

Camp, R. A. (2013) *Political Recruitment across Two Centuries: Mexico, 1884–1991*, Austin: University of Texas Press.

Campbell, H. (2009) *Drug War Zone: Frontline Dispatches from the Streets of El Paso and Juárez*, Austin: University of Texas Press.

Cano, A. (2014a) 'Aprehenden a Mireles y otros 69 por portar armas prohibidas', *La Jornada*, 28 June.

— (2014b) 'El Ejército los armó para que echaran a los templarios', *La Jornada*, 3 July.

— (2014c) 'La Marina llegó a la costa 9 años después que La Familia Michoacana', *La Jornada*, 16 February.

— (2014d) 'A Mireles "que ni lo embarren; él nunca ordenó la avanzada"', *La Jornada*, 14 May.

Caramante, A. and A. Benites (2012) 'Corregedoria suspeita que policiais venderam dados de PMs a bandidos', *Folha de São Paulo*, 13 November.

Carlsen, L. (2014) 'Mexico's oil privatization: risky business', www.cipamericas. org/archives/12170, accessed 8 July 2014.

Casillas, R. (2012) 'Redes visibles e invisibles en el tráfico y la trata de personas en Chiapas', *Migración y Seguridad: nuevo desafío en México*, Mexico: CASEDE.

Castellanos, L. (2013a) 'Guerrero: pese a conflictos, hacen asamblea policías comunitarias', *El Universal*, 24 February.

— (2013b) 'Masacre de Acteal cumple 16 años', *El Universal*, 22 December.

— (2014) 'Ostula va por autogobierno indígena: el retorno de los comunitarios desterrados', *El Universal*, 16 March.

Castillo García, G. (2012) 'Bajo investigación, todos los agentes adscritos al aeropuerto de la ciudad de México', *La Jornada*, 28 June.

Cavalcanti, M. (2009) 'Do barraco à casa: tempo, espaço e valor(es) em uma favela consolidada', *Revista Brasileira de Ciências Sociais*, 24(69).

— (2014) 'Value between the "favela" and the "pavement"', in B. Fischer, B. McCann and J. Auyero (eds), *Cities from Scratch: Poverty and Informality in Urban Latin America*, Durham, NC, and London: Duke University Press.

Cavalcanti, R. (2013) 'Edge of a barrel: gun violence and the politics of gun control in Brazil', *British Society of Criminology Newsletter*, 72.

CEPAL (2012) *Panorama social de América Latina 2012*, Santiago de Chile: Comisión Económica para América Latina y el Caribe.

Chalhoub, S. (1996) *Cidade febril: cortiços e epidemias na corte imperial*, São Paulo: Companhia das Letras.

Cochet, H. (1991) *Alambradas en la sierra: un sistema agrario en México. La Sierra de Coalcomán*, Mexico City: CEMCA, El Colegio de Michoacán and ORSTOM.

Colombo, S. (2014) 'Tráfico volta a assombrar cidade colombiana', *Folha de São Paulo*, 7 June.

Comaroff, J. and J. L. Comaroff (2000) 'Millennial capitalism: first thoughts on a second coming', *Public Culture*, 12(2).

Comisión Nacional para el Desarrollo de los Pueblos Indígenas (2010a) *Indicadores sociodemográficos de la población total y la población indígena, 2010: Chiapas*, www.cdi.gob.mx/cedulas/2010/CHIA/chia2010.pdf, accessed 13 June 2014.

— (2010b) *Indicadores sociodemográficos de la población total y la población indígena, 2010: Michoacán*, www.cdi.gob.mx/cedulas/2010/MICH/mich2010.pdf, accessed 19 June 2014.

CONEVAL (2013) *Informe sobre la pobreza en México 2012*, Mexico City: Consejo Nacional de Evaluación de la Política de Desarrollo Social.

Conn, C. (2013) 'Guerrero's indigenous community police and self-defense groups', *Upside Down World*, upsidedownworld.org/main/mexico-archives-79/4163-mexico-guerreros-indigenous-community-police-and-self-defense-groups, accessed 6 May 2013.

Consejo Ciudadano para la Seguridad Pública y Justicia Penal, A.C. (2012) 'San Pedro Sula (Honduras) la ciudad más violenta del mundo; Juárez, la segunda', www.seguridadjusticiaypaz. org.mx/sala-de-prensa/541-san-pedro-sula-la-ciudad-mas-violenta-del-mundo-juarez-la-segunda, accessed 18 March 2012.

— (2014) 'Por tercer año consecutivo, San Pedro Sula es la ciudad más violenta del mundo', www.seguridad justiciaypaz.org.mx/biblioteca/finish/5-prensa/177-por-tercer-ano-consecutivo-san-pedro-sula-es-la-ciudad-mas-violenta-del-mundo/o, accessed 23 April 2014.

Cordero Díaz, B. and C. Figueroa Ibarra (2011) 'Triturando a la humanidad: capitalismo, violencia y migración en el tránsito por México', in D. Villafuerte Solís and M. d. C. García Aguilar (eds), *Migración, seguridad, violencia y derechos humanos: lecturas desde el sur*, Mexico City: Miguel Ángel Porrúa.

Cornwall, A. and K. Brock (2005) 'What do buzzwords do for development policy? A critical look at "participation", "empowerment" and "poverty reduction"', *Third World Quarterly*, 26(7).

Corvo, Á. C. (2014) 'Poderes viejos y vecinos nuevos: la disputa por los recursos naturales en el norte de Quiché', comunitariapress.wordpress. com/2014/07/14/poderes-viejos-y-nuevos-vecinos/, accessed 16 July 2014.

Costa, A. C. (2011) 'Ex-presidente da Associação de Moradores da Rocinha é preso', *O Globo*, 2 December.

Costa, A. C., D. Barreto and P. Rebello (2012) 'Polícia prende suspeito de participar da morte de PM na Rocinha', *O Globo*, 14 September.

Costa Vargas, J. H. (2013) 'Taking back the land: police operations and sport mega-events in Rio de Janeiro', *Souls*, 15(4).

Covarrubias, A. (2013) 'Aguirre: éxodo,

por crimen organizado', *El Universal*, 20 July.

Covarrubias, A. and J. Cervantes (2013) 'Exigen justicia en Ayotzinapa', *El Universal*, 13 December.

Craske, N., L. Crean, B. Flinn, R. Howitt, E. MacAskill, E. O'Connell, D. Stransfield and L. White (1998) *Chiapas, before It's Too Late*, Bristol: Chiapas Support Group.

Da Cunha, E. (1984) *Os Sertões*, São Paulo: Três Publishing.

Da Cunha, N. V. (2012) 'Vivienda popular y seguridad pública: el proceso de pacificación en las favelas de Río de Janeiro', in *Dimensiones de habitat popular latinoamericano*, Quito: FLACSO, CLACSO, Instituto de la Ciudad.

Damasceno, N., R. Leite, R. Berta and W. Borges (2013) 'Após longo histórico de queda, homicídios dolosos têm o maior aumento mensal desde 2009', *O Globo*, 8 March.

Damián, F. (2014) 'Bajaron 16% homicidios dolosos en 2013: Campa', *Milenio*, 3 June.

Dantas Neto, P. F. (2006) *Tradição, autocracia e carisma: a política de Antônio Carlos Magalhães na modernizacão da Bahia (1954–1974)*, Belo Horizonte: Universidade Federal de Minas Gerais.

Dart, T. (2014) 'Running from gangs and fear, the migrant children who are now America's problem', *Observer*, 13 July.

Dávila, P. (2014) 'Michoacán: los Nahuas de Aquila, atacados desde todos los frentes', *Proceso*, 1962, 8 June.

De la Peña, G. (2006) 'A new Mexican nationalism? Indigenous rights, constitutional reform and the conflicting meanings of multiculturalism', *Nations and Nationalism*, 12(2).

De Soto, H. (2000) *The Mystery of Capital: Why Capitalism Triumphs in the West and Fails Everywhere Else*, New York: Basic Books.

De Vos, J. (2002) *Una tierra para sembrar sueños: historia reciente de la Selva Lacandona*, Mexico City: Ciesas.

Decat, E. and A. Matais (2012) 'Acordo

entre partidos faz CPI do Cachoeira acabar semindiciados', *Folha de São Paulo*, 19 December.

Dias, M. (2014) 'A violência aplaudida', *Carta Capital*, 789, 5 March.

Dourado, T. (2014) 'Com greve, PMs ganham revisão de código de ética e gratificação cresce', *G1 Bahia*, g1.globo.com/bahia/noticia/2014/04/com-greve-pms-ganham-revisao-de-codigo-de-etica-e-gratificacao-cresce.html, accessed 17 April 2014.

Druck, G. (2011) 'Trabalho, precarização e resistências: novos e velhos desafios?', *Caderno CRH*, 24(1).

Duffield, M. (2010) 'The liberal way of development and the development–security impasse: exploring the global life-chance divide', *Security Dialogue*, 41(1).

Eça, J. (2011) 'Envolvido em morte de meninas se entrega', *Jornal A Tarde*, 4 January.

Elencar, E. (2013) 'Beltrame: caso Amarildo não arranha imagem das UPPs', *O Globo*, 5 October.

Escalona Victoria, J. L. (2010) 'En los márgenes del zapatismo: Veracruz y Saltillo, dos poblados tojolabales (Las Margaritas)', in M. Saavedra Estrada and J. P. Viqueira (eds), *Los indígenas de Chiapas y la rebelión zapatista: microhistorias políticas*, Mexico City: El Colegio de México.

Esquivel, J. (2014a) 'Tamaulipas: "limpia" de narcos tolerada por el gobierno', *Proceso*, 1962, 8 June.

— (2014b) 'En Juárez, paz pactada, pero viene una "limpia"', *Proceso*, 1960, 25 May.

Estrada Saavedra, M. A. (2013) 'Entre utopía y realidad: historia de la Unión de Ejidos de la Selva', *LiminaR. Estudios Sociales y Humanísticos*, 4(1).

Estrada Saavedra, M. E. (2005) 'The "armed community in rebellion": Neo-Zapatismo in the Tojolab'al Cañadas, Chiapas (1988–96)', *Journal of Peasant Studies*, 32(3).

Farmer, P. (2003) *Pathologies of Power: Health, Human Rights, and the New War on the Poor*, Berkeley: University of California Press.

Farmer, P., P. Bourgois, N. Scheper-Hughes, D. Fassin, L. Green, H. K. Heggenhougen, L. Kirmayer and L. Wacquant (2004) 'An anthropology of structural violence', *Current Anthropology*, 45(3).

Feltran, G. (2010a) 'Crime e castigo na cidade: os repertórios da justiça e a questão do homicídio nas periferias de São Paulo', *Caderno CRH*, 23(58).

— (2010b) 'The management of violence on the São Paulo periphery: the repertoire of normative apparatus in the PCC era', *Vibrant*, 7(2).

FEMOSPP (2005) *Draft Report, Chapter 6: la guerra sucia en Guerrero (Fiscalía Especial para Movimientos Sociales y Políticos del Pasado)*, Washington, DC: National Security Archive, www2.gwu.edu/~nsarchiv/NSAEBB/NSAEBB180/060_Guerra%20Sucia.pdf, accessed 23 July 2013.

— (2006) *Informe Histórico a la Sociedad Mexicana (Fiscalía Especial para Movimientos Sociales y Políticos del Pasado)*, Mexico City: Procuraduría General de la República.

Ferguson, J. (1990) *The Anti-Politics Machine: 'Development', Depoliticization, and Bureaucratic Power in Lesotho*, Cambridge: Cambridge University Press.

Ferreira, L., M. R. A. de Machado and M. R. Machado (2012) 'Massacre do Carandiru: vinte anos sem responsabilização', *Novos Estudos-CEBRAP*, 94.

Fitting, E. (2006) 'The political uses of culture: maize production and the GM corn debates in Mexico', *Focaal*, 48.

Fleury, S. (2012) 'Militarização do social como estratégia de integração – o caso da UPP do Santa Marta', *Sociologias*, 14(30).

Flores, J. C., A. Valadez and R. Villalpando (2014) 'Denuncian comuneros michoacanos desvío de regalías pagadas por minera', *La Jornada*, 24 May.

Freeman, J. (2012) 'Neoliberal accumulation

strategies and the visible hand of police pacification in Rio de Janeiro', *Revista de Estudos Universitários*, 38(1).

Fukuda-Parr, S. (2003) 'New threats to human security in the era of globalization', *Journal of Human Development*, 4(2).

Galdeano, A. P. (2010) 'Civil society, violence and public safety: new issues, old dilemmas', *Vibrant*, 7(2).

Galemba, R. (2012) 'Taking contraband seriously: practicing "legitimate work" at the Mexico–Guatemala border', *Anthropology of Work Review*, 33(1).

Gallagher, K. and R. Porzecanski (2010) *The Dragon in the Room: China and the Future of Latin American Industrialization*, Stanford, CA: Stanford University Press.

García Davish, F. and F. Miranda (2014) 'Suman más de 700 mil toneladas de mineral incautado', *Milenio*, 11 June.

Garduño, R. (2014) 'La PGR conoció una averiguación contra Abarca por triple homicidio desde 2013', *La Jornada*, 10 November.

Garzón, J. C. (2008) *Mafia & Co: The Criminal Networks in Mexico, Brazil, and Colombia*, Washington, DC: Woodrow Wilson International Center for Scholars.

Gledhill, J. (1999) 'Official masks and shadow powers: towards an anthropology of the dark side of the state', *Urban Anthropology*, 28(3/4).

— (2002) 'Una nueva orientación para el laberinto: la transformación del Estado mexicano y el verdadero Chiapas', *Relaciones*, 90.

— (2003) 'Neoliberalismo e ingobernabilidad: caciquismo, militarización y movilización popular en el México de Zedillo', *Relaciones*, 24(96).

— (2004) *Cultura y desafío en Ostula: cuatro siglos de autonomía indígena en la Costa-Sierra Nahua de Michoacán*, Zamora: El Colegio de Michoacán.

Gledhill, J. and M. G. Hita (2014) '¿Las redes de organización popular aún pueden cambiar la ciudad? El caso de Salvador, Bahía, Brasil', in M. di Virgilio and M. Perelman (eds), *Ciudades latino-americanas: desigualdad, segregación y tolerancia*, Buenos Aires: CLACSO.

Goldstein, D. M. (2003) *Laughter out of Place: Race, Class, Violence and Sexuality in a Rio Shantytown*, Berkeley: University of California Press.

— (2012) *Outlawed: Between security and rights in a Bolivian city*, Durham, NC, and London: Duke University Press.

Gomide, R. (2011) 'Assaltos não aconteciam na Rocinha com tráfico, dizem moradores', *Ultimosegundo*, ultimosegundo.ig.com.br/brasil/rj/assaltos-nao-aconteciam-na-rocinha-com-trafico-dizem-moradores/n1597410789553.html, accessed 9 January 2012.

Gomora, D. (2014) 'Activistas de EU sellan frontera a migrantes', *El Universal*, 11 July.

González de la Rocha, M. (2004) 'De los "recursos de la pobreza" a la "pobreza de los recursos" y a las "desventajas acumuladas"', *Latin American Research Review*, 39(1).

Gordilho Souza, A. (2000) *Limites do habitar. Segregação e exclusão na configuração urbana contemporânea de Salvador e perspectivas no final do século XX*, Salvador: Edufba.

— (2007) 'Regularização fundiária na nova política municipal de habitação de interesse social em Salvador', *Revista VeraCidade*, 2.

Gómez, E. and E. Henríquez (2014) 'El sur de Veracruz, triángulo de las Bermudas para los migrantes', *La Jornada*, 18 June.

Grayson, G. W. (2010) *La Familia Drug Cartel: Implications for US–Mexican Security*, Carlisle Barracks, PA: Army War College Strategic Studies Institute.

Grayson, G. W., S. Logan and C. Lindsey (2012) *The Executioner's Men: Los Zetas, Rogue Soldiers, Criminal Entrepreneurs, and the Shadow State They Created*, Piscataway, NJ: Transaction Publishers.

Grillo, I. (2012) *El Narco: The Bloody Rise of Mexican Drug Cartels*, London: Bloomsbury.

Guimarães, N. A. (2006) 'Trabalho em transição: uma comparação entre São Paulo, Paris e Tóquio', *Novos Estudos-CEBRAP*, 76.

Handelman, D. (2005) 'The extended case: interactional foundations and prospective dimensions', *Social Analysis*, 49.

Handzic, K. (2010) 'Is legalized land tenure necessary in slum upgrading? Learning from Rio's land tenure policies in the Favela Bairro Program', *Habitat International*, 34(1).

Harvey, D. (2007) 'Neoliberalism as creative destruction', *ANNALS of the American Academy of Political and Social Science*, 610(1).

Hautzinger, S. J. (2007) *Violence in the City of Women: Police and Batterers in Bahia, Brazil*, Berkeley: University of California Press.

Hernández, A. (2012) *Los señores del narco*, Mexico City: Grijalbo.

Hernández Castillo, A. R. (2002) 'National law and indigenous customary law: the struggle for justice of indigenous women in Chiapas, Mexico', in M. Molyneux and S. Razavi (eds), *Gender Justice, Development and Rights*, Oxford: Oxford University Press.

Hernández Navarro, L. (2014) 'Guerrero: el asedio contra la CRAC-PC', *La Jornada*, 24 June.

Hita, M. G. and J. E. Gledhill (2010) 'Antropologia na análise de situações periféricas urbanas', *Cadernos Metrópole*, 12(23).

Holston, J. (2009) 'Dangerous spaces of citizenship: gang talk, rights talk and rule of law in Brazil', *Planning Theory*, 8(1).

IGBE (2012) *PNAD (Pesquisa Nacional por Amostra de Domicílios) 2011*, Rio de Janeiro: Instituto Brasileiro de Geografia e Estadística.

Isacson, A., M. Meyer and G. Morales (2014) *Mexico's Other Border: Security, Migration, and the Humanitarian Crisis at the Line with Central America*, Washington, DC: Washington Office on Latin America, www.wola.org/publica-tions/mexicos_other_border, accessed 20 June 2014.

Ivo, A. (2008) *Viver por um fio: pobreza e política social*, São Paulo and Salvador: Annablume and CRH/UFBA.

Jasso Martínez, J. J. (2010) 'Las demandas de las organizaciones purépechas y el movimiento indígena en Michoacán', *LiminaR. Estudios Sociales y Humanísticos*, VIII(1).

Jopson, B. and R. Harding (2014) 'AFL-CIO finds hope in inequality debate', *Financial Times*, 2 July.

Joseph, G. M. and D. Nugent (eds) (1994) *Everyday Forms of State Formation: Revolution and the Negotiation of Rule in Modern Mexico*, Durham, NC, and London: Duke University Press.

Jütersonke, O., R. Muggah and D. Rodgers (2009) 'Gangs, urban violence, and security interventions in Central America', *Security Dialogue*, 40(4/5).

Kaldor, M. (2012) *New and Old Wars: Organized Violence in a Global Era*, 3rd edn, Stanford, CA: Stanford University Press.

Leahy, J. (2013) 'Brazil opens prison doors to investors', *Financial Times*, 29 January.

Leblon, S. (2012) 'O bangue-bangue paulista: a cidade quer saber', *Carta Maior*, www.cartamaior.com.br/templates/postMostrar.cfm?blog_ id=6&post_ id=1130, accessed 6 November 2012.

Lewis, P. (2014) 'Obama seeks fast deportation of tens of thousands of child migrants', *Guardian*, 30 June.

Leyva Solano, A. and A. Burguete Cal y Mayor (2011) 'Remunicipalization in Chiapas: between peace and counterinsurgency', in X. Leyva Solano and A. Burguete Cal y Mayor (eds), *Remunicipalization in Chiapas: Politics and the Political in Times of Counter-Insurgency*, Mexico City: CIESAS and IWGIA.

Leyva Solano, X. and G. Ascencio Franco (1996) *Lacandonia al filo del agua*, Mexico City: Fondo de la Cultura Económica.

Lima, J. A. (2014) 'A PM-SP revela sua

ideologia em nota oficial', *Carta Capital*, www.cartacapital.com.br/sociedade/a-pm-sp-revela-sua-ideologia-3626.html, accessed 11 April 2014.

Linger, D. T. (1992) *Dangerous Encounters: Meanings of Violence in a Brazilian City*, Stanford, CA: Stanford University Press.

Lomnitz-Adler, C. (1992) *Exits from the Labyrinth: Culture and Ideology in the Mexican National Space*, Berkeley: University of California Press.

López Castro, G. and S. Zendejas Romero (1988) 'Migración internacional por regiones en Michoacán', in T. Calvo and G. López Castro (eds), *Movimientos de población en el occidente de México*, Zamora: El Colegio de Michoacán AC.

Lucero Estrada, D. (2011) 'Señora Isabel y Señora Reyna Ayala Nava executed in Xaltianguis, Guerrero', *El Enemigo Común*, elenemigocomun.net/2011/07/execution-senoras-xaltianguis-guerrero/, accessed 13 July 2013.

Maeckelbergh, M. (2011) 'Doing is believing: prefiguration as strategic practice in the alterglobalization movement', *Social Movement Studies*, 10(1).

Maldonado Aranda, S. (2013) 'Stories of drug trafficking in rural Mexico: territories, drugs and cartels in Michoacán', *European Review of Latin American and Caribbean Studies*, 94.

Malkin, V. (2001) 'Narcotrafficking, migration, and modernity in rural Mexico', *Latin American Perspectives*, 28(4).

Martins, M. A. (2014) 'Número de homicídios dolosos aumenta 16,7% no Rio de Janeiro', *Folha de São Paulo*, 27 February.

Martins, M. A. and D. Brito (2012) 'Rio reforça segurança para inaugurar UPP da Rocinha', *Folha de São Paulo*, 21 September.

Martins, R. (2012) 'O crime não descansa', *Carta Capital*, 724(10).

Martín, F. (2014) 'Se enfrentan miembros de EZLN y CIOAC', *El Universal*, 4 May.

Martínez, E. and S. Ocampo (2013) 'March-an contra autodefensas en Michoacán', *La Jornada*, 20 June.

Martínez, S. (2014a) 'Castillo ha pecado de ingenuo y se ha dejado comer el mandado', *La Jornada*, 15 June.

— (2014b) 'Soy un preso político, sostiene Mireles Valverde', *La Jornada*, 7 July.

Martínez, S. and E. Martínez Elorriaga (2014) 'En Michoacán no habrá soberanía mientras esté El Virrey: Selene Vázquez', *La Jornada*, 22 June.

Martínez Elorriaga, E. (2011) 'Ostula y Cherán pactan realizar elecciones por usos y costumbres', *La Jornada*, 28 September.

— (2013a) 'Desplazados por la delincuencia, más de 1,500 habitantes de Tancítaro', *La Jornada*, 25 November.

— (2013b) 'En Aquila nos armamos contra el crimen organizado', *La Jornada*, 15 August.

— (2014a) 'Afirma Valencia Reyes que dejará alcaldía de Tepalcatepec por presiones de Castillo', *La Jornada*, 13 February.

— (2014b) 'Exigen indagar reunión de hijo de Vallejo con La Tuta', *La Jornada*, 16 June.

— (2014c) 'Rinde protesta Jara Guerrero al gobierno de Michoacán', *La Jornada*, 21 June.

Maurer, B. (2002) 'Repressed futures: financial derivatives' theological unconscious', *Economy and Society*, 31(1).

McCabe, D. (2014) 'State Department awarded Blackwater more than $1 billion after threat on investigator's life', *Huffington Post*, www.huffingtonpost.com/2014/07/10/blackwater-state-department-contracts_n_5572355.html, accessed 11 July 2014.

McNeish, J.-A. (2013) 'Extraction, protest and indigeneity in Bolivia: the TIPNIS effect', *Latin American and Caribbean Ethnic Studies*, 8(2).

Mendes, H. (2014) 'Tráfico tenta criar espaço no Bairro da Paz, diz tenente; criança é morta', *G1 Bahia*, g1.globo.com/bahia/noticia/2014/01/trafico-tenta-criar-espaco-no-bairro-da-paz-diz-tenente-crianca-e-morta.html, accessed 31 January 2014.

Mendes Jr, L. A. (2014) 'Impunidade do Carandiru estimula novos massacres', *Carta Capital*, www.cartacapital.com. br/sociedade/impunidade-do-carandiru -estimula-novos-massacres-8610.html, accessed 7 April 2014.

Meneses, R. (2013) '"Pats" podem ter ligação com Fal: polícia suspeita que jovens são "mulas" do bando de um dos chefões da facção', *Jornal Massa!*, 12 April.

Meneses, R. et al. (2012) 'Cintra deu queixa de ameaça contra Osmar', *Jornal A Tarde*, 1 February.

Méndez, A. (2014) 'Cae medio hermano de El Chayo', *Milenio*, 10 February.

Michel, V. H. (2014a) 'Honduras: por culpa del narco, la crisis de niños', *Milenio*, 12 July.

— (2014b) 'Policías en Acapulco torturan a detenido', *Milenio*, 2 April.

Misse, M. (1997) 'As ligações perigosas: mercado informal ilegal, narcotráfico e violência no Rio', *Contemporaneidade & Educação. Revista semestral temática de Ciências Sociais e Educação. Ano II*, 2(1).

— (2007) 'Illegal markets, protection rackets and organized crime in Rio de Janeiro', *Estudos Avançados*, 21(61).

Mitchell, T. (2011) *Carbon Democracy: Political Power in the Age of Oil*, London and New York: Verso.

Moberg, M. (2003) *Banana Wars: Power, Production, and History in the Americas*, Durham, NC, and London: Duke University Press.

Moguel, J. (1994) 'The Mexican left and the social program of Salinismo', in W. A. Cornelius, A. L. Craig and J. Fox (eds), *Transforming State–Society Relations in Mexico: The National Solidarity Strategy*, La Jolla: Center for US-Mexican Studies, University of California, San Diego.

Moksnes, H. (2012) *Maya Exodus: Indigenous Struggle for Citizenship in Chiapas*, Norman: University of Oklahoma Press.

Molloy, M. (2013) 'Mexico's national crime statistics show no significant decline in homicides and disappearances', James

A. Baker III Institute for Public Policy, blog.chron.com/bakerblog/2013/10/ is-drug-related-violence-in-mexico- on-the-decline/, accessed 24 October 2013.

Moodie, E. (2011) *El Salvador in the Aftermath of Peace: Crime, Uncertainty, and the Transition to Democracy*, Philadelphia: University of Pennsylvania Press.

Morales, A. and S. Oterol (2014) 'Indagan a Mireles por droga; sus cuentas, bajo sospecha', *El Universal*, 1 July.

Mosso, R. (2014) 'El Chayo, vivo ... hasta ayer', *Milenio*, 10 March.

Muedano, M. (2014) '"El Abuelo" se integra a Fuerza Rural', *El Universal*, 11 May.

Muñoz Ramírez, G. (2012) 'Paramilitares nos emboscaron, aclaran comuneros de Cherán', *La Jornada*, 20 April.

— (2014) 'Me quieren matar o enloquecer, acusa Nestora Salgado; cumple un año en prisión', *La Jornada*, 21 August.

Muñoz Ríos, P. (2014) 'En 9 meses EU aprehendió a 52 mil menores que viajaban solos', *La Jornada*, 20 June.

Nelson, D. M. (2005) 'Life during wartime: Guatemala, vitality, conspiracy, milieu', in J. Inda (ed.), *Anthropologies of Modernity: Foucault, Governmentality and Life Politics*, Malden, MA, and Oxford: Blackwell.

Nordstrom, C. (2007) *Global Outlaws: Crime, Money, and Power in the Contemporary World*, Berkeley: University of California Press.

Norget, K. (2010) 'A cacophony of autochthony: representing indigeneity in Oaxacan popular mobilization', *Journal of Latin American and Caribbean Anthropology*, 15(1).

Noronha, C. V. (2008) 'Criminalidad urbana y acciones de los escuadrones de la muerte en la Bahía (Brasil): de la impunidad a la pena máxima', *URVIO- Revista Latinoamericana de Seguridad Ciudadana*, 4.

Nugent, D. (2012) 'Commentary: Democracy, temporalities of capitalism, and dilemmas of inclusion in Occupy movements', *American Ethnologist*, 39(2).

Nuijten, M. (2003) *Power, Community and the State: The Political Anthropology of Organisation in Mexico*, London: Pluto.

Nunes, M. and J. S. Paím (2005) 'Um estudo etno-epidemiológico da violência urbana na cidade de Salvador, Bahia, Brasil: os atos de extermínio como objeto de análise', *Cadernos de Saúde Pública*, 21(2).

Ocampo Arista, S. (2013a) 'Crimen político, el asesinato de miembros de la UP, afirma viuda', *La Jornada*, 5 June.

— (2013b) 'Familias de pueblos de Guerrero huyen de sus casas ante amenazas de muerte', *La Jornada*, 19 July.

Olmos, J. G. (2014) 'Vallejo: un gobernador por el narco y para el narco', *Proceso*, 1964, 22 June.

Olney, P. (2004) 'Global order, local chaos: explaining paramilitary violence in Chiapas, Mexico and Colombia', *Low Intensity Conflict and Law Enforcement*, 12(2).

Oswald, V. (2014) 'Um reino nada unido de nobres e plebeus', *O Globo*, 19 April.

Otero-Briz, M. (2014) 'Era difícil caminar sin los programas del gobierno', *Milenio*, 19 March.

Overmyer-Velázquez, R. (2011) *Folkloric Poverty: Neoliberal Multiculturalism in Mexico*, University Park: Pennsylvania State University Press.

Paes Machado, E. P. and C. V. Noronha (2002) 'A polícia dos pobres: violência policial em classes populares urbanas', *Sociologias*, 4(7).

Pagnan, R., G. Uribe, A. Monteiro and M. C. Carvalho (2014) 'Ex-presidário, ex-foragido excomungado', *Folha de São Paulo*, 1 June.

Paiva, G. (2014) 'Pezão: ataques às UPPs preocupam devido à aproximação da Copa', *O Globo*, 26 May.

Pansters, W. (1997) 'Theorizing political culture in modern Mexico', in W. Pansters (ed.), *Citizens of the Pyramid: Essays on Mexican Political Culture*, Amsterdam: Thela.

— (2012) 'Zones of state-making: violence, coercion and hegemony in twentieth century Mexico', in W. Pansters (ed.), *Violence, Coercion, and State-making in Twentieth-century Mexico: The Other Half of the Centaur*, Stanford, CA: Stanford University Press.

Patterson, K. (2012) 'The contradictions of the "new" Juárez', CIP-Americas Program, www.cipamericas.org/archives/8410, accessed 28 November 2012.

Pearson, S. (2012) 'Brazil's crack cocaine boom', *Financial Times Beyondbrics Blog*, blogs.ft.com/beyondbrics/2012/09/11/brazils-crack-cocaine-boom/#axzz265Rd7RKy, accessed 11 September 2012.

Penglase, B. (2009) 'States of insecurity: everyday emergencies, public secrets, and drug trafficker power in a Brazilian favela', *PoLAR: Political and Legal Anthropology Review*, 32(1).

— (2011) 'Lost bullets: fetishes of urban violence in Rio de Janeiro, Brazil', *Anthropological Quarterly*, 84(2).

Perlman, J. (2010) *Favela: Four Decades of Living on the Edge in Rio de Janeiro*, Oxford: Oxford University Press.

Petrich, B. (2014) 'Julio César Mondragón sólo disfrutó su paternidad 15 días', *La Jornada*, 12 November.

Pérez Ramírez, T. (2009) 'Memoria histórica de la insurrección cívica purépecha en 1988', *Política y cultura*, 31.

Phillips, T. (2011) 'Rio World Cup demolitions leave favela families trapped in ghost town', *Guardian*, 26 April.

Piketty, T. (2014) *Capital in the Twenty-first Century*, Cambridge, MA: Harvard University Press.

Pochman, M. (2009) *A volta da mobilidade social*, www.ipea.gov.br/portal/index.php?option=com_content&view=article&id=521&Itemid=2, accessed 18 October 2011.

Poy Solano, L. (2013) 'Estamos preparados para la resistencia, advierten maestros indígenas de Guerrero', *La Jornada*, 8 June.

Provost, C. (2014) 'El Salvador groups accuse Pacific Rim of "assault on democratic governance"', *Guardian*, 11 April.

Ramírez Sánchez, M. A. (2012) 'We are all government: Zapatista political community and libertarian politics in history and practice', Unpublished PhD thesis, University of Manchester.

Rasch, E. D. (2012) 'Transformations in citizenship: local resistance against mining projects in Huehuetenango (Guatemala)', *Journal of Developing Societies*, 28(2).

Ribeiro, G. L. (2006) 'Economic globalization from below', *Etnográfica*, 10(2).

Ribeiro, L. (2012) 'Cai atacadista do pó', *Correio da Bahia*, 24 November.

Ribeiro Delgado, F., R. E. Ferreira Dodge and S. Carvalho (2011) *São Paulo sob achaque: corrupção, crime organizado e violência Institucional em maio de 2006*, São Paulo: Justiça Global and Harvard University.

Rocha, C., S. Schmidt and S. Ramalho (2013) 'Taxa de homicídios em UPPs é quase 1/3 da média nacional', *O Globo*, 7 December.

Rodgers, D. (2012) 'Haussmannization in the tropics: abject urbanism and infrastructural violence in Nicaragua', *Ethnography*, 13(4).

Rodrigues, R. and V. Longo (2014) 'Precisava?', *Correio da Bahia*, 18 April.

Rojas, R. (2014) 'Declara CRAC-PC ilegítima la reunión que convoca el ex coordinador Eliseo Villar', *La Jornada*, 6 April.

Rojas, R. and F. Camacho (2014) 'Oleada de críticas a las declaraciones superficiales de Robles contra indígenas', *La Jornada*, 3 May.

Rolnik, R. (2012) 'Remoções forçadas em tempos do novo ciclo econômico', *Carta Maior*, www.cartamaior.com.br/templates/materialImprimir.cfm?materia_id=20790, accessed 1 September 2012.

Rovai, R. (2013) 'Black blocs, o assassinato do menino Douglas e o inferno anunciado', *Carta Maior*, www.cartamaior.com.br/?/Editoria/Direitos-Humanos/Black-blocs-o-assassinato-do-menino-Douglas-e-o-inferno-anunciado-/5/29376, accessed 15 December 2013.

Rubin, J. W. (1996) 'Decentering the regime: culture and regional politics in Mexico', *Latin American Research Review*, 31(3).

Salvadori, F. and W. Cardoso (2014) 'Guerra à periferia', *Carta Capital*, www.cartacapital.com.br/sociedade/guerra-a-periferia-9038.html, accessed 6 June 2014.

Sandoval, E. (2012) 'Economía de la fayuca y del narcotráfico en el noreste de México. Extorsiones, contubernios y solidaridades en las economías transfronterizas', *Desacatos*, 38.

SanMartin, F. (2012) 'PM teria distúrbios, alega defensor', *Jornal A Tarde*, 14 February.

Sánchez, J. (2013) 'Anomalías "inundan" Zona Diamante', *El Universal*, 20 October.

Sánchez, L. (2013) '"Topos": los esclavos del narco', *El Universal*, 24 March.

Sánchez Díaz, G. (1979) *El suroeste de Michoacán. Estructura económico-social, 1821–1851*, Morelia: Universidad Michoacana de San Nicolás de Hidalgo.

Scahill, J. (2008) *Blackwater: The Rise of the World's Most Powerful Mercenary Army*, New York: Nation Books.

Schneider, J. and P. T. Schneider (2003) *Reversible Destiny: Mafia, Antimafia, and the Struggle for Palermo*, Berkeley: University of California Press.

Serapião, F. (2014) 'Crime em lugar do estado', *Carta Capital*, 789, 5 March.

Serrano Alvarez, P. (1997) 'El sinarquismo mexicano: expresión conservadora de la Región Centro-Oeste: síntesis de su historia', *Contrastes*, 9/10.

Sheriff, R. E. (1999) 'The theft of Carnaval: national spectacle and racial politics in Rio de Janeiro', *Cultural Anthropology*, 14(1).

Silva, S. (2014) 'Clima tenso deixa 7 mil sem aula na Zona Oeste', *Meia Hora*, 27 May.

Smale, A. (2014) 'Roots of Bosnian protests lie in peace accords of 1995', *New York Times*, 14 February.

Smith, N. (2002) 'New globalism, new urbanism: gentrification as global urban strategy', *Antipode*, 34(3).

Soares, L. E. (2006) 'Segurança pública: presente e futuro', *Estudos Avançados*, 20(56).

Souza, J. (2009) *A ralé brasileira: quem é e como vive*, Belo Horizonte: Editora UFMG.

Speed, S. and J. F. Collier (2000) 'Limiting indigenous autonomy in Chiapas, Mexico: the state government's use of human rights', *Human Rights Quarterly*, 22.

Stanford, L. (2000) 'The globalization of agricultural commodity systems: examining peasant resistance to international agribusiness', in A. Haugerud, P. M. Stone and P. D. Little (eds), *Commodities and Globalization: Anthropological Perspectives*, Lanham, MD: Rowman & Littlefield.

Stiglitz, J. E. (2012) *The Price of Inequality*, London: Allen Lane.

Suarez Dillon Soares, S. (2008) *O ritmo de queda na desigualdade no Brasil é adequado? Evidências do contexto histórico e internacional*, Brasilia: Instituto de Pesquisa Econômica Aplicada, www.ipea.gov.br/portal/images/stories/PDFs/TDs/td_1339.pdf, accessed 12 June 2011.

Taussig, M. T. (1999) *Defacement: Public Secrecy and the Labor of the Negative*, Stanford, CA: Stanford University Press.

— (2005) *Law in a Lawless Land: Diary of a 'Limpieza' in Colombia*, Chicago, IL: University of Chicago Press.

Tavares, V. (2014) 'Interview with Luiz Eduardo Soares: A sociedade em seu conjunto terá de mudar, porque é ela quem autoriza, hoje, a barbárie policial', www.luizeduardosoares.com/?p=1195, accessed 11 July 2014.

Telles (2010) *A cidade nas fronteiras do legal e ilegal*, Belo Horizonte: Argumentum.

Thomé, C. (2014) 'Governo age contra milícias no programa Minha Casa', *Jornal A Tarde*, 4 April.

Torres, A. C. and A. Werneck (2012) 'Ex-comandante da UPP do São Carlos é preso por envolvimento com o tráfico', *O Globo*, 16 February.

Trejo, G. (2012) *Popular Movements in Autocracies: Religion, Repression, and Indigenous Collective Action in Mexico*, New York: Cambridge University Press.

Tsing, A. (2000) 'Inside the economy of appearances', *Public Culture*, 12(1).

Turati, M. (2014) 'Inacción militar que olió a complicidad', *Proceso*, 1984, 9 November.

Turati, M. and F. Castellanos (2012) 'Rebelión contra la mafia michoacana', *Proceso*, 1864, 21 July.

Ulloa Bornemann, A. (2007) *Surviving Mexico's Dirty War: A Political Prisoner's Memoir*, trans. A. Camacho de Schmidt and A. Schmidt, Philadelphia, PA: Temple University Press.

UNDP (1994) *Human Development Report 1994*, New York and Oxford: Oxford University Press.

— (2013) *The Rise of the South: Human Progress in a Diverse World*, New York: United Nations Development Programme.

Valporto, O. (2013) 'Violência em baixa', *Correio da Bahia*, 9 August.

Van der Ploeg, J. D. (2010) 'The food crisis, industrialized farming and the imperial regime', *Journal of Agrarian Change*, 10(1).

Villafuerte Solís, D. (2005) 'Rural Chiapas ten years after the armed uprising of 1994: an economic overview', *Journal of Peasant Studies*, 32(3).

— (2011) 'Políticas de seguridad y migración trasnacional en la frontera sur de México', in D. Villafuerte Solís and M. d. C. García Aguilar (eds), *Migración, seguridad, violencia y derechos humanos: lecturas desde el sur*, Mexico City: Miguel Ángel Porrúa.

Villarpando, V. (2013) 'Atenção ao Nordeste', *Correio da Bahia*, 7 July.

Vincent, D. P. (2014) 'The Trans-Pacific Partnership: environmental savior or regulatory carte blanche?', *Minnesota Journal of International Law*, 23(1).

Viqueira, J. P. (1999) 'Los peligros del Chiapas imaginario', *Letras libres*, 1(1).

Vogt, W. A. (2013) 'Crossing Mexico: structural violence and the commodification of undocumented Central American migrants', *American Ethnologist*, 40(4).

Vulliamy, E. (2010) *Amexica: War along the Borderline*, London: Bodley Head.

Wacquant, L. (2007) 'Territorial stigmatization in the age of advanced marginality', *Thesis Eleven*, 91.

— (2009) *Punishing the Poor: The Neoliberal Government of Social Insecurity*, Durham, NC, and London: Duke University Press.

Waiselfisz, J. J. (2012) *Mapa da violência 2012: os novos padrões da violência homicida no Brasil*, São Paulo: Instituto Sangari.

— (2014) 'Prévia do *Mapa da Violência 2014. Os jovens do Brasil*', www.mapadaviolencia.org.br/pdf2014/Previa_mapaviolencia2014.pdf, accessed 27 May 2014.

Watts, J. (2014) 'Priced out of booming favelas, Brazil's poor say occupation is the only option', *Guardian*, 13 May.

Weinberg, B. (2000) *Homage to Chiapas: The New Indigenous Struggles in Mexico*, London: Verso.

Welsbrot, M. (2013) 'Why the world should care about Honduras' recent election', *Guardian*, 3 December.

Wendel, B. (2012) 'Traficantes que fogem das bases da Polícia buscam atuar em outros bairros', *Correio da Bahia*, 15 September.

— (2013) 'Colocaram a arma na mão dele, diz amigo de rapaz morto no Nordeste de Amaralina', *Correio da Bahia*, 14 June.

— (2014) 'Corpo carbonizado é mesmo de Geovane', *Correio da Bahia*, 20 August

Williams, M. E. (2001) *Market Reforms in Mexico: Coalitions, Institutions, and the Politics of Policy Change*, Lanham, MD: Rowman & Littlefield.

Wilson, J. (2013) 'The urbanization of the countryside: depoliticization and the production of space in Chiapas', *Latin American Perspectives*, 40(2).

Wolf, R. C. (2004) *Trade, Aid, and Arbitrate: The Globalization of Western Law*, Aldershot: Ashgate.

World Bank (2011) *World Development Report 2011: Conflict, Security and Development*, Washington, DC: World Bank.

Wrede, C. (2014) 'À espera de um polo', *Meia Hora*, 1 June.

Wright, D. S. (2014) 'Blackwater founder Eric Prince to advise Chinese firms in Africa', *Fire Dog Lake News*, news.firedoglake.com/2014/07/07/blackwater-founder-erik-prince-to-advise-chinese-firms-in-africa/, accessed 11 July 2014.

Zaluar, A. (2010) 'Turf war in Rio de Janeiro: youth, drug traffic and hyper-masculinity', *Vibrant*, 7(2).

Zaluar, A. and C. Barcellos (2012) 'Mortes prematuras e conflito armado pelo domínio das favelas no Rio de Janeiro', *Revista Brasileira de Ciências Sociais*, 28(81).

Zaluar, A. and I. Siqueira Conceição (2007) 'Favelas sob o controle das milícias no Rio de Janeiro', *São Paulo em Perspectiva*, 21(2).

Zeiderman, A. (2013) 'Living dangerously: biopolitics and urban citizenship in Bogotá, Colombia', *American Ethnologist*, 40(1).

INDEX

Bonfim Lopes, Antonio Francisco (Nem), 51
Bosnia, 22; conflict in, 13–14
Brazil: crack cocaine market in, 88;
    economic development of, 2, 4, 208;
    evictions in, 15 (of poor from town
    centres, 18); Gini coefficient of, 5;
    incarceration of poor black people
    in, 25; issue of corruption in, 214–15;
    public security in, 24, 26; violence-
    related issues in, 29–63 *see also*
    homicide, rates of, in Brazil
'Brazil without Misery' programme, 5
Brazilian Democratic Movement Party
    (PMDB), 26, 48
Brazilian Social Democratic Party (PSDB),
    43, 46, 105, 107
BRICS countries, project for multilateral
    investment bank, 213
Brigada Campesina de Ajusticiamiento
    (BCA) (Mexico), 120
Brizola, Leonel, 47
buses, burning of, 40, 105
Bush, George W., 202

Caballeros Templarios, Los, 28, 171–3, 175,
    179, 181, 186–8, 192
Cabañas, Lucio, 116–17, 118–24, 136; death
    of, 124
cable cars, installation of, 50, 60
cable TV, illegal connections to, 53
Cabral, Sergio, 48, 55
Cachoeira, Carlinhos, 215
Calabar neighbourhood, 91–103 *passim*
Calderón, Felipe, 11, 33, 109, 111, 115, 133, 151,
    168–9, 178, 185
Calles, Plutarco Alias, 154
Camacho Solis, Manuel, 137
Camarena, Enrique (Kike), 156
Camino das Árvores district (Salvador),
    100
Canahuancera, La, 180, 182; land invasion,
    176–7; renaming of, 177
Candomblé religion, 79, 90
Canudos millenarian community, 37
Carandiru penitentiary (Brazil), massacre
    in, 39
Cárdenas, Cuauhtémoc, 126, 165
Cárdenas, Lázaro, 108, 118, 153, 154, 155,
    160, 162
Cárdenas Batel, Lázaro, 166, 175

Cardoso, Fernando Henrique, 5, 212
Carillo Fuentes family, 33
Carneiro, João Henrique, 64
Carnival, police work during, 96
Casa Legal programme (Brazil), 65
Castillo Cervantes, Alfredo, 182, 187, 189,
    190, 191, 192–3, 194, 211
Castro, Xiomara, 205
Catholic church, 90, 160; rituals
    undermined by insecurity, 184; shelter
    for migrants in Mexico, 145
CCTV surveillance technologies, 77
Central Independiente de Obreros
    Agrícolas y Campesinos Histórica
    (CIOAC-H) (Mexico), 135
Central Intelligence Agency (CIA),
    operations in, 13
Chávez, Hugo, 205
Chávez, Uriel, 188, 193
Cherán (Michoacán), 173; autonomy
    movement, 175–6, 185
Chiapas (Mexico), 21, 213; as locus of
    counter-insurgency, 27, 130–46; as
    region of passage for migrants to USA,
    144; effects of US policy on, 203–4;
    illegal economy in, 142–3; seen as
    indigenous state, 148
child labour, legislation against, 70
children, killing of, prohibition of, 40
Chile, economic growth in, 4
China: demand for Latin American
    minerals, 180, 208
choque de ordem, 66
churches, as exit strategy from world of
    crime, 43–4
Ciénega de Chapala (Mexico), 153, 155, 156
Cidade de Deus *favela*, 34, 55; attack on
    UPP base in, 56
Cintra, Mr, 78
Ciudad Juárez (Mexico), 216; homicide
    rates in, 30; reducing violence in, 34
class, issues of, 7
clientelism, 108, 110, 139
climate change, 12
Coalition of Workers, Peasants and
    Students of the Isthmus (COCEI), 149
cocaine, 80, 156, 164, 166, 167; processing
    of, 161 *see also* crack cocaine
Cochabamba, issue of water privatization
    in, 150